Great Thinkers A–Z

Also available from Continuum:

What Philosophers Think, edited by Julian Baggini and Jeremy Stangroom
What Philosophy Is, edited by Havi Carel and David Gamez

Great Thinkers A–Z

Edited by Julian Baggini and Jeremy Stangroom

continuum
LONDON • NEW YORK

Continuum
The Tower Building, 11 York Road, London SE1 7NX
15 East 26th Street, New York NY 10010

www.continuumbooks.com

First published 2004

British Library Cataloguing-in-Publication Data
A catalogue record for this book is available from the British Library.

ISBN: 0-8264-7326-1 (hardback)
     0-8264-6742-3 (paperback)

Typeset by Kenneth Burnley, Wirral, Cheshire
Printed and bound in Great Britain by MPG Books Ltd, Bodmin, Cornwall

Contents

Acknowledgements

Editing a book like this can be trying. Working with 63 people, all of whom have a slightly different idea of what an intelligent non-specialist is able to understand, what a deadline means, and how strict one should be about word limits, is a recipe for frustration and irritation. But contributors can make this less of a hell by accepting guidance and revision gracefully, responding to requests at ridiculously short notice and making sure they do their work well. In this respect we have been fortunate and we'd like to thank all the contributors to this book for working with us to produce what we hope is a volume of enduring value both to interested general readers and students of philosophy.

We'd also like to thank John Shand for his helpful comments on the introduction, Tristan Palmer for his assistance at conception, Hywel Evans for his midwifery and Rowan Wilson for ante and post natal care.

In memory of Lori Fells, whose kindness and good humour will be long remembered by her friends in the philosophical community.

Introduction:
Great Thinkers A–Z: A User's Guide

The great thinkers profiled in this volume are one hundred of the people whose ideas have done the most to shape the western philosophical tradition. Only a fool, however, would claim that they are the *top* one hundred such thinkers. Probably around half of the people included here would find their way into any similar volume. Beyond that, everyone will have his or her own opinion about who should be in and who should be out. A common reaction to a glance down the index will surely be, 'How could they have left *x* out and put *y* in?!'

We would be happy with such a reaction, for our purpose in collecting together these snapshots of the great thinkers is to include all the celebrated names whose place in the canon demands their inclusion, along with an eclectic mix of other thinkers who represent the many styles and strands of philosophy. While all the thinkers in this latter group are undoubtedly important, we do not claim that they are greater than others who have been left out, merely that together they form a representative showcase for the movements of thought of which they are parts.

Although the ideas dealt with in this volume are often quite complex, we have endeavoured to make sure that no difficulties are the result of unnecessary obscurity or use of a technical vocabulary. Such difficult passages as remain should be negotiable with close and careful reading.

For ease of reference, the entries are arranged alphabetically. We have, however, provided a chronological index as well as nine thematic guides. The purpose of this introduction is to provide an overview to put these guides and the entries themselves into a variety of contexts.

2,500 years in as many words

Over two and a half millennia lie between the birth of the earliest philosopher in this book and its year of publication. To provide a historical overview in the confines of this short introduction therefore requires devoting approximately one word for every year covered. The task may seem impossible. But philosophy is a slow moving subject and it is in fact possible to trace some of the most significant developments in thought to give a brief, if selective, potted history of the subject.

The earliest philosopher in this collection is Pythagoras, who was born around 550 BCE. Pythagoras is an excellent example of a thinker at the very dawn of philosophy, and indeed science. Pythagoras, like the Milesian philosophers of the sixth century BCE, was just beginning to realise how the world and its workings could be understood rationally, mechanistically and impersonally. Up until then, explanations for natural phenomena postulated mysterious, personalized, supernatural forces such as gods.

Pythagoras spotted mathematical regularities in nature, and found he could reason from these to provide accounts of geometry and musical pitch. The template for future philosophy was thus being laid down. Equipped only with the powers of reason and observation, Pythagoras was fumbling towards a rational method that was much more powerful than myth at explaining how the world is as it is.

But Pythagoras was still a man of his time, and alongside this new rationalism was a more old-fashioned mysticism. His theories of the reincarnation of the soul are much more speculative and do not have the same rational and experimental foundations as his mathematics. But even here, Pythagoras provides an early example of the philosophical impulse to give an account of being, even though his philosophical method was too immature to move much beyond speculation.

The other early Greek philosophers continued this process of grappling towards a philosophical mode of thinking about the world. Most histories of philosophy will run through the thought of a good few of them. But most of their ideas are of historic interest only, even when they find a later echo, such as with Democritus's atomic theory. Philosophy only really starts to warm up when we get to the big three ancient Greeks: Socrates, Plato and Aristotle.

It is with these three thinkers that philosophy really started to take up the shape it would hold to the present day. All three helped refine the methods of rational enquiry, in particular with the method of interrogation known as *elenchus* practised by Socrates and recorded by Plato;

and with Aristotle's development of formal logic. But perhaps even more importantly, here we first get a sense of the problem that would be central to philosophy: the problem of certainty.

In many ways, the history of philosophy can be seen as the quest to establish how we can know anything at all and the extent to which such knowledge can be certain. Plato and Socrates certainly seemed to think that knowledge required certainty; that beliefs which are uncertain just cannot be knowledge. Hence Socrates' claim that he knew nothing, for he did not think he could be certain of any of his beliefs. Against this, Aristotle seemed to have a more relaxed attitude, claiming we should only seek the degree of certainty each subject matter allowed. Hence we can have a firm proof in mathematics, but must content ourselves with balances of probability in political theory.

Jumping ahead for a moment, we find that this debate rages throughout the history of philosophy. The claims of certainty were made most optimistically by the seventeenth-century rationalists, notably Descartes, Spinoza and Leibniz, who thought that all human knowledge could be established on firm foundations and demonstrated with the same precision as a mathematical proof. But this optimism soon faded, led by the criticisms of empiricists such as Locke and Hume. The story there onwards is one of declining faith in the possibility of certainty in human knowledge. In the nineteenth century, for example, the American pragmatists, such as Dewey, James and Peirce, were arguing that, crudely, what is true is what works, and that to demand any more from knowledge – such as certainty – is futile. Even attempts at establishing a delimited certainty, such as Russell and Whitehead's project of analysing the logical basis of mathematics, met with failure.

The debate is very much alive today. A wide array of thinkers, usually termed 'postmodernist' by critics but not by themselves, are pessimistic about the claims of reason. Foucault, for example, sees knowledge as being intimately connected with power and thus a tool of oppression as much as a means of understanding. Similarly, Lacan talks of language as the 'symbolic order' that constrains our thinking rather than enables it.

Yet even these philosophers are not simply dismissing rationality. After all, they themselves employ rational arguments to make their cases. Rather, they are trying to come to terms with what one might think of as the mature realization that rationality, though vital to human understanding, is constrained in ways which the early modern and ancient philosophers could not imagine. In trying to understand these constraints, contemporary philosophers are no less keen than their predecessors on harnessing the power of rational argument to develop human understanding.

American and British thinkers, often following in the empiricist and pragmatic traditions, are also generally more sanguine about the limitations of reason. They seem more impressed by what rationality can do than worried by what it can't and are happy to live with a lack of certainty without too much hand-wringing about where that leaves rational method. So it should certainly not be thought that contemporary philosophy is universally characterized by a struggle to come to terms with the death of certainty. After all, some might say David Hume taught us how to live with that loss three centuries ago.

Returning to philosophy after the Greeks, for several centuries religious thought intermeshed with philosophy as the power of the church in western society grew. For several centuries after the Roman, Seneca, it is hard to find a philosopher who wasn't as much a theologian. Arguably, this suppressed philosophy, for if rational method is used in the service of religious belief, and must therefore take religious tenets as its founding principles, it cannot be philosophy, since philosophy must start by sweeping away the assumptions which underlie normal habits of thought. So although there is much of interest in the writings of Plotinus, Augustine, Aquinas, Duns Scotus and, in the Islamic world, Avicenna, philosophy proper does not fully emerge again until the middle of the second millennium CE with the emergence of renaissance humanism, exemplified in the person of Erasmus.

From this point onwards, philosophy began its second and most productive phase. Montaigne revived the ancient Greek tradition of secular writing on living the good life; Bacon outlined the basis of scientific method; Machiavelli and Hobbes began modern political philosophy, examining the roles of leaders and the state; Descartes reinvigorated the quest for certainty, and along the way distinguished mind and body in terms which have framed the debate to the present day; Locke's 'way of ideas' introduced the notion that all we are directly aware of is the contents of our minds, thus opening the door to both the modern problem of scepticism and Berkeley's idealism. All the major threads that continue to run in philosophy to this day were first picked up in the middle centuries of the last millennium.

However, western philosophy was not to remain a unified discipline. By the mid twentieth century, there would be distinctive 'continental' and 'Anglo-American' or 'analytic' schools in philosophy. The depth and nature of this division are much contested. Although the rift did not appear until much later, it is generally agreed that its origins can be traced back to Kant, perhaps the most important philosopher of the modern era.

Kant's philosophy is labyrinthine in its complexity, but at its heart is a strikingly simple idea, what he called his 'Copernican revolution in metaphysics'. This is the claim that philosophy up until his time had made the mistake of believing that it was the job of our concepts to conform to the nature of the world. The world provides the mould and we must cast our concepts to fit that mould as seamlessly as possible. Kant, however, claimed this was to get things precisely the wrong way around: it is the world that must conform to our concepts. It is the mind which is a kind of mould and the world only become intelligible to us to the extent that it can fit that mould.

This idea can seem bizarre, but it is not hard to make it sound more intuitively plausible. After all, our scientific understanding of the world has it made up of sub-atomic particles which are themselves perhaps best understood as energy. The world we actually see is simply the result of the fact that we are constituted to be sensitive to certain aspects of the world and to experience them in certain ways. So, for example, we hear some forms of radiation, see others and don't notice many others at all. The world 'as it is' is thus not what we perceive. Rather, we perceive a construction created by our own minds and bodies to which the world as it is makes a causal contribution.

Kant goes much further than this, however. His distinction is not between the world of appearances and the world revealed by science, but between the world as it appears to us, including as it appears through science, and the unknowable world as it is (the noumenal world). For example, he argued that time and space themselves are not part of the noumenal world but are aspects of our minds which frame experience and make it possible. Hence his Copernican revolution leaves the world in itself completely unknowable: even science is about the world as experience, not as it really is.

Kant died in 1804, at least a hundred years before the continental/ analytic divide became a reality. But many believe that the divide is rooted in differing responses to Kant. In France and Germany in particular, the dominant school in twentieth-century philosophy was phenomenology. Phenomenology has its roots in Dilthey and Brentano, but its first great thinker was Husserl. If Kant was right and it is our minds which make the world and not vice versa, then shouldn't philosophy's primary subject be consciousness and the role it plays in world-making? This is the kind of thinking that motivated phenomenology. Philosophy should turn its attention inward to consciousness, not outward towards the world. This is the basic methodological premise that would guide the work of many of Germany's and France's great thinkers in the years to come, such as Heidegger, Sartre and Beauvoir. It is also implicit in the work of the many philosophers who have used psychoanalysis in their philosophizing, such as Lacan, Deleuze and Cixous.

This route was generally resisted in Britain and America. Like the continentals, and partly in response to Kant, they too tended to turn away from the idea that the world in itself should be the object of philosophy. But the nature of conscious experience seemed to provide too opaque a basis for rigorous philosophical thinking, and instead attention turned to the two main structures of abstract thought: language and logic. This seemed to be a way of heeding Kant's warnings about the futility of probing into the world in itself without robbing philosophy of a clear, systematizable subject matter.

Versions of this story are still in circulation. To recap: the claim is that the continental/analytic divide is rooted in different responses to Kant, which, at the turn of the nineteenth and twentieth centuries, led to a logical-linguistic turn in Anglo-American philosophy and a phenomenological turn in continental Europe. These responses to Kant fostered different styles of philosophizing: logical analysis in Britain and America and a more literary, impressionistic attempt to capture the nature of lived experience in continental Europe.

The story, however, doesn't stand up to close scrutiny. It is rooted in truth, but it grossly overstates the importance of logical analysis in Anglo-American philosophy and understates it in continental Europe. But perhaps most importantly it fails to account for the fact that in recent western philosophy as a whole there has been a common concern with language. If one looks at the late nineteenth- and twentieth-century thinkers in this volume who have dealt with the nature of language and meaning, the names straddle the Atlantic and the English Channel: Frege, Saussure, Russell, Wittgenstein, Lacan, Quine, Ayer, Davidson, Deleuze, Derrida, Searle, Cixous, Kripke.

This common concern with language has certainly not led to much of a dialogue between philosophers who, on the one hand, mainly read French and German authors and, on the other, mainly read works of Britons and Americans. But the idea that the sociological divide is wider than any philosophical one is gaining ground. Michael Dummett, for example, a leading 'hard-nosed' analytic philosopher of language, draws on Husserl as readily as he does Russell. Jacques Derrida, a paradigmatically 'continental' thinker, has drawn on the works of the quintessentially Oxford philosopher J. L. Austin. One of the contributors to this volume, Christopher Norris, is as happy discussing Saussure as he is Quine. Another, Jaroslav Peregin, has written a book outlining the similarities between French structuralism and American linguistic holism.

This is not to claim there are no real divisions in philosophy that correspond roughly to certain geographical borders. Psychoanalysis is a bona fide philosophical tool in much of continental Europe. For analytic philosophers, Freud and his heirs are *persona non grata*. Political philosophy is a branch of analytic philosophy, whereas in continental Europe it is more accurate to say the philosophical is political. Analytic philosophy of mind is as marginal in 'continental' philosophy as phenomenology is in analytic departments. Readers of this volume will almost certainly detect differences in approach between analytic and continental philosophers. But it is perhaps not too optimistic to still see these differences as eddies and tides within the one discipline – philosophy – and not as two different oceans. That this volume includes continental and analytic philosophers, and yet still has some coherence, is testimony to that hope.

Theory of Knowledge
In addition to a chronological index in Appendix A, we also provide nine thematic guides in Appendix B. These suggest recommended routes through selected entries for those wishing to gain an overview of each theme and how it has developed through the history of philosophy. It

should be stressed that this is a tool designed for the specific content of this volume and in no way should the guides be taken as authoritative lists of the top thinkers in each topic area.

The first such theme is the theory of knowledge (epistemology). This is arguably about the most fundamental philosophical question of all: what is knowledge and can we ever have it? As we saw in the historical overview, the Ancient Greeks were already divided between those who thought knowledge required certainty and that it was attainable (such as Socrates and Plato) and those who took a more pragmatic view (such as Aristotle).

One division which has run though this debate is between those thinkers who have argued that reason acting independently could be a source of knowledge (rationalists) and those who thought all knowledge had to be derived from experience (empiricists). Modern empiricism began with Bacon and was developed though the writings of Locke and Hume. The great rationalist hero was Descartes, who was followed by Spinoza and Leibniz.

Kant occupies a more difficult to locate middle ground. He followed the rationalists in insisting that the mind itself gives form to experience and thus it is by studying the operations of the intellect that we understand the basic forms of experience, such as time and space, which make knowledge possible. But he also follows the empiricists by arguing that the only world we can know is the one given to us by experience. The world in itself is beyond our comprehension.

Just as philosophers have envied the precision of mathematics and sought to model philosophy on its methods, so more recently have many in the empiricist tradition come to see science as providing the proper model for knowledge. In this spirit Comte introduced positivism to modern philosophy: the view that the only statements that can be held to be true are those which can be verified by experience. Comte was followed by the Vienna Circle of logical positivists, which included Carnap, and it was a young A. J. Ayer who introduced the doctrines of the Circle to Britain and, ultimately, America.

A further important movement in epistemology is American pragmatism, as championed by Peirce, Dewey and James. Pragmatism circumvents the question of whether knowledge is of the world or not by insisting that to say 'I know x' is really to say that believing x allows one to be successful in predicting or manipulating the world. For the pragmatists, it is futile to worry about whether or not knowledge can be certain or whether what we claim to know accurately represents the world as it is. We should simply content ourselves with what works. Pragmatism has been a strong influence in American philosophy ever since and can be seen in the work of Quine, Putnam and Rorty.

Metaphysics

The second big field in philosophy is metaphysics, which is no less grand than the study of the fundamental nature of being. Some of the most important metaphysical questions concern the nature of time, matter, causation and identity.

Pythagoras's early attempts at metaphysics look a little crude now and seem to be based more on speculation than sound reasoning. Aristotle's metaphysics too has aged, although his distinctions between the different types of causation are still useful when disentangling confusions that arise from claims that one thing caused another.

Perhaps the most ambitious metaphysician of all time was Spinoza. His masterwork, *Ethics*, proceeded in the manner of a geometric proof and provided a complete account of the nature of mind, matter, God and much else along the way. Although few now accept his overall system, much of his argument that mind and matter are really two aspects of the one substance continues to be of interest today.

Metaphysics is where you'll find some of philosophy's more exotic creations, among them idealism, first developed in detail by Bishop George Berkeley. Berkeley argued that the universe is essentially mental in nature and that there was no such thing as matter, if we took that to mean some non-mental substance that sustained being. Berkeley's view sounds like nonsense, but he argued it was common sense and there is still something invigorating about examining his careful arguments and considering their profound implications.

What some find so beguiling about metaphysics is also what makes some people so dismissive of it. Each of the great metaphysicians in this book – including Hegel, Schopenhauer, Bergson, Santayana – offers a complete system, a way of understanding the whole of being. This vast reach strikes many as being intellectually extravagant. Is it really possible for philosophical reasoning to justify a belief such as in the real existence of all possible worlds, as was claimed by perhaps the greatest recent metaphysician, David Lewis? Much as we might admire the ambition of such thinkers and exhilarate in following the arguments that lead them to such conclusions, the prevailing contemporary mood is to consider such adventures flights of fancy rather than credible descriptions of the nature of the world, despite a recent rebirth of interest in metaphysics

Moral Philosophy

The third core subject of philosophy, along with epistemology and meta-physics, is ethics, or moral philosophy. The question of how we should live has always been central to philosophy, and plays an important part in the philosophy of Plato and Aristotle. Indeed, moral philosophy has continued to be done within the framework established by the Ancient Greeks. Seneca's moral philosophy, for instance, is firmly in the tradition of the Stoics, who emphasized the maxim that it is not what happens to you but how you react that chiefly determines whether you live a contented or miserable life. This is a good example of how ethics in antiquity was centrally concerned with the question of how human life could flourish, not with delineating a set of rules and prohibitions for human conduct. Moral guidelines served the purpose of maximizing life's potential: they had no independent value.

One enduring question in ethics has been the relationship between reason and morality. Is right conduct a demand of rationality? Hume argued that it was not. Rather, our emotions are what motivate action, including kind action, and reason's job is merely to calculate the means and work through the consequences. As he put it, 'Reason is, and ought only to be, the slave to the passions.' Many have found this 'emotivism' disturbing, since to base morality on nothing more than human feeling seems to give ethics too fragile a foundation. But the view continues to have many adherents.

Perhaps the most influential moral theory of the last two hundred years is utilitarianism. Utilitarianism comes in various versions, but all have in common the view that actions are right in so far as they have consequences which improve the lot of human beings (and sometimes also other sentient creatures) and wrong in so far as they make their situation worse. Bentham is the founder of utilitarianism, Mill did the most to popularize and develop it, Sidgwick provided perhaps the most intellectually complete account of it and Peter Singer, in the last thirty years, has vigorously applied it to issues of life, death and animal welfare.

But perhaps the most important development in modern ethics has not been any positive moral theory at all, but the spread of moral scepticism. Here, Nietzsche stands out as the most important influence. Nietzsche questioned the whole idea of morality, arguing that we operate within the framework of Christian ethics, which really only keeps us all in our place rather than helping us to maximize our potential. He argued that we should slough off the yoke of traditional morality altogether. Yet it is far too crude to say this makes him anti-ethics. Indeed, in many ways he is arguing for a return to the Ancient Greek idea of ethics as a guide to human flourishing.

After Nietzsche ethics certainly did not come to an end. G. E. Moore made one of the most important theoretical contributions to ethics in history when he argued that 'the good' can never be analysed in terms of other, non-moral concepts. His views presented a challenge to those who think that morality is about what is 'natural' or 'conducive to happiness'.

During the last century, however, there was some concern that moral philosophy had become too detached from the experience of lived life. Such a criticism could not be directed at Gandhi, who showed it was possible to meld moral theory and moral engagement.

In continental Europe, ethics has been more integrated with philosophy as a whole and doesn't have the same autonomy as it does in the Anglo-American world. Nowhere is this more evident than in the work of Levinas, who argued that morality is at the heart of all philosophy, and that the traditional western philosophical desire for a total system is morally as well as intellectually flawed.

Political Philosophy

Political philosophy could not have got off to a more ambitious start than with Plato's *Republic*: an attempt to describe, or prescribe, the perfect state. Although the *Republic* is a brilliant work, in many ways it manifests all the ways in which political philosophy can go wrong. It starts with a *tabula rasa*, rather than the world as it existed at the time, and we know now from bitter experience what happens when leaders think they can build society anew from a 'year zero'. It entrusts power to a protected élite – the philosopher-kings – and as Lord Acton said, 'Power tends to corrupt, and absolute power corrupts absolutely.' And the template is a product of theoretical discourse, not an engagement with the messy realities of the world, and we know what happens when ideology drives policy.

A much more worldly political philosopher than Plato is Machiavelli. Perhaps too worldly, for his pragmatism has struck many as at least amoral and perhaps even immoral. The idealism of Plato and the brutal realism of Machiavelli thus stand as polar opposites, between which all other political philosophy can be located.

Hobbes shared Machiavelli's bleak view of human nature, but also some of Plato's ambition to describe a complete state. Like Hobbes, Rousseau took as his starting point how human beings would behave in an unregulated state of nature. But unlike Hobbes, Rousseau thought that the situation of the 'noble savage' was one of bliss, albeit one we cannot now return to. Many have followed Hobbes and Rousseau in constructing their political philosophies in terms of an imaginary contract between citizen and state. Most recently, Rawls rewrote the social contract to provide a justification for liberal social democracy. Rawls is the most eminent of recent political philosophers in the Anglo-American world, whose closest challenger is Nozick, an advocate of a minimal state libertarianism which chimes with the view many Americans in particular have of their country as the home of liberty.

Many political philosophers have been involved in actual as well as theoretical philosophy. Paine was one of the intellectual forces behind the American revolution and that country's subsequent constitution. Bentham was a leading social reformer in the late eighteenth and early nineteenth centuries. Marx inspired the world's biggest ever revolutionary movement, although the extent to which the various communist regimes actually implemented his ideas is contended. And Gandhi led Indian resistance to British imperial rule in a movement of non-violent protest that has been an inspiration in a century of bloody conflict.

Political philosophy has also been a part of public intellectual life in continental Europe. Adorno was an early pioneer in the Frankfurt school, whose 'critical theory' has become an integral part of political discourse, especially in Germany, where Habermas continues the tradition.

Foucault's once revolutionary dissection of the uses of power by means of language and social practice has also become, in diluted form at least, part of a set of common assumptions among educated citizens who are on constant guard against manipulation by their political leaders.

Philosophy of Religion

The great philosophers of religion can be divided between the apologists and the natural theologians. Apologists start from a belief in God and attempt to reconcile that belief with the demands and challenges of reason. Belief in God is not demanded by reason, but is consistent with it. The natural theologians attempt to demonstrate that God must exist using standard techniques of philosophical argumentation. The division is neat; the problem is in applying it.

Augustine and Avicenna, for example, both present arguments for the existence of God. But it is not clear that these are self-standing. Rather, they seem to serve as rational supports for a belief that is fundamentally rooted not in reason but in experience.

Other philosophers are easier to classify. Duns Scotus, Schelling and Spinoza were natural theologians, although none of them supported orthodox religious creeds. Butler and Pascal, on the other hand, were apologists. Pascal derided the traditional arguments for the existence of God while maintaining that reason could be used in the service of faith.

The middle position is occupied by thinkers such as Vico and Santayana, who emphasized the limits of reason to reach any kind of understanding of the fundamental nature of reality. On this view, belief in God is not some special area of human knowledge that lies outside the scope of rationality. Rather, rationality always sells us short, and so we are obliged to rely on non-rational sources, such as faith, conviction or instinct, to resolve questions of ultimate reality. This kind of approach is also found in James's pragmatism and Kierkegaard's existentialism.

Phenomenology

Phenomenology is probably the most important movement in modern French and German philosophy. Two vital precursors to phenomenology proper are Dilthey and Brentano. Dilthey's concept of the 'objective mind' anticipated the phenomenological concern with conscious experience as the locus for understanding both human nature and the world we inhabit. Brentano's concept of 'intentionality' was also to play a crucial role in the phenomenologists' conception of the relationship between mind and world. Mind is intentional in Brentano's sense because it is the nature of conscious experience to be *of* something. This essential link between mind and what it is aware of is crucial to motivating the phenomenological project of making the study of conscious experience central to philosophy.

Phenomenology proper begins with Husserl, who undertook a project, in the spirit of Descartes, to cast aside all the assumptions we make when we speak of the world and talk only of that of which we have certain knowledge: our own conscious experience. Only then can we reconstruct what it means to say, for example, that an object such as a chair exists, when evidently all we can be sure of is that we see a chair.

In very different ways, Bergson and Heidegger added an emphasis on our experience of time as being central to how we experience ourselves and the world. Merleau-Ponty added to the lengthening list of factors critical to phenomenological analysis our sense of being embodied.

Phenomenology also played an important part in French existential-ism. For example, Sartre's conception of the individual consciousness as being permanently detached from the world of things, and therefore absolutely free, is based at root on a radical reworking of the notion of intentionality. And Beauvoir, in much of her work, was interested in how individual consciousnesses confront each other in the social world, a common theme in the writings of phenomenologists, and indeed one which stretches back at least as far as Hegel.

Philosophy of Mind

Phenomenology can be seen as a form of philosophy of mind. Yet what is called the 'philosophy of mind' in British and American universities is quite different.

Contemporary philosophy of mind has its roots in Descartes, who argued that mind and body must be two distinct substances – a theory known as dualism. But while there seem to be good reasons for thinking that body and mind aren't the same thing, there are huge problems in thinking of them as distinct. In particular, how can mind and body interact, which they surely do, if they are two totally different kinds of substance?

Spinoza thought he had the answer: mind and body aren't two substances at all. They are simply two aspects of the same substance. Ryle's solution was that Descartes had simply thought about the problem in the wrong terms. Mind and body are different, but not different substances. It makes sense to think of body as a kind of substance, but mind is not a thing. Rather, we say something has a mind when it is able to do certain things.

Ryle's thesis raises the question of what mind is anyway. Perhaps the problem with the mind/body problem is that we don't have a good grip on what mind is. As we have seen, Brentano thinks that the characteristic feature of mind is that it is directed at objects other than itself. Dennett took up this idea, arguing that this isn't so much a truth about minds as a truth about how we view agents with minds. We say something is conscious if it is fruitful to think of it as being an intentional system. Nagel has argued that what distinguishes conscious from nonconscious beings is that there is something it is like to be conscious, whereas there is nothing it is like to be, say, a rock.

The question of what makes something conscious is becoming more pressing as we anticipate the possibility of artificial intelligence. Turing argued that any machine that was able to respond to interrogation in the same or a similar way as a human would have to be thought of as conscious. Since we cannot ever enter the mind of another person, we would have to give such a machine the same benefit of the doubt as we do other people, who we only think of as conscious on the basis of how they behave.

Against this view, Searle has argued that a merely computational device, one that simply processes information according to rules, can never have understanding, a thesis he defends with his famous Chinese room argument.

The mind-body problem is very much alive in contemporary philosophy. Two extremes of the debate are represented by Churchland and Putnam. Churchland has consistently held the straightforward and unfashionable view that there is no more to minds than brains. Putnam, on the other hand, has altered his view over the years, and represents the kind of philosopher for whom no simple answer to the mind-body problem is available but who believes it is worth trying to understand consciousness as clearly as possible anyway.

Philosophy of Language

In Britain, America and continental Europe, the last hundred years or so have been marked by a 'linguistic turn': an increased preoccupation with seeing language as central to philosophical understanding. The turn probably began with Frege, whose famous distinction between the sense of a word (roughly, its meaning) and its reference (roughly, the thing it refers to) has framed debates in the philosophy of language ever since.

Sense and reference was but the first of a whole series of distinctions that would come to be made in the field. Saussure, for example, distinguished between signifiers (word) and signified (concept). Russell distinguished between descriptions (such as 'the capital of France') and the proper nouns which are really just shorthands for them (such as 'Paris'). Wittgenstein introduced the idea that meaning is given by the way in which a word is used, rather than by some mental picture, which his earlier philosophy postulated. Ryle came up with the notion of a 'category mistake', which is what happens when, for example, we mistake a way of *doing* something for a something: for example, when we think of team-spirit not as a way of pulling together, but as some kind of ghostly presence. And Kripke coined the term 'rigid designator' to explain how certain words have their meanings fixed by what they are invented to name, even though our understanding of what those things are can change radically over time.

As the philosophy of language developed, many philosophers began to come round to the view that language provides a kind of framework within which all understanding is located, and that there is no way to get behind language to conceptualize the world 'as it is'. Quine's 'semantic holism' is part of this broad approach. Lacan is also of the same spirit, but for him this has a political dimension, since language provides the 'symbolic order' which can restrict our thoughts and help maintain the status quo. For Lacan, language limits us, but we must fight against the limits of language.

Chomsky also saw a political dimension in his highly technical linguistics. His thesis that the basic structures of language are innate is a challenge to those behaviourists who think that the human mind is essentially a blank slate that can be 'programmed' by society as it sees fit, a view which opens the door to frightening possibilities of social control.

But perhaps the philosopher whose work on language has been most famous, or notorious, is Jacques Derrida. His idea of deconstruction – not quite a theory, nor a method – infuriates and enthrals in equal measure, with people tending to line up either as ardent admirers or as critics who accuse him of obscurantism. Yet few philosophers, if any, have had such an influence across the humanities and social sciences as Derrida, for better or for worse.

Philosophy and Science

The relationship between philosophy and science is itself the subject of much philosophizing. As the historical overview earlier suggests, they share a common origin, in that both were made possible by the acceptance that the universe can be understood by means of rational enquiry.

Indeed, for many years there was no distinction between philosophers and scientists; and scientists continued to be known as natural philosophers until only a few centuries ago. Thinkers like Descartes and Leibniz also undertook scientific investigations.

Scientific method has been a subject for philosophy since Bacon described empiricism: the means of forming scientific hypotheses on the basis of experimentation and observation. Comte went further and argued that claims which could not be supported by experimentation or observation were not even worthy of serious consideration. Carnap and Popper worked very much in the tradition of Comte's positivism, while Peirce also privileged the scientific viewpoint as providing the model and yardstick for proper knowledge.

Yet the most widely-read modern theorist of scientific method is much more sceptical about the status of scientific knowledge. Kuhn is a debunker of the myth of science as making steady, continuous progress. Rather, he argues that science works within certain 'paradigms' – temporary frameworks of assumptions and core tenets within which 'normal science' is done. But at key moments, these paradigms are shown to be inadequate to explain observable phenomena, or else reveal internal contradictions. Then the paradigm must change and a new era of different normal science begins.

Two scientists have also had a profound influence not just on philosophy, but on the whole of western thought. Darwin's theory of evolution has changed people's thinking in just about every area of philosophy. Ethics, political philosophy, epistemology, philosophy of mind, philosophy of religion – all have at least to take account of Darwin's powerful thesis, probably the most potent idea in human history.

Einstein's theory of relativity has had a more local impact, but no less a profound one. Certainly metaphysics, philosophy of mind and epistemology have felt its shockwaves.

There are then many ways of reading this book, in whole or in part. Its one hundred pieces are like parts of a jigsaw puzzle that can be put together in different ways to reveal very different shapes and patterns. This is fitting, for the history of philosophy is extremely rich and there are many stories to be told about it, not just one, nor just the ten we have sketched in this introduction. These great thinkers can be seen as one hundred characters in search of an author. See what stories you can find to tell about them.

Theodor Adorno

1903–1969   Jack Furlong

A critic of modern jazz, a key theoretician of the left and a leader in the most celebrated academic institute of the last century, Theodor Weisengrund Adorno combined the intense speculative focus of a German academic with the feel for the concrete of a French aesthete. Along the way, he also unwittingly became a model – and a foil – for Anglo-American culture critics.

As a teenager, Adorno spent many Saturday afternoons poring over **Immanuel Kant**'s *Critique of Pure Reason* with Siegfried Kracauer, who encouraged him to read philosophy in its socio historical context and to apply philosophical and sociological tools to understand such cultural artefacts as film. Not surprisingly, as an undergraduate, he applied himself to philosophy, psychology and sociology and, after spending three years studying music in Vienna with avant-garde composers, he completed his doctoral degree requirements and began writing. His work over the span of forty years never lost the connectivity of art, philosophy and cultural criticism that so enthralled him in his early reading of Kant with Kracauer.

Adorno wrote most of his mature works under the aegis of the celebrated Institute for Social Research. He officially joined in 1938, but his relationship with its guiding spirit and founder, Max Horkheimer, began in the 1920s when they took courses together. Along with several others, they began a collaborative research programme within the Institute called the Frankfurt School of Critical Theory. Under Horkheimer and Adorno, the school dedicated itself to producing research characterized by the systematic rejection of closed philosophical and political systems, and a commitment to ongoing study and criticism of current oppressive sociopolitical structures. Less interested in **Marx**'s reductionist critique of capitalism than traditional Marxists, the Frankfurt School sought to expand his criticisms of bourgeois culture. Less preoccupied with praxis (revolutionary action) than with theoretical insight into oppressive structures and processes, the school was often charged by more orthodox Marxists with élitism and passivity. This accent on culture and the charge of élitism have marked Adorno's career.

Adorno would put himself in the same group as **Hegel**, Marx and others who used the form of argumentation known as dialectics to unmask the hypocrisies and absurdities of the political and social status quo. Contemporary bourgeois life requires that all of its aspects be controlled – the statehouse, the family, the church, the airwaves, the marketplace. This 'administered world' needs homogenized certainties, concepts taken for granted unfailingly, in order to maintain total control. Hence, says Adorno, modern regimes 'reify' – make into a thing – and quantify what cannot be fashioned into permanent concepts and identities, but which nonetheless prove useful to those who rule. For Adorno, the most tragic manifestation of this 'administered world' was the Holocaust, in which even human beings themselves were 'reified' – counted, recorded and, eventually, 'consumed'.

Dominating regimes must run according to political theories made of clear, determined concepts and predictable logic – a closed system. Philosophy for Adorno contests this desire for conceptual and systematic finality, for philosophical concepts resist their own closure. So understood, philosophy is dialectics, or 'thought driven by its own insufficiency.' The identical gets its wholeness only through the non-identical; the universal only through particulars. 'Thought as such,' Adorno maintains, 'is an act of negation, of resistance to that which is forced upon it.' Philosophy must constantly criticize itself, preventing the negative energy of thinking from getting short-circuited by conformity.

Art, too, like philosophy, can liberate people from the claustrophobia of power. 'Works of art,' states Adorno, 'are . . . social products which have discarded the illusion of being-for-society, an illusion tendentiously maintained by all other commodities.' To the extent that art gives people what they expect, it becomes a commodity.

This theme appears vividly in Adorno's best-known book, *Dialectic of Enlightenment* (1947), co-authored by Horkheimer. The authors first describe how the Enlightenment concept of reason became an efficient tool for social and political administrations to ensure the compliance of the administered at all levels of discourse and practice. 'Through the countless agencies of mass production and its culture the conventionalised modes of behaviour are impressed on the individual as the only natural, respectable, and rational ones. He defines himself only as a thing.' Even art becomes commodified, an example of 'instrumental reason', producing what the authors call 'the culture industry'.

Though written in the 1940s this critique has not lost its relevance: speaking about what they saw as a growing monopoly, Adorno and Horkheimer claimed that 'Movies and radio need no longer pretend to be art. The truth that they are just business is made into an ideology in order to justify the rubbish they deliberately produce.' Widely anthologized, this chapter on the culture industry has inspired and guided the relatively new field of culture studies in the social sciences and humanities.

In the last year of his life, Adorno became embattled with radical students, and charges of élitism unfortunately made his last few months stressful. Yet Adorno's reputation survived to the extent that, currently, he is often claimed as a precursor to postmodern and post-structuralist thought.

Suggested reading
Adorno, T. 1991. *The Culture Industry: Selected essays on mass culture.* London: Routledge.
O'Connor, B. 2000 (ed.). *The Adorno Reader.* Oxford: Blackwell.
Horkheimer, M. & Adorno, T. W. 1976 [1947], *Dialectic of Enlightenment.* London: Continuum.

St Thomas Aquinas
1225–1274 Jon Phelan

St Thomas Aquinas was born into a noble family near the small town of Aquino which lies between Naples and Rome. He became a Dominican friar in 1244 and was a heavyweight scholar in both senses of the word. Weighing around twenty stone it is rumoured that this doctor of the church worked at a desk specially designed to fit around his corpulence. Despite a peripatetic life of preaching and teaching, Aquinas penned over two million words of in-depth theology, his best known works being the *Summa contra Gentiles* (1258–60) and the *Summa Theologiae* (1267–73). A *summa* (summary) was a comprehensive exposition of doctrine.

In these works faith and reason are harmonized into a grand theologico-philosophical system which inspired the medieval philosophical tradition known as Thomism and which has been favoured by the Roman Catholic church ever since. There are many areas of interest to philosophers in Aquinas' writings, such as his theory of knowledge, his analysis of causality, his writings on God (the 'five ways' and the doctrine of analogy) and his teleological theory of ethics.

Aquinas made an important contribution to epistemology (theory of knowledge), recognizing the central part played by sense perception in human cognition. It is through the senses that we first become acquainted with existent, material things. St Thomas held that the dependence objects have on something which transcends them is disclosed to the observer through the contemplation of material things. Just as our knowledge depends not on innate ideas but on perceiving the material world, the same material world is dependent on a productive agent for its existence. Aquinas thought the proposition 'everything which begins to exist through the agency of an already existent, extrinsic thing' to be a fact beyond doubt.

In the *Summa Theologiae*, Aquinas records his famous Five Ways which seek to prove the existence of God from the facts of change, causation, contingency, variation and purpose. These arguments can be neatly expressed in the form of 'syllogisms' as below:

Way 1
1. The world is in motion.
2. All changes in the world are due to some prior cause.
3. There must be a prior cause for this entire sequence of changes, i.e. God.

Way 2
1. The world is a sequence of events.
2. Every event in the world has a cause.
3. There must be a cause for the entire sequence of events, i.e. God.

Way 3
1. The world might not have been.
2. Everything that exists in the world depends on some other thing for its existence.
3. The world itself must depend upon some other thing for its existence, i.e. God.

Way 4
1. There are degrees of perfection in the world.
2. Things are more perfect the closer they approach the maximum.
3. There is a maximum perfection, i.e. God.

Way 5
1. Each body has a natural tendency towards its goal.
2. All order requires a designer.
3. This end-directedness of natural bodies must have a designing force behind it. Therefore each natural body has a designer, i.e. God.

Aquinas devotes a further part of his philosophical writing to the problem of religious language. He accepts that God-talk may be literal or metaphorical but believes that in its literalness it is never univocal or equivocal, but rather analogical. That is to say, a phrase such as 'God is omnipotent, omniscient and compassionate' represents a relation between what we mean by these terms and the divine nature. God's nature corresponds to and is in ratio with these terms, yet is still literal in that it reveals to us something about God.

Unlike some of his contempories, Aquinas was sympathetic towards and influenced by **Aristotle**, whom he customarily refers to as 'the philosopher'. In a similar vein to Aristotle, Aquinas formulates a teleological theory of ethics (one that explains ethics in terms of its aim or goal) known as Natural Law.

Aquinas assumes that God created the world, that the world reveals his purpose and that the fulfilment of that purpose is the supreme good to be sought: '[Natural law] is the participation of the human person in the divine law of God.' Elsewhere he declares that Natural Law is 'nothing other than the light of understanding infused in us by God whereby we see what is to be done and what is not to be done'. This exercising of rational conscience has been at the forefront of Roman Catholic teaching for centuries, though it is not the sum total of it.

Aquinas' theory of ethics, his writings on God and other metaphysical issues provide a unique contribution to philosophical thought and led Anthony Kenny to call him 'one of the dozen greatest philosophers of the western world'.

Suggested reading

Aquinas, T. 1998. *Selected Philosophical Writings*. Oxford: Oxford Paperbacks.

Copleston, F. C. 1991. *Aquinas. An Introduction to the Life and Work of the Great Medieval Thinker*. Harmondsworth: Penguin.

Kenny, A. 1979. *Aquinas*. Oxford: Oxford University Press.

Hannah Arendt

1906–1975 **William W. Clohesy**

Hannah Arendt is widely recognised as among the most original and profound political thinkers of the twentieth century as well as one of the most controversial. Arendt produced no systematic political theory but dealt with a series of interrelated topics including totalitarianism, the public and private realms, the structure of public action, and the modern loss of the public realm of politics through preoccupation with economic well-being. Arendt's work is controversial because of her abstraction, examples, and startling observations and conclusions regarding recurring themes. Even her strongest defenders find much that needs qualification and revision in her work. Such controversy would have pleased Arendt, for she did not intend to found a school of thought with disciples, but to attempt to 'think what we are doing' in our public and private lives. Arendt intended her work to stimulate further thought in others as it did in herself. The vast literature on Arendt is a tribute to her success at provoking others to think.

Arguably her most fundamental theme concerns human plurality and natality: humans are unique individuals with distinctive perspectives and potentials for action and with the birth of each person a new beginning enters the world. When people exchange opinions and decide how to act together so as to affect their common world, they generate the power whereby they begin something, and so display freedom. Arendt's thought is in great measure an examination of the ways in which plurality and initiative are supported or thwarted today.

The twentieth century saw numerous brutal attacks on individuality. Through depression, statelessness and war, a great mass of people found themselves superfluous: displaced, lonely and vilified. Arendt, as a

German Jew, knew superfluity first-hand. Born in 1906 to a German Jewish family, Arendt studied with the eminent philosophers **Martin Heidegger** and Karl Jaspers, and wrote her dissertation on **Augustine**'s concept of love under Jaspers' direction. Threatened by the rise of National Socialism, Arendt fled Germany for Paris in 1933. With the fall of Paris, she was briefly interned but escaped to the United States where she wrote and taught until her death in 1975.

In *The Origins of Totalitarianism* (1951), Arendt holds that Hitler's and Stalin's regimes are instances of a new form of government – totalitarianism – which differs from an older, superficially similar form – tyranny – the rule by one for his own sake at the expense of the populace. Totalitarianism is a social movement driven by a thoroughly developed, mythic ideology that offers to the masses of the displaced and lost the certainty of a thoroughgoing, consistent account of the world, rooted in race or class struggle. Ideologies offer the masses a refuge from the complex, confusing reality in which they can gain no footing because, in their loneliness, they lack interlocutors with whom to achieve a common perspective for thought and action. Totalitarian ideologies hold sway through terror that violently eliminates not only those who contest them, but those who hold them due to personal conviction, for conviction betrays the potential for criticism of the fiction. Terror in totalitarianism, by diminishing and subduing believers and destroying critics, creates supporters who have shed their legal rights and duties as citizens and their responsible freedom as moral agents. Totalitarianism seeks to destroy human individuality and ingenuity by rendering humans an animal species whose members are no more than specimens. Totalitarianism manifests evil by fostering unthinking obedience in banal, utterly predictable believers who serve as bureaucratic cogs in a machine of terror eradicating the humanity of everyone – including the rulers.

Arendt's discovery of totalitarianism's threat to human individuality leads her to articulate the meaning of individuality and ingenuity, above all in political action. Arendt pursued these matters systematically in *The Human Condition* (1958). Humans live biologically in the cycles of daily metabolism and of birth, reproduction and death. Humans also live as individuals because they achieve identities through actions, words and deeds done before others, and their lives form narratives for those who witness them. In politics individuals shine forth through their public actions for their polity.

Arendt draws several crucial distinctions traceable to ancient Athens for understanding politics. People inhabit both a private realm as family members, where economic activities maintain life, and a public realm where they speak and act together as citizens. Human activity has three forms: labour – producing what must be consumed for life, such as food or wages; work – making enduring objects; and action – intervening in the flow of events, by which citizens display freedom and courage by facing their world's challenges. Arendt warns that, ever since the rise of market society, work and especially labour have dominated life with a corresponding eclipse of action, so that politics, even in democracies, is inexorably changing into economic administration while the shared public world, the space for action whereby individuals can appear, threatens to vanish.

Suggested reading

Arendt, H. 1973 [1951]. *The Origins of Totalitarianism*. San Diego: Harvest.
Arendt, H. 1998 [1958]. *The Human Condition*. Chicago: University of Chicago Press.
Baehr, P. 2003. (ed.) *The Portable Hannah Arendt*. Harmondsworth: Penguin.

Aristotle
384–322 BCE   **Rosalind Rawnsley**

Aristotle was one of the world's greatest thinkers, whose profound influence on western philosophy and philosophical terminology continues to this day. Born in Stagira, at that time in Macedonia, in 384 BCE, the son of a doctor who was physician to the Royal Family, he studied for 20 years at **Plato**'s Academy in Athens, before being invited by King Philip II of Macedon to become tutor to his son Alexander ('the Great').

Returning to Athens in 335 BCE, Aristotle founded his own philosophical school, the Lyceum, and his surviving works are considered to be his lecture notes, collected and edited by his pupils and others during the centuries after his death. His best known philosophical works are the *Metaphysics*, *de Anima* (on the Soul), *Politics*, and *Ethics*. Aristotle's interests did not however end with philosophy – he wrote extensively on topics as diverse as education, psychology, grammar and linguistics, and on different aspects of science, particularly biology, and he put forward a cosmology to explain the movements of the heavenly bodies which was not superseded until Ptolemy. But as Jonathan Barnes points out, Aristotle has not always had a good press. Because his works were never edited for publication as connected narratives, Aristotle is difficult to read. Perhaps partly for this reason, since antiquity his writings have been the subject of endless critical analysis and comment, a process still gathering momentum at the beginning of the twenty-first century.

Aristotle's writings (the *Nicomachean* and *Eudemian Ethics* in particular) inspired **St Thomas Aquinas**, who in his great work *Summa Theologiae* set out to reconcile Aristotle's system of logic and natural law with the Christian worldview and, through Aquinas, the pagan Aristotle can be seen to have influenced Roman Catholic theology through the centuries to the present day.

In the *Metaphysics* Aristotle is concerned to discover the first principles or causes of things (*arche*). The true essence of a thing consists in its function rather than in the matter of which it is made. With this principle in mind, as a biologist, Aristotle was primarily interested in discovering how things are as they are, rather than why they exist as they do. Rejecting Plato's theory of forms or ideas, he considered that a thing which does not physically exist cannot in any coherent sense be susceptible to discussion. His scientific works are thus attempts, grounded in empirical observation, to account for phenomena.

However, as scientists are still inclined to do, Aristotle was not above selecting evidence to fit his pre-existing pet theories. Nonetheless, Aristotle was a meticulous observer of the natural world and some of his recorded observations of fish and other sea creatures were not subsequently rediscovered and proved until the middle of the nineteenth century. His taxonomy of plants and animals anticipates that of Linnaeus.

His two ethical treatises are fundamentally enquiries into how the individual may best achieve a good life. Such a life, Aristotle considers, cannot be lived in isolation, but only in the context of society or the *polis*. This being the case, the *Politics* considers what type of society or *polis* will best enable the individual to live a good or moral life, rather than what might be the duty of the individual towards the state as a discrete entity, as in modern political theory. Aristotle thinks of his political treatise as being of practical use to actual legislators, rather than simply as a blueprint for the ideal state. As a pragmatist he therefore considers what type of constitution would work best given the existing constraints of his place and time. The claimed interdependence of master and slave, discussed at length early in *Politics*, gets Aristotle onto difficult ground, and he fails to justify slavery as it was practised in the ancient world. In later 'books' of *Politics*, Aristotle suggests the form of an educational system for the ideal *polis* and criticizes the hypothetical 'ideal' state, as postulated by Plato.

Finally, Aristotle may be safely claimed as the founder of the science of logic, and his writings on this subject (*Prior* and *Posterior Analytics*, *Topics*, *On Sophistical Refutations*, among others) had a profound influence on medieval Islamic and European thought for two thousand years. 'Logic' was to all intents and purposes synonymous with Aristotelian logic. Aristotle identifies two types of argument. The first is what today would be called a 'valid' argument, in which the conclusion is necessarily drawn from the premises. For example:

All philosophers are human beings.
Aristotle is a philosopher.
Therefore Aristotle is a human being.

The second is the argument from induction, or drawing a general claim from a number of instances. For example:

My cat Tolstoy has whiskers.
Aristotle's cat Alexander had whiskers.
Dr. Johnson's cat had whiskers.
Therefore all cats have whiskers.

The uses of argument are discussed in *Posterior Analytics*, and one conclusion that Aristotle draws is that scientific knowledge can only be knowledge of causes. This brings his theory full circle to his preoccupation with the *arche* or first principle of all things.

Suggested reading
Aristotle. 1986. *De Anima (On the Soul)*. Harmondsworth: Penguin.
Aristotle. 1976. *The Nichomachean Ethics*. Harmondsworth: Penguin.
Barnes, J. 1995. (ed.) *The Cambridge Companion to Aristotle*. Cambridge: Cambridge University Press.

St Augustine of Hippo

354–430   Robin Wood

Augustine can be considered as the last great figure of the ancient world and the first of the medieval. He was at once a philosopher, a theologian and a Christian bishop involved in the day-to-day practical affairs of church administration. He was a prolific writer and it would be difficult to overestimate his influence upon Western Christendom, both for good and ill. On the positive side, he emphasized the sheer grace of God freely offered to human beings and the essential goodness of creation, but on the negative there is a darker picture concerning arbitrary predestination and a less-than-healthy attitude to sex and the body. This was perhaps due to the fact that the three determining influences in his life – Manichaeism, Neo-Platonism, and Christian orthodoxy – were never fully reconciled in his mind.

Augustine was born at Thagaste in Numidia. His mother Monica was a devout Christian whose beliefs left a deep impression on her son. He taught rhetoric successively at Thagaste, Carthage, Rome, and Milan and for nine or ten years embraced the philosophy of the Manichees with their sharp dualistic outlook on good and evil. This was when he was between 19 and 29, although it left an enduring mark on his thought. He was also greatly influenced by 'certain books of the Platonists', probably Latin translations of **Plotinus**'s *Enneads*, and Porphyry's *On the Retreat of the Soul*.

At Milan he came under the influence of Bishop Ambrose, and in Milan Cathedral at Easter, 387, after a long intellectual and moral struggle, in which he states that he was influenced by Cicero's *Hortensius*, he was baptized along with his friend Alypius. He then returned to Africa and became a priest, and in 395 Bishop of Hippo, which office he occupied until his death.

His conversion had a dramatic dimension. There was a child playing in the garden in Milan, saying 'Take and read, take and read'. The passage from the Bible that his eyes fell upon was Romans XIII, 13–14: 'Let us conduct ourselves becomingly as in the day, not in revelling and drunkenness, not in debauchery and licentiousness, not in quarrelling and jealousy. But put on the Lord Jesus Christ and make no provision for the flesh to gratify its desires.'

His treatises *De Immortalitate Animae* (*On the Immortality of the Soul*, 387) and *De Libero Arbitrio* (*The Free Choice of the Will*, 387–395) show his philosophical cast of mind. In the latter, he discusses the vexed question of free will and divine foreknowledge. After his appointment as bishop his writings became more theological and he was involved in disputes with the Manichees, Pelagian heretics, and the Donatist schismatics. During the latter part of his life, as well as being occupied with the Pelagians, who denied that human beings need God's grace in order to be good, he wrote two great works: the fifteen books of the *De Trinitate* (*On the Trinity*, 399–426) and the twenty-two books of the *De Civitate Dei* (*City of God*, 413–427). The former, with its concept of the divine quality of love binding the three persons of the Godhead together, still exercises a profound influence; and the latter, inspired by the fall of Rome in 410, when some blamed Christianity for the disaster, presents the concept of two cities, the city of the world whose citizens may prosper in this life but not afterwards, and the city of God whose citizens, even if they suffer in this life, are nevertheless ultimately vindicated by God.

Perhaps Augustine's best-known work is his *Confessions*, written (some thirteen years after his conversion) in the year 397, an acknowledged masterpiece of introspective autobiography in which he reveals, in the form of a long prayer to God, his own personal (and perhaps humanity's?) longing and restlessness for knowledge and experience of God. It contains his famous saying 'You [O God] have created us for yourself and our heart is restless till it finds its rest in you.' Another saying, perhaps not so well known but fundamental to Christian theology, is his assertion that in the writings of the Platonists he read many congenial things, 'but that the word was made flesh and dwelt among us, I read not there'.

All the evidence suggests that Augustine was a man of intense sensibility with a profound awareness of and trust in the God who comes in Christ. He is part of the living stream of the Christian tradition, and perhaps one of the continuing tasks for Christian philosophy is to discern and treasure what is enduring in his thought and to jettison some of its darker aspects.

Suggested reading

Augustine. 1998 [397]. *The Confessions*. Oxford: Oxford University Press.
Brown, P. 2000. *Augustine of Hippo* (revised edition). Berkeley: University of California Press.
Lancel, S. 2002. *St. Augustine*. London: SCM Press.

Avicenna
980–1037   Sajjad Rizvi

Abu 'Ali Husayn ibn Sina, better known in Europe as Avicenna, is arguably the most influential philosopher of the pre-modern era. Born near Bukhara in Central Asia, he is best known as a physician whose major work the *Canon* continued to be taught as a medical textbook in Europe and in the Islamic world until the early modern period, and as a philosopher whose major work the *Cure* had a decisive impact upon European scholasticism.

Avicenna is well known as the author of one of the most influential proofs for the existence of God. The argument runs as follows. Our perceptual experience of the world confirms that things exist, and that their existence is non-necessary because we notice that things come into existence and pass out of it. Existence that does not exist by virtue of itself cannot arise unless it is made necessary by a cause. A causal chain must culminate in one un-caused cause because one cannot posit an infinite series of causes. Therefore, the chain of existents which do not exist through themselves must culminate in and find its causal principle in a sole self-subsistent existent that is necessary. This, of course, is the same as the God of religion.

Avicenna's theory of knowledge was also highly influential. According to him, humans were not born with any innate knowledge of the world.

Humans attain knowledge and understanding through acquaintance with and experience of objects in the world. From those experiences, they abstract universal concepts. For example, you see a horse and note what properties and features it possesses. From this experience, you derive the concept of a horse and when you encounter another object with similar features, you recognize it to be a horse. More complex notions and knowledge require that you add together concepts abstracted in the mind to produce further concepts. Observations lead to the formulation of concepts; amalgamation of concepts leads to the formulation of more complex concepts. Take the example of the horse again. We can understand more complex concepts of a horse depending on, say, its uses or its colour, or its species.

The most important question which arises is, how can we verify that the concepts we have abstracted from our experiences are correct? How can we say that it is true that a horse is always an animal with four legs, for example? According to Avicenna, there are two ways of verifying our claims. First, we must correctly extrapolate concepts from our experiences and arrange those concepts in a form of argument which is valid in order to produce complex concepts. Second, we must guarantee that we are not mistaken in our experience and that our concept of a horse is indeed a valid concept. That guarantor must be independent of the ability of humans to make mistakes; it must be infallible and must transcend our experiences and our world, drawing its knowledge of things from their absolute source in a higher perfectly intelligible world, of which our world is a weak image. Avicenna calls this transcendent guarantor and source for human knowledge the 'Active Intellect'. This higher source illuminates the human mind and bestows upon it true knowledge through an act of conjunction whereby the human mind encounters the higher mind in episodes where it seeks verification of what it knows. As the Active Intellect is linked to the perfect knowledge of God, it is ultimately God who bestows true knowledge upon humans.

Avicenna's epistemology is predicated upon a theory of soul (or an inner essence that in modern parlance might be called a 'self') that is independent of the body and capable of abstraction. This proof for the soul in many ways prefigures the Cartesian *cogito* by some 600 years. It is the so-called 'flying man' argument or thought experiment. If a person were created in a perfect state, but blind and suspended in the air and unable to perceive anything through his senses, would he be able to affirm the existence of his soul? Suspended in such a state, he cannot affirm the existence of his body because he is not empirically aware of it, thus the argument may be seen as affirming the independence of the soul from the body. But in that state he cannot doubt that his soul exists because there is a subject that is thinking, thus the argument can be seen as an affirmation of the self-awareness of the soul. This argument does raise an objection, which may also be levelled at **Descartes**: how do we know that the knowing subject is the soul?

Avicenna's major achievement was to propound a systematic philosophical defence of religion rooted in the theological tenets of Islam, and its success can be gauged by the recourse to Avicennan ideas found in the subsequent history of philosophical theology in Islam. In the Latin West, his metaphysics and theory of the soul had a profound influence on scholastic arguments and, as in the Islamic East, were the basis for debate and argument until the early modern period.

Suggested reading
Goodman, L. E. 1992. *Avicenna*. London: Routledge.
Gutas, D. 1988. *Avicenna and the Aristotelian Tradition*. Leiden: Brill.
Street, A. D. 2004. *Avicenna*. Cambridge: The Islamic Texts Society.

A. J. Ayer
1910–1989   Jon Phelan

Will Ayer be remembered as a great thinker? In a moment of uncharacteristic humility during an interview on 27 April 1989, Alfred Jules Ayer cited himself in the first division of philosophers rather than the premiership. To judge whether this was a fair description we need to examine his main contributions to the subject.

Ayer was passionate about philosophy. His tour de force *Language, Truth and Logic* (1936), written when he was only twenty-four on the advice of confidant Isaiah Berlin, was a work of missionary zeal. It sought to rid philosophy of the metaphysical waffle that Ayer believed had plagued the subject since **Plato**. Ayer wished to give philosophy the same epistemic status and certainty as science, which he believed was the greatest achievement of the human intellect. Science was able to answer questions, whereas much of the philosophical enterprise concerning 'the meaning of life', aesthetics, ethics and religion seemed imprecise, indecisive and faintly ludicrous.

Like other members of his family, the young philosopher loved puzzles and crosswords. Crosswords had an answer that one could work out. It was unclear, however, whether many philosophical dilemmas had, or could ever have, a solution. In order to separate the wheat of meaningful philosophical issues from the chaff of nonsensical ones, Ayer devised the Principle of Verification, which says that a statement is meaningful if and only if it is true by definition or provable by experiment.

Propositions which are true by definition are logically necessary truths such as 'your mother's mother is your grandmother'. Empirically verifiable statements are ones that are provable by experiment. If one wished to prove whether magnesium burns with a white flame, for instance, there is an empirical procedure to follow in order to find out. The verification principle thus provides clear demarcation criteria to distinguish between sense and nonsense.

What raised the hackles of Ayer's contemporaries was that according to his methodology most religious, metaphysical and moral statements were judged factually meaningless. Ayer was called the most wicked man in Oxford. His moral philosophy became known as Emotivism because it claimed that moral language merely expressed the speaker's emotions or feelings. Thus if I were to say 'war is wrong', I would be giving vent to my personal distaste of war and nothing more. This non-cognitive, meta-ethical theory influenced Hare's prescriptivism and is an easy bedfellow of relativism and nihilism. Ayer and Hare agreed that ethical codes sought only to win approval from an audience.

Ayer championed epistemology (theory of knowledge), philosophy of language and the philosophy of science as worthwhile disciplines. He explained the proliferation of metaphysics by suggesting that its proponents had made a category mistake. While it is a useful shorthand to assign a catch-all description such as 'tree' to a collection of sense experiences, these descriptions do not exist as separate entities in their own right. Discrete sensory phenomena, which have been called the flashcards of experience and atoms of perception, are all there is and to believe that anything else has a real and separate existence is misguided.

Ayer's theory of perception is termed linguistic phenomenalism. Just as Ayer believed that all moral statements could be translated into statements concerned with emotions, he believed that all statements concerning perception could be translated into sentences made up of verifiable, discrete experiences of 'sense data'.

According to Ayer, the role of philosophy was to preside over the work of scientists and assist in matters of categorization and justification. Ayer's philosophy of science has been described as positivistic instrumentalism. Just as he rejected moral realism and perceptual realism, so he argued against the scientific realist position which claims that science discovers truths about reality. Instead, for Ayer, science works like a predictive machine that processes data and produces an accurate and useful output but whose content is essentially unknowable.

Philosophically, Ayer danced on the surfaces of things; in real life he danced the samba. He loved socializing and was reported as being a charismatic if slightly self-absorbed bon viveur. His academic career took him from Eton to Oxford where, after a spell in the British Intelligence Service during the Second World War, he became a fellow. Ayer revivified the philosophy department at University College London, lectured around the world and became Wykeham Professor of Logic at Oxford University in 1960.

But will he be remembered as a second-rate philosopher? Although he is credited as bringing the philosophical school known as logical positivism to Britain, his achievement is viewed by some as parochial. His main work *Language, Truth and Logic* was written with such youthful enthusiasm that it contains repetitive errors. Indeed, logical positivism seems to contain many flaws. In addition, Ayer drew so much on his philosophical heroes in the empiricist tradition – **Hume**, **Berkeley** and **Russell** – that one is hard pushed to specify his original contribution to the subject. The key tenets of his thought, however, still sound a resonance through the British analytic tradition to this day, where he continues to have many admirers.

Suggested reading
Ayer, A. J. 1936. *Language, Truth and Logic*. London: Victor Gollancz.
Ayer, A. J. 1981. *The Central Questions of Philosophy*, Harmondsworth: Penguin.
Macdonald, G. & Wright, C. 1986 (eds). *Fact, Science and Morality*, Oxford:
    Blackwell.

Francis Bacon

1561–1626   Jan Broadway

Francis Bacon owes his place in intellectual history to his exploration of the fundamental principles of scientific thought and his role in popularising experimental science. He gave the study of natural philosophy prestige through his literary ability and personal standing as a member of Jacobean England's ruling élite. He wrote well, which meant that his scientific works were widely read and admired, despite the judgement of James I on one of his books that it 'is like the peace of God, that passeth all understanding'.

The youngest son of Queen Elizabeth I's Lord Keeper and nephew to Lord Burghley, her chief minister, Bacon grew up at the heart of the political and intellectual establishment. A Cambridge student at the precocious age of 12, he was subsequently sent to France in the household of the English ambassador. Although he returned in 1579 on the death of his father and remained in England thereafter, this experience and his contacts from an early age with well-travelled courtiers made Bacon less insular than the majority of his English contemporaries. He completed his education for a career in public service by studying common law at Gray's Inn. Throughout his life Bacon was engaged in politics and the practical affairs of government and he eventually became Lord Chancellor. His writings on natural philosophy formed only part of his literary output, which also encompassed history, law and moral essays. His attempt to forge a new philosophy which would lead to an understanding of how the world worked – a project he called the Great Instauration or Renewal – was conducted against this background and unsurprisingly was never completed.

Denied by Elizabeth I the advancement he felt he deserved, Bacon hoped to gain favour with James I by appealing to his pride in his intellect and learning. In *Of the Proficiencie and Advancement of Learning* (1605) he set out in detail a plan for the overhaul of education and research in England. He dedicated the book to the king, who he hoped would endorse its programme and appoint him to oversee the project. Bacon argued that the dominance of Aristotelian logic in the universities was an impediment to the advancement of knowledge and that the educational system needed reform to allow a new scientific method based on observation to develop. This work provided an intellectual underpinning to the practical promotion of scientific education represented by the newly founded Gresham College and its lectureships in astronomy, divinity, geometry, law, music, physic and rhetoric.

In *Novum Organum* (1620), Bacon summarized the results of his exploration of the fundamental principles of scientific thought. He demonstrated the inadequacies of Aristotelian science and of reasoning based on logical deduction from causes rather than the observation of effects. He also criticized empiricists who inferred general rules from particular instances and built conclusions liable to be overturned by a contrary example. He proposed an alternative philosophy, based on the postulation of universal laws on the basis of observation tempered by the exercise of the scientist's rational deductive faculty.

Early experimentalists were often regarded with suspicion and charged with irreligion or atheism. From his position within the Jacobean establishment Bacon combated this prejudice against experimentation. He argued that as God revealed himself to Man both through the Scriptures and through the created universe, the study of Nature was not contrary to religion. His positing of a twofold Truth – the truth of religion and the truth revealed through the study of God's creation – was a means of protecting the pursuit of scientific knowledge from the prejudice and conservatism of theologians. He was a powerful propagandist for the practical application of natural philosophy.

Bacon published *Novum Organum* at the height of his public career, having become Lord Chancellor in 1618. He was created Viscount St Albans in 1621, but was shortly afterwards impeached for bribery, a victim of Jacobean political factionalism. He died five years later still in disgrace. In the next generation John Aubrey recorded the story that he had died after catching a cold while stuffing a chicken with snow as part of an impromptu experiment in refrigeration. The popularity of this apocryphal story, which is still retold, demonstrates how Bacon had become synonymous with practical experimentation as the way to advance scientific knowledge. By endowing experimentalism with respectability he helped to create the environment in which scientific advances would flourish in the seventeenth century.

Suggested reading

Vickers, B. 2002 (ed.). *Francis Bacon: The Major Works*. Oxford: Oxford University Press.
Jardine, L. & Stewart, A. 1998. *Hostage to Fortune: The Troubled Life of Francis Bacon*. London: Victor Gollancz.
Zagorin, P. 1998. *Francis Bacon*. Princeton: Princeton University Press.

Simone de Beauvoir
1908–1986   Sally J. Scholz

Simone de Beauvoir is the most important feminist philosopher of the twentieth century. Her monumental study of woman, *The Second Sex* (1949), ignited a new wave of feminist activism and became the foundation for feminist theories in philosophy, political science, psychology, sociology and many other disciplines. But her influence reached far beyond feminism. The 'Grande Dame' of existentialism articulated her unique conception of freedom as ambiguity in the *Ethics of Ambiguity* (1948) and made significant contributions to phenomenology and politics as well.

According to Beauvoir, existence is marked by ambiguity in that meaning 'must be constantly won'. Whereas the more common existential position holds that existence is absurd or meaningless, Beauvoir's optimistic existentialism posits meaning for the individual through a freely chosen project that engages with the freedom of others. Human nature or essence, and other metaphysical notions, are rejected. The individual exists and, in existing, must choose a project that engages freedom; all values spring from freedom. The project must not be thought of as a static end-point or final goal. Instead, the authentic project constantly turns back to freedom thereby opening the future for the individual. Each action or decision the individual undertakes is directed toward this project, dynamically recreating the project as it aims at it. But there is also a tendency to flee freedom or opt for a project that allows the individual to adopt a static identity and thus avoid the responsibility and fear of having to choose. In existentialist terminology, 'existence' means that a consciousness assumes its responsibility to act freely whereas 'being' is the static identity of a thing.

Beauvoir's first novel *L'Invitée* (*She Came to Stay*, 1948) explores the relationship between consciousnesses and set the foundation for her ethics and feminist theory. If each individual is responsible for giving meaning to existence, how do we account for the existence of an *other* consciousness also freely choosing? Do individuals assume other individuals are mere objects in their world? Ultimately, each individual must realise that an existence that is limited to itself cannot find meaning; freedom is realized in relation with others. Moreover, it is with the same movement that one recognizes one's own freedom and tries to free others. Beauvoir emphasizes the need for liberation saying, 'To will oneself free is to will others free.'

While the novel details the individual other and the *Ethics of Ambiguity* demonstrates the method of existentialist ethics binding humans together through freedom, *The Second Sex* discusses the social Other in relationships of oppression. In particular, Beauvoir scrutinizes the oppression of women. The Other is a social group that may not recognise itself as such, but is set apart because of difference from the group in power. In defining itself, the powerful group necessarily excludes others. The characteristics that mark others as different account for the structure of oppression. Regardless of its origin, oppression limits the ability of the oppressed to exercise their freedom.

Beauvoir uses the term 'situation' to indicate aspects of a person's existence that may inhibit the ability to freely choose and pursue a project. Situation entails everything from how an individual's body is perceived to what career opportunities are available. If the situation becomes sufficiently embedded, it takes on the appearance of being natural. Such is the case with women, Beauvoir argued. They had become mystified by the 'eternal feminine,' the notion that there is a particular way to *be* as a woman.

In her most famous book, Beauvoir addresses the question, 'What is a Woman?' She argues that there is no 'eternal feminine' or essence that would define woman. On the contrary, 'One is not born, but rather becomes, a woman.' The freedom limiting situation within which females are raised creates the appearance of a natural inferiority. Told they are inferior, women become inferior.

Beauvoir uses the Hegelian terms 'transcendence' and 'immanence' to discuss the situation of women. Transcendence describes the ability of the individual to freely pursue a project, thereby acting on the world in an important way. Immanence is the condition of endless repetition of mundane tasks that do not impact history. While each person should participate in both immanent and transcendent activities, oppression may keep some from exercising their transcendence. The key to understanding woman's oppression is that her situation relegates her to a sphere of activity that cuts off transcendence. Moreover, because woman's otherness appears as a natural inferiority, women become complicit in their own oppression, often choosing to deny their freedom rather than risk embracing it.

In order for women to create themselves anew in liberty, they must throw off the mystification that makes their situation appear natural and choose projects that open the future of possibilities. Non-exploitive work within a socialist system would provide the conditions for such liberation and create true solidarity among men and women.

Suggested reading
Beauvoir, S. de. 1952 [1949]. *The Second Sex*. New York: Bantam Books.
Beauvoir, S. de. 1948 [1947]. *The Ethics of Ambiguity*. Secaucus, NJ: Citadel Press.
Beauvoir, S. de. 1954 [1943]. *She Came to Stay*. New York: W.W. Norton & Company.

Walter Benjamin
1892–1940   Roger Taylor

On 27 September 1940, Walter Benjamin, Jew, Marxist, his flight from the Gestapo blocked at Port Bou on the Franco-Spanish border, took a lethal dose of morphine. Five years earlier he had published the essay

'The Work of Art in the Age of Mechanical Reproduction'. Forty-two years after his death, his magnum opus, *The Arcades Project*, was published. These two works alone are sufficient to establish his reputation. Some now say, belatedly, he was one of the very great minds of the twentieth century. Benjamin would have resisted this veneration. As he said, 'It is more arduous to honour the memory of the nameless than that of the renowned. Historical construction is devoted to the memory of the nameless.'

Consider the difference between making a painting and taking a photograph. And consider these activities not abstractly but in context: for instance, the easel painting for connoisseurship and collection, and the newspaper photo. Different historical circumstances give rise to a range of competing concepts with which we think about what makes a work a work of art. In 'The Work of Art in the Age of Mechanical Reproduction', Benjamin revealed and explored a number of such concepts: 'uniqueness', 'authenticity', 'original', 'aura', 'reproduction', 'copy', 'ritual', 'cult', 'exhibition', 'concentration', 'distraction'. In bourgeois aesthetics these concepts are used to construct essentialist and discriminatory theories of art. Benjamin, though, understands the emptiness of questions about whether or not photography and film can be art. Those who raise such questions elevate *some* film, *some* photography, to the art world by finding analogies with 'aura', 'high-mindedness', 'sacredness'. These elevations are élitist. They look down on and are dismissive of popular culture despite, as Benjamin illuminates so brilliantly, its challenge to and replacement of redundant cultural norms.

Benjamin realizes these questions are not substantive, but that they are historically significant. Their concepts are transitory and historical, not universal. In the art world, the universality of art is assumed, but the prehistoric drawing of an elk on a cave wall was 'first and foremost, an instrument of magic' and 'only later did it come to be recognized as a work of art'. He follows through in detail one central conception of a work of art, its uniqueness, its authenticity, all subsumable under 'aura'. This conception ties the work of art to the notion of a unique particular, having a unique presence in time and space as well as a specific history of ownership and attention. This is all cast aside in an age of mechanical reproduction. Identical copies make a nonsense of the authenticity of the original, the precious, singular object. As Benjamin says, to ask for an authentic print from a photographic negative makes no sense. The older tradition is 'shattered' by the mechanical reproduction of works of art, its concepts 'outmoded', 'withered', the attempts to preserve them essentialist, even fascist. The concept of art is open and changing. Brilliantly, Benjamin shifts aesthetics from a debate about canons of taste to a mapping of different modes of sense perception, modes that signify real changes in psyche and society. Our lives come to be conducted through visual reproduction.

We witness the dominance of film over literature. New media 'demand a specific kind of approach' and 'free floating contemplation is not appropriate to them'. The camera permeates deeply the web of reality, revealing multiple fragments assembled under new laws. Close-ups, slow motion and hidden details introduce the mass audience to 'unconscious optics'. Painting maintains a natural distance from reality, and it pictures reality as a totality, ideologically whole. With film the masses fixate on fractions, a person reaching for a spoon, or a lighter. No sooner has the eye grasped a scene than it is already changed. Film's public is absent-minded, distracted, like unruly kids at school: philistine. For Benjamin, film promotes revolutionary criticism of traditional concepts of art. The masses respond positively to the film *Gold Rush*, but are hostile to arty cinema and inflated ideologies of art.

The human psyche and collective unconscious immediately preceding these twentieth-century changes is the subject of *The Arcades Project*. Nearly 1,000 pages are devoted to the life of 'commodity fetishism' (a concept from the early chapters of **Marx**'s *Das Kapital*) in Paris's first shopping arcades. The life of the virtual begins; the Parisians resist their commodification by acquiring fantasy identities: detectives, street fighters, desperadoes (like Belmondo in *A Bout de Souffle*). A process has begun, swirling through photos, cinema, television and – post-Benjamin – to avatars and Internet games. In this way Benjamin brings into focus something much larger than art. His account was prescient, spot on. His brief is not prognostic about the art of a classless society. Instead he exhaustively and deeply explores the developmental tendencies of art under present conditions of production. Subsequently, Warhol's copies are symptomatic of a withered 'aura' desperately attempting to stay abreast.

Suggested reading
Benjamin, W. 1999 *The Arcades Project*. Cambridge, Mass.: Harvard University Press.
Benjamin, W. 1985 [1969]. *Illuminations*. New York: Schocken Books.
Smith, G. 1989 (ed.). *Benjamin: Philosophy, Aesthetics, History*. Chicago: University of Chicago Press.

Jeremy Bentham

1748–1832   **Bart Schultz**

Jeremy Bentham was the greatest of the classical utilitarians and one of the strangest men who ever lived. This champion of the greatest happiness of the greatest number insisted that after his death he be dissected, preserved and displayed, to serve the cause of reason both by supporting medical dissection and by leaving his 'Auto-Icon' as an inspirational relic. He can still be viewed today, at University College London.

A precocious boy, Bentham entered Queen's College, Oxford, at the age of twelve, and it was on a return visit there in 1768 that he discovered the key utilitarian notion of promoting the greatest happiness in Priestly's *Essay on the First Principles of Government*. He would claim, in his article on 'Utilitariansm', that it was by this pamphlet that his 'principles on the subject of morality, public and private together, were determined'. His readings of Helvetius and Beccaria, not to mention **Hume** and the *philosophes*, were also crucial in making utilitarian legal reform the centre of his life.

Bentham's most famous work remains *An Introduction to the Principles of Morals and Legislation* (1789). Against theological utilitarianism and lunatic asceticism, he held that maximizing happiness involves summing up pleasures and pains to determine which action yields the greatest net pleasure in this world.

Obsessed with working out every detail of effective utilitarian legal and penal institutions, his writings ranged widely, from his 'Panopticon' prison scheme, to his 'Chrestomathic' schools, to his rules of judicial evidence, to his proposed constitutions for countries across the globe. When various monarchs resisted his efforts to enlighten them, he converted to democracy, and the Reform Act of 1832 owed much to the Benthamite influence.

The practical work of Benthamism was mostly carried out by Bentham's disciples, James Mill and his son **John Stuart Mill**, and other so-called philosophical radicals, who pushed his ideas in such organs as the *Westminister Review*. Still, as his heir apparent J. S. Mill put it: 'The father of English innovation, both in doctrines and in institutions, is Bentham: he is the great subversive or, in the language of continental philosophers, the great critical thinker of his age and country.' No one could match Bentham's scorn for the unscientific and the infelicitous: 'Natural rights is simple nonsense: natural and imprescriptible rights, rhetorical nonsense, nonsense upon stilts.' Despite this aversion to 'the pestilential breath of fiction' in law and morals, Bentham was made an honorary citizen of France, where he enjoyed a great reputation.

The Revd Sydney Smith twitted 'that Bentham thought people ought to make soup of their dead grandmothers', and analogous slanders can be found in everyone from Dickens and **Marx** to **Michel Foucault** and the faculties of most university English departments. Even Mill complained that Bentham was 'one-eyed', seeing only the unpoetic, business side of life, and not much of a philosopher.

Yet Bentham has an eerie way of embarrassing his critics as well as his followers. The great gay critic Foucault, who mistook the Panopticon scheme for a larger vision of social control, failed to recognize not only Bentham's actual social vision but also his role in the history of sexuality: it was Bentham who penned the very first call for the de-criminalization of male love in the English language. It also turns out that Bentham can be largely exonerated of charges that he represented the ideology of British imperialism. The more imperialistic Mills misrepresented Bentham on this and other topics, as when the younger Mill charged him with finding the pleasure of 'pushpin was as good as poetry' (Bentham only meant from the standpoint of the state).

As for philosophy, Bentham made it into **Quine**'s 'five milestones' of empiricism for his formulation of the method – crucial to analytical philosophy – of 'paraphrasis', such that 'to explain a term we do not need to specify an object for it to refer to, nor even specify a synonymous word or phrase; we need only show . . . how to translate all the whole sentences in which the term is to be used'.

Lastly, it was Bentham who urged that: 'the blackness of the skin is no reason why a human being should be abandoned without redress to the caprice of a tormentor. It may one day come to be recognised that the number of the legs, the villosity of the skin, or the termination of the *os sacrum* are reasons equally insufficient for abandoning a sensitive being to the same fate.'

Suggested reading

Bentham, J. 1996 [1789]. *An Introduction to the Principles of Morals and Legislation*. Oxford: Clarendon Press.

Schultz, B., and Varouxakis, G. 2004 (eds). *Classical Utilitarianism and Questions of Race and Empire*. Lanham: Lexington Books.

Rosen, F. 2004. *Classical Utilitarianism from Hume to Mill*. London: Routledge.

Henri Bergson

1859–1941   **Lewis Owens**

Henri Bergson's quasi-mystical work is dominated by his insistence that any attempt to understand the human self by using static concepts of the intellect will fail to reveal its dynamic and changing character. Due to unceasing thoughts, feelings and passions, there is constant change within the inner self that cannot be adequately described by the static axioms of the intellect.

As a result, Bergson rejects the 'mathematical' notion of time which demarcates between past, present and future and offers his own fluid concept of 'real-time' or 'duration'. Using a metaphor of a rolling snowball constantly accumulating new snow, Bergson claims that memory consists, not in recalling events that have long past, but in the past living on in the future. This experience of duration cannot be contained within intellectual concepts – it is to be lived, experienced, rather than abstractly thought. For Bergson, this ability of the inner self to change and grow suggests a dynamic principle which accounts for such creative behaviour. Although the intellect is closely related to individual consciousness, and is able to formulate general truths, it is unable to grasp the inner nature of things because it freezes reality into digestible and analysable concepts.

To account for the dynamics of change within the self, as well as the emergence of the intellect, Bergson examines biological phenomena and the evolution of living organisms. He rejects mechanistic and materialistic accounts of evolution (e.g. Lamarckian and Darwinian), as they fail to account sufficiently for the evident dynamic process of life. Instead, Bergson claims there to be life-force (*élan vital*) which desires life to free itself from the domination and constrictions of matter and to achieve self-consciousness; it therefore accounts for creative evolution and the emergence of instinct and intellect in living things.

The *élan vital* began as a dim spark which willed to become alive; therefore, it distinguishes living things from those that are dead. Thrusting up through diverging branches of the evolutionary tree and differing species of nature (vegetable, animal), it seeks the best route to achieving self-consciousness. The *élan* has progressed through plant and animal evolution before locating the channel of human consciousness. However, although the self is essentially spiritual, dynamic and creative, it serves to weigh down the *élan* in periods of stagnation and sterility. Bergson uses another metaphor of a jet of steam that surges upwards before its loss of energy forces it to descend. The upward stream signifies the ascent of the *élan* whilst its descent represents congealed spirit – materiality – which prevents its continuing upward spurt.

The *élan vital* and matter are not two independent entities. Matter is congealed spirit that has lost the energy to continue its surge upward towards self-consciousness; it is thus devoid of life. Perpetually creative life therefore attempts to 'unmake itself' in the sense of freeing itself from the matter into which it has congealed. Life attempts to surge upwards, matter serves to weigh it down and the faculty of the intellect is specifically related to this restriction of the *élan*. The intellect is fundamentally characterized by a natural inability to comprehend life. The processes of matter and the related faculty of the intellect are therefore inverse to that of life. The *élan vital* has a need for creation and thus attempts to insert as much indeterminacy into matter as possible in order to overcome its fatigue.

As well as the faculty of intellect, humanity also shares with the animal world the capacity for instinctual behaviour. However, although instinct is able to act spontaneously and grasp the fluidity of life freed from the distorting constrictions of the intellect, it is self-conscious. Hence, both the intellectual and instinctual faculties within humanity are unable to account sufficiently for the dynamic principle in life. Both the intellect and instinct serve in manipulating matter and hence weigh life's *élan* down. Bergson proceeds to invoke a third faculty which the *élan vital* has been working to produce, a faculty that will combine the advantages of the intellect and instinct in its ultimate transcendence of both: *intuition*. Intuition consists of instinct becoming self-conscious; life becomes conscious of itself directly and immediately, not through the static concepts of the intellect. Intuition empathizes with all beings and manifests itself in situations of intense human experience, action, joy and sadness.

Bergson therefore prioritises intuition as the channel from which life's vital impulse can continue its ascent; only intuition can fully enable the vital impulse in life to ascend to higher levels of consciousness. Nevertheless, despite the attempt of the *élan vital* to produce beings which can maintain this intuitive empathy with life, even if this requires the surpassing of what is regarded as 'human', intuition still remains at present only a weak light in the darkness of the intellect.

Suggested reading

Bergson, H. 1997 [1934]. *The Creative Mind*. New York: Citadel Press.
Bergson, H. 2002. *Key Writings*. London: Continuum.
Mullarkey, J. 1999 (ed.). *The New Bergson*. Manchester: University of Manchester Press.

George Berkeley
1685–1753   Jonathan Walmsley

Bishop George Berkeley is widely regarded as a loony. This diagnosis of psychosis is in spite of his evident wit, wisdom and wile whilst writing on topics as diverse as the calculus, natural law, optics, politics, poverty and, somewhat incongruously, tar-water. Why then was Berkeley seen as having taken leave of his senses? Ironically, it was because he beseeched us to pay strict attention to the evidence of their testimony.

Berkeley made a quite remarkable claim: there is no such thing as matter. Put so bluntly, this sounds ridiculous. No trousers or Meccano?

No chifferobes or lariats? This must be manifest derangement. Not quite. Berkeley was an undergraduate of Trinity College Dublin. A few years prior to his matriculation, William Molyneaux, another Dubliner, entered into an exchange of letters with **John Locke**. Molyneaux was impressed with his correspondent's lately published work, the *Essay concerning Human Understanding*. Molyneaux enjoined all of Dublin's literati to embrace the book. Thus by the time Berkeley came to Trinity, the only book on the curriculum worth studying was Locke's majestic text.

Berkeley's claims were reactions to and extensions of Locke's empiricism. Locke's principal principle was that the foundations of our knowledge were ideas perceived by sensation. Berkeley agreed with this fundamental assumption and, on this basis, took a survey of everything that could exist. He concluded that they were those things either perceived or perceiving – our ideas or ourselves. But what of matter? According to Locke, matter was the unperceived cause of our ideas. Moreover, it was inert and senseless – the very antithesis of the spiritual. It neither perceived itself nor was perceived by others. How then, asked Berkeley, could it be said to exist? To say that it existed was simply a contradiction – to exist was to perceive or to be perceived and 'matter' evidently did neither.

What, then, were radiators and ball-point pens? Such things always were, replied Berkeley, 'collections of sensations'. What is it to say that 'there was a note in G flat'? That it was *heard*. What is it to say that 'there was a shade of cerise'? That it was *seen*. What is it, at the end of the day, to say 'there was a pump-action shotgun'? That it was seen, heard, felt, tasted and smelt. Without these there would simply be no shotgun. The shotgun just is the collection of sights, sounds, smells, tastes and textures. Aside from the fact that the idea of inscrutable matter is inherently contradictory, there is no need to posit it as responsible for these sensations – after all, what does this matter add that was not there already? We were quite happy with the shotgun as seen, heard and tasted, etc., without tagging on some 'matter' which serves no useful purpose whatsoever. Matter is simply redundant.

This, Berkeley claimed, was mere common sense – what are objects over and above what we take them to be in everyday life? What, more to the point, are the products of these everyday interactions but our perceptions of these objects? It is only when you start introducing 'matter' that you begin to worry about the verity of the senses and trouble yourself with scepticism. By ridding the world of matter, Berkeley hoped to relieve philosophy of this burden.

But, it was objected, if all an object amounts to is a collection of sensations, what happens to it when there is no-one around doing any perceiving? Furthermore, how it is that these sensations of smell, colour, taste and so on always 'hang together' so well? How does it so happen that when I see the shape and colour of the shotgun, it is always accompanied by the texture and smell I am accustomed to? Why do our sensations warn us of things that are harmful? Bishop Berkeley thought the answer rather obvious. These good and advantageous things speak of a benevolent author, one moreover much more powerful than ourselves. What could be responsible for ideas but another spirit – for where can ideas exist but in minds? There simply must be a massively powerful mind that is benevolent in the extreme. God is responsible for these benefactions. God stands on perpetual perceptual sentry duty for objects when no-one else is looking.

This brief summary of Berkeley's thought is surely not enough to convince the reader of the truth of Berkeley's views, nor will it convey the subtlety of their exposition. It does not adequately expatiate upon Berkeley's enduring influence. It in no way captures the quality of Berkeley's writing, for he was surely as eloquent a man of letters as he was a philosopher and George Berkeley was as sophisticated and intelligent a philosopher as the British Isles have ever produced. But the most notable lack in this short introduction is a failure to convey the sheer beauty of Berkeley's vision. He was a deeply religious man and the place for God in his system, as the benevolent immanent cause of the entire world, is intimate, awesome and compelling. His was a consistent Christian vision that even the most hard-headed atheist cannot fail to respect.

Suggested reading

Berkeley, G. 1991. *Philosophical Works*. London: Everyman Paperback Classics.
Stoneham, T. 2002. *Berkeley's World: an examination of the three dialogues*. Oxford: Oxford University Press.
Winkler, K. P. 1989. *Berkeley: An Interpretation*. Oxford: Clarendon Press.

Franz Brentano

1838–1917   **Glen Koehn**

Franz Brentano is best known for the way in which he proposed to distinguish mental from physical phenomena. He was born in Germany and taught at Wuerzburg and the University of Vienna. He took holy orders but later resigned from the Catholic priesthood, in part over his rejection of papal infallibility. An impressive teacher, he influenced a number of individuals who went on to become prominent, among them **Edmund Husserl**, Alexius Meinong, Kasimir Twardowski and the first president of Czechoslovakia Thomas Masaryk. Through his students and his writings he had a significant effect on philosophy in central Europe and elsewhere.

The written works of Brentano fall into two groups: those which he published himself, and a larger number of posthumously edited fragments on various topics. In 1874 he published the first part of *Psychology from an Empirical Standpoint,* later followed by a second volume. These books record his attempts to classify and analyse basic mental acts. He believed that 'descriptive psychology' – a kind of philosophical theory of mental activity – is of great importance to the theory of knowledge and to philosophy generally. For example, rather than viewing logic as the study of formal languages and their relationships, Brentano conceived of logic as the science of the mental activities of right judging and inferring.

In the *Psychology*, Brentano argues that all and only mental acts have a representational nature, a *directedness* toward some object which 'intentionally in-exists', in the act. This is his famous distinction of mental acts from their objects and his criterion of intentionality for characterizing mental phenomena. For instance, a thought is always a thought of something, and even a pain arising from a cut or a burn is a painful representation of a spatial location, usually on the body.

While representing (*Vorstellen*) is the most fundamental type of mental activity, there are two other main types of mental act: judging (*Urteilen*), and activity of the affections (*Gemütstätichkeit*) i.e. loving and hating taken in a broad sense. Judging and acts of loving and hating depend upon representations, but acts of representing need involve neither judging nor acts of loving and hating. In turn, acts of representing and of judging make acts of loving and hating possible. For Brentano, to judge is always to accept or reject the object of some representing activity.

The threefold classification of mental acts plays a role in Brentano's theory of value. For him, true judgements are acts of right intellectual acceptance, while intrinsically good things are those which are rightly loved. The values of truth and of moral goodness thus admit of an analogous treatment.

In his so-called reist phase, after about 1905, Brentano turned against theories which posit abstract entities. There is a single highest genus, that of concrete things, and only a thing in this sense can be an object of mental representation. His mature view of universals (such as roundness or numbers) was that we can have thoughts only of concrete objects, though we represent them in more or less general ways.

On Brentano's reist theory, thinking that a thing exists amounts to representing the thing itself and accepting it rather than representing an abstract object called 'existence'. This is consciously reminiscent of **David Hume**'s view which construed the idea of a thing's existence as simply the idea of that thing itself. Further, for Brentano, to deny that something exists is to reject the thing itself. In rejecting a centaur we are not rejecting an existing idea or an abstract object. However, a difficulty for reism arises from the status of non-existent objects, since it is difficult to see how a non-existent thing can be rejected if there is nothing to reject.

Over his lifetime Brentano produced several books on the Greek thinker **Aristotle**, including the early *On the Many Senses of Being in Aristotle* (1862), and the late work *Aristotle and His World View* (1911). His interpretations are influenced by the views of **Leibniz** and stress the systematic and theological tendencies of Aristotelian thought.

Brentano set himself against the prevailing winds of idealism in German philosophy, and he strove for a more scientific and empirical method of inquiry. His writing style gives some hint of what his students found so impressive, for he takes pains to express himself accurately while judiciously posing and rebutting objections to his own views. He is attentive to ordinary usage yet argues that it must be reformed and regimented at times to make its philosophical commitments explicit.

Suggested reading
Brentano, F. 1973 [1874]. *Psychology from an Empirical Standpoint*. London: Routledge.
Chisholm, R. M. 1986. *Brentano and Intrinsic Value*. Cambridge: Cambridge University Press.
Jacquette, D. 2003. *The Cambridge Companion to Brentano*. Cambridge: Cambridge University Press.

Joseph Butler

1692–1752   Steven F. Bernstein

Bishop Joseph Butler was a moral philosopher and theologian. Until the late nineteenth century, he was one of the most widely read of moral philosophers. His ethical ideas are most completely expressed in his classic work *Fifteen Sermons Preached at Rolls Chapel*, published originally in 1726.

While Butler is a Christian apologist, he offers a largely secular account of what we today refer to as human moral psychology. His theory is practical, and largely an empirical or scientific account of human nature. Butler's approach is practical because he sees that the judgements of conscience affect conduct, and so he is less interested in theoretical issues which lack practical importance. By showing empirically that the practice of virtue is part of natural human psychology and necessary for achieving happiness and living a good life, Butler believes he will reach a wider audience.

The linchpin of Butler's theory is the claim that a moral agent acts according to his nature by recognizing his conscience as providing authoritative and conclusive reasons for acting. Butler believes that man is good by nature and by following his nature he acts virtuously and will live a good life; while acting against his nature is unnatural and the source of viciousness. This belief about human nature goes back at least to the Stoics. Butler maintains, however, that no one has provided an adequate account of what it means to follow one's nature, and so forwards a systematic theory to remedy this failing.

Butler views human nature as a system of various principles of action and motivation; a system of principles which concerns happiness, pain, appetites, passions, and the reflective powers which lead to virtuous or vicious behaviour. Some of these principles motivate self-interested action, while others motivate actions which concern public interest, manifesting a regard for others. Butler believes that the principles of human nature participate in a hierarchical relationship with conscience as the supreme and most authoritative principle.

Psychological egoists such as **Hobbes** claim that we are never really motivated by concern for the interests of others. Hobbes believes that references to benevolence are nothing more than disguised claims of ambition. In order to show that benevolence and ambition are distinct motivating forces, Butler found it necessary to refute Hobbes. Believing he had been successful, Butler theorizes that there are particular principles which function to motivate the satisfaction of desires or appetites. These lowest principles enable persons to satisfy a desire for external objects without specifying the means of satisfaction. There is also the general principle of reasonable self-love, a principle which is reflective: it is guided by reason and motivates the satisfaction of reasonable self-interest. Butler further claims that a general principle such as reasonable self-love is superior in kind to a desire or appetite, and so has 'authority' regardless of the strength of the desire.

The distinction between power and authority is central to Butler's theory of human nature. He claims that it is self-evident that the satisfaction of a particular desire at the expense of one's interest is a violation of one's nature, even if that desire has great strength or power. It is unnatural because self-love is concerned with a person's 'reasonable' interest, and to violate one's reasonable interests by mere power is 'disproportional'. By disproportional Butler means that it is unnatural to allow a lower, more powerful principle to override a superior and more authoritative one.

Conscience is the highest or most authoritative principle and the source of judgements of right action. Conscientious judgements are the source of the moral law, provide the conclusive requirements of duty and, at the same time, motivate right action. As Butler suggests, 'It is by this faculty, natural to man, that he is a moral agent and law to himself: by this faculty, I say, not to be considered merely as a principle in his heart, which is to have some influence as well as others: but considered as a faculty in kind and in nature supreme over all others, and which bears its own authority of being so.' This means that while both self-love and conscience are reflective faculties, they employ reason differently, and in the case of conflict between them, a moral agent understands that the determinations of conscience are authoritative. By developing the right kind of character a man conforms to the dictates of his conscience by recognizing the natural hierarchy of his nature. In so doing, he acts as a moral agent, which is a necessary condition for living a good life.

We generally do regard our conscience as authoritative and often become conflicted when we violate its dictates. We are of course left with the question: Is Butler correct in believing that there is a general consensus and consistency between and among the conscientious judgements of human beings?

Suggested reading

Butler, J. 1983. *Five Sermons*. Indiana: Hackett.
Cunliffe, C. 1992 (ed.). *Joseph Butler's Moral and Religious Thought*. Oxford: Clarendon Press.
Penelhum, T. 1985. *Butler*. London: Routledge.

Albert Camus

1913–1960   Jonathan Walmsley

Albert Camus was born into Algerian poverty, the son of an illiterate mother and a father who would shortly die in the First World War. A promising boy, fond of sun, sea, writing, girls and football, his studies toward a bright academic future were cut short by tuberculosis. Camus knew that his incurable illness would likely kill him. The young man, who loved everything of life, now faced an arbitrary annihilation.

How, then, to live? How to reconcile the conflict of human aspiration with an indifferent world? This juxtaposition Camus labelled the 'absurd' – the mismatch of what we want from the world (order, reason, answers) and what it can provide us (nothing). Aware of the human tendency to project desires onto the universe through means of 'transcendent' religious or political myth, Camus refused to dissolve the disjunction between man and world. We should not pretend the world has intelligible meaning, nor should we kill ourselves – we must unflinchingly sustain consciousness of the absurd with no respite. Camus' essay, *Le Mythe de Sisyphe* (*The Myth of Sisyphus*, 1942), presented four exemplars – seducer, actor, conqueror, artist – who act to extract all they can from life. Free from a belief in 'another life', they pursue their own ends relentlessly and without distraction.

So too Mersault, the protagonist of Camus' narrative *L'Etranger* (*The Stranger*, 1942). Conscious at all times of his own existence and the joy that he derives from it, Mersault finds himself confronting and then killing an Arab through force of circumstance. He refuses to pretend he was responsible, or feel remorse, and society condemns him to death. When a chaplain comes to visit him the night before his execution, Mersault attacks the pretence of life after death and vigorously asserts the happiness he has experienced in this life alone.

The Second World War trapped Camus in Paris, where he became editor of the resistance newspaper *Combat*. Nazi nihilism, not ruled out by mere consciousness of the absurdity of life, demanded principled exclusion. We must live without hope, but not without value – humanity itself, Camus held, is the end and the measure of life. A fictional chronicle of the plague's visitation on Oran, and a parable of the occupation, *La Peste* (*The Plague*, 1947) showed that the labour to maintain life and alleviate suffering sufficed as an end in itself. The town's inhabitants each sought their own way of adjusting to the chance slaughter of infection, but it was the resolution of the plague fighters, who risked their own lives struggling against the disease, that illustrated Camus' view of the dignity and worth of humanity.

Camus codified the political aspect of his humanism in *L'Homme Révolté* (*The Rebel*, 1951). Whilst there is no transcendence and 'everything is permitted', suicide was inconsistent with the absurd. Human life has value and murder, of any sort, is therefore anathema. Thus, even in rebellion against injustice, revolt must never lead to political totality – murder cannot be justified by future utopias. As a reasoned call for political moderation, and a detailed obliteration of totalitarian Stalinism, Camus' work was savaged by his contemporaries, **Jean-Paul Sartre** foremost amongst the critics. The two men, once associates, could not now have been further apart. Where Camus was working class, humanist, moderate, studied, charming and attractive, Sartre was self-hating bourgeoisie, egotistical, extremist, polemical, vituperative and quite ugly. The public dispute about *L'Homme Révolté* separated the two men irretrievably.

Camus' political and personal sensibilities were tested to the limit by the Algerian independence movement. As a young journalist, Camus had called attention to the economic and political plight of the Algerian Arabs and was sympathetic to their desire for autonomy. However, he felt himself to be Algerian and sought a political accommodation which did not require the forcible expulsion of the colonists. When both French and Arab forces resorted to extra-military tactics in what was now a war of independence, Camus called for a truce from both sides against harming civilians. It was in this context that he inadvertently summarised his ethical position. At a rally, he was asked to choose between his mother, still living in Algiers, and justice. He chose his mother. Human feeling was more important than any abstract principle.

Camus was awarded the Nobel Prize for Literature in 1957. He died in a car crash three years later, his final incomplete novel, *Le Premier Homme* (*The First Man*, 1994) thrown intact from the wreck. Though not an academic 'philosopher', Camus has enduring resonance in our post-Christian world – his writings and actions provide a guide to living without hope.

Suggested reading
Camus, A. 2000 [1942]. *The Myth of Sisyphus*. Harmondsworth: Penguin.
Camus, A. 1989 [1942]. *The Stranger*. London: Vintage Books.
Camus, A. 2000 [1951]. *The Rebel*. Harmondsworth: Penguin.

Rudolf Carnap

1891–1970   **Julian Willard**

'A towering figure' is how **W. V. O. Quine**, himself one of the greatest twentieth-century philosophers, described Carnap: 'I see him as the dominant figure in philosophy from the 1930s onward, as **Russell** had been in the decades before.' A German-born philosopher who moved to America in 1935, Rudolf Carnap was one of the leaders of the Vienna Circle, a movement commonly referred to as Logical Positivism. Its members – including Moritz Schlick, Otto Neurath, Herbert Feigl and Hans Hahn – aimed to solve particular problems in the philosophy of mathematics and the physical and social sciences. Carnap himself made important contributions to semantics, the philosophy of science, probability and inductive logic.

A central creed of logical positivism, in part inspired by **Wittgenstein**, was the verification principle – that sentences gain their meaning by specification of the means by which we determine their truth or falsity. The Circle's manifesto, which Carnap completed with Neurath and Hahn, articulated a philosophical standpoint which was to reverberate around English-speaking universities for a generation: 'If anyone asserts, "There is a God", "The primary cause of the world is the Unconscious" . . . we do not say "What you say is false"; rather, we ask him "What do you mean by your statements?"' And since these assertions are neither testable against experience, nor analytic – somehow true by definition – it follows that they are meaningless.

A. J. Ayer was the most widely known advocate of logical positivism in the English-speaking world. He aggressively proclaimed the central importance of science to philosophy, and rejected theology and metaphysics with a flourish as factually meaningless. But it was Carnap who rose to the challenge of spelling out exactly how philosophy can make use of the scientific procedures of empirical observation and confirmation to construct a meaningful picture of the world. In *Pseudoproblems of Philosophy* (1928) he argued that many age-old philosophical problems are vacuous – a result of mere linguistic muddle. For example, while the thesis of realism asserts the reality of the external world, and that of idealism denies this reality, both statements are actually devoid of factual content: 'Statements which cannot, in principle, be supported by experience are meaningless.'

Carnap maintained that human knowledge of the social and physical world can be analysed in terms of phenomenalistic language, the 'immediately given' of sense experience. Whereas Bertrand Russell had talked about deriving the world from experience by logical construction,

Carnap, in *The Logical Structure of the World* (1928), actually set about trying to realise this monumental empiricist task, applying the new logic developed by his 'father figures' Russell and **Frege** to problems in the philosophy of science. Although the book failed to achieve its ambitious goal – and he was never afraid to change his beliefs in response to pertinent reasons – in the attempt Carnap demonstrated how much philosophy stood to gain from the careful employment of technical logic and scientific understanding.

An essential part of Carnap's radical empiricism was his adherence to a distinction between synthetic and analytic sentences. Intuitively there might seem to be a significant difference between what in the jargon are known as 'synthetic' sentences, that can be assessed a posteriori by appeal to sense experience (I can determine whether 'there's an elephant in my kitchen' is true or not by taking a look), and 'analytic' sentences, whose 'a priori' assessment depends solely upon the meanings of the words and their grammatical structure (the dullest example in the literature being 'bachelors are unmarried'). While this distinction has been widely criticized in recent years, Carnap's version is tempered with the claim that one's basic logical commitments can be justified only on pragmatic grounds, and we should be tolerant towards alternative frameworks. In a classic paper 'Empiricism, Semantics, and Ontology,' he articulated and developed the striking claim that ontological questions – questions about the ultimate nature of reality – are best understood as practical issues about the choice and structure of a language, with no further appeal to theoretical rationality: 'The acceptance or rejection of abstract linguistic forms . . . will finally be decided by their efficiency as instruments, the ratio of the results achieved to the amount and complexity of the efforts required.' Many philosophers have found this metaphysical neutrality frustrating, but Carnap was too calm and selfless a thinker to be seduced by a desire to engage in unwarranted and super-ficially impressive polemic.

In his championing of the cardinal philosophical virtues of clarity and logical rigour, and with his substantive contributions to probability theory, semantics and the philosophy of science, Carnap is unquestion-ably one of the most significant philosophers of the last century.

Suggested reading

Carnap, R. 2003 [1928]. *The Logical Structure of the World and Pseudoproblems in Philosophy*. Chicago: Open Court.

Carnap, R. 1995 [1966]. *An Introduction to the Philosophy of Science*. New York: Dover Publications.

Schilpp, P. A. 1984. *The Philosophy of Rudolf Carnap*. Chicago: Open Court.

Noam Chomsky

1928–   **Christopher Norris**

Noam Chomsky is an MIT-based linguist and cognitive psychologist whose thinking in these fields has been more influential (and controversial) than any other such body of work in recent times. He is also a prominent left-wing dissident and implacable critic of US government policy on numerous foreign and domestic issues during the past three decades.

In linguistics, Chomsky is best known for his theory of transformational-generative grammar, first developed in his 1957 book *Syntactic Structures*. This holds that human beings have an innate capacity for acquiring, using and interpreting language, one that transcends any differences of culture or individual psychology. In his early review of B. F. Skinner's *Verbal Behaviour* Chomsky mounted a full-scale attack on the then dominant school of American linguistic thought. Here he showed that no behaviourist account based on a stimulus-response model of language acquisition could possibly explain the rapidity and ease with which children learn to utter well-formed grammatical sentences, often sentences more complex than any to which they have been exposed in their learning environment. Rather, they must possess an innate competence which allows them to generate a huge (open-ended) variety of novel expressions from a finite and strictly specifiable range of basic syntactic forms.

Such were the three main arguments – from 'nativism', 'poverty of the stimulus', and linguistic 'creativity' – that Chomsky deployed to powerful effect against Skinner's behaviourist approach. Thus the task of linguistics was to specify the various transformational-generative mechanisms which enabled speakers and interpreters to assign a determinate meaning to this or that surface string of lexical items. These included the active/passive transformation – that is, the capacity to grasp that a pair of sentences such as 'Alison read the book' and 'the book was read by Alison' have the same underlying structure despite their disparity of surface form. Ambiguous expressions (like 'flying model aircraft can be a challenge!') are shown to result from the fact that a single surface grammatical form has two quite distinct underlying structures, one of which assigns the meaning: 'it can be a challenge to fly model aircraft!', while the other is construed: 'model aircraft that fly can be a challenge!'. Also there is the ability to distinguish nonsensical but grammatically well-formed strings (such as 'colourless green ideas sleep furiously') from strings that possess neither semantic coherence nor grammatical structure (such as 'sleep colourless green furiously ideas'). Chomsky's point is that language-users are vastly more resourceful – or less at the mercy of environmental factors – than could ever be explained by stimulus-response models of linguistic or cognitive grasp.

There are some large philosophical, ethical, and socio-political issues bound up with this debate about the scope and nature of linguistic creativity. Thus behaviourism treated human beings as malleable creatures whose beliefs and conduct were entirely shaped by their passive response to ambient physical or verbal stimuli. In which case (Skinner urged) they had better be subject to the right sorts of stimuli – or social conditioning – so as to ensure their compliance with acceptable norms. For Chomsky, such arguments are not just philosophically bankrupt but also a pretext for the worst, most repressive forms of mass-indoctrination or thought-control. They deny the competence and the right of each individual to form their own, critically considered judgement on issues of moral conscience as regards (say) the US record of involvement in conflicts from Vietnam to Iraq, or the effective suppression of dissident voices through 'voluntary' control of media access by compliant editors and journalists. Behaviourism merely elevates this habit of passive acquiescence to the status of a full-scale programmatic doctrine in the social and human sciences, a doctrine, moreover, with thinly veiled punitive sanctions attached.

In *Cartesian Linguistics* (1966) and other works Chomsky invokes an alternative philosophical tradition, one that counters this denial of freedom and responsibility by stressing the inherent rationality of mind and its freedom to exercise powers of autonomous judgement. Among the central figures are **Descartes** and the Port-Royal logician-grammarians of the seventeenth century, thinkers who placed a high valuation on just those distinctively human attributes. There are certain problems here, not only as concerns that original project, but also with Chomsky's claim to derive substantive ethico-political values from such a narrowly rationalist epistemology. Perhaps this explains his more recent reluctance to be drawn on the topic, no doubt reinforced by conservative opponents who are apt to say that if a link exists between Chomsky's linguistic theories and his political views, then the theories had better be junked along with the politics. More constructively it might be suggested that Chomsky should have looked to the later (post-Kantian) tradition of Enlightenment thought as a source of philosophical and ethico-political inspiration. Nevertheless his work stands as a powerful riposte to some of the shabbier intellectual complicities of our time, as well as having made an immensely original contribution to linguistics and cognitive psychology.

Suggested reading
Chomsky, N. 1966. *Cartesian Linguistics*. New York: Harper & Row.
Chomsky, N. 1978. *Language and Politics*. Montreal: Black Rose Books.
Peck, J. 1987 (ed.). *The Chomsky Reader*. New York: Pantheon.

Paul Churchland

1942–   **Hans Dooremalen**

What is the nature of mental states and processes? Will my mind survive the disintegration of my physical body? These are some of the important questions which have occupied Paul Churchland. Much of his most famous work is concerned with the mind-body problem, solutions to which range between two main positions. On the one hand, there are dualist theories, which claim that the mind exists and is different from the body. On the other hand, there are materialist theories of mind, which hold that mental states and processes are nothing more than states and processes of the brain. This is Churchland's position. He is a reductionist or an eliminative materialist. This means that the mental can be explained in terms of the physical, in such a way that the mind is shown not to exist at all (and hence is 'eliminated').

Churchland's arguments for this position are based on neuroscientific evidence. He bases his ideas on the theory in cognitive science known as 'connectionism'. When we see an object – for instance, a face – our brains transform the input into a pattern of neuron-activation somewhere in the brain. The neurons in our visual cortex are stimulated in a particular way, so a pattern emerges. The patterns differ, of course, with each face (or other objects), which means that we can distinguish faces on the basis of slight differences. According to Churchland, there is one pattern that represents the prototypical face, which is the average of a lot of faces you have seen. This prototype has no big nose, nor a small one, but a normal sized nose. The same goes for all its other features. Churchland shows by this prototype that face recognition, and by extension all object recognition, is something for which no consciousness is necessary. On a purely physical basis we can recognize objects. This claim is supported by work with a parallel computer system made by Garrison Cottrell's group at the University of California, which is designed to recognize faces. This computer has, of course, no consciousness and doesn't know the meaning of the input, but it is still almost 100 per cent successful in recognizing faces. As our brains work in the same way, we don't have to postulate consciousness to explain how we recognize objects.

Another important point about these connectionist networks is that they can recognize faces which are partly covered. This shows that the computer system or the brain is able to complete the picture of the input; that is, that it is able to recognize part of a pattern and then complete it. What we have here is a primitive form of a very important feature of the human capacity to gain knowledge from limited experience. Again, Churchland shows that this feature can be explained without an appeal to notions such as consciousness or meaning. If he is correct, it is a very strong argument for reductive or eliminative materialism: we can do without consciousness and meaning and still have the capacity to reason.

Of course not everyone agrees with Churchland's reductionist position, which eliminates the necessity of personal conscious experience. **Thomas Nagel**, for example, points out that the awareness that a bat has of the world has a distinct, subjective feel, and that this is not captured in physical descriptions of the bat. We don't know what it is like to be a bat, because we don't have the experiences a bat has. We can extend this argument: I don't know what it is like to be you, because you have your own experiences. So experience, and therefore consciousness, cannot be reduced to something physical.

Churchland's reply to this attack is that everyone has his or her personal neuronal network, his or her own internal resources for gaining knowledge about his or her own sensory activities and cognitive states. But this does not mean that there is something nonphysical about those states. So there is nothing which suggests that there is something about sensory and cognitive states which transcends understanding by the physical sciences. I can know what it is like to be a bat, but I cannot know it in the way the bat does. Churchland concludes that 'there is nothing supraphysical, nothing beyond the bounds of physical science here.'

Suggested reading

Churchland, P. 1984. *Matter and Consciousness*. Cambridge, Mass.: MIT Press.
Churchland, P. 1995. *The Engine of Reason, the Seat of the Soul*. Cambridge, Mass.: MIT Press.
McCauley, R. 1996. (ed.) *The Churchlands and their Critics*. Oxford: Blackwell.

Hélène Cixous

1937–   **Megan Laverty**

Hélène Cixous is recognised, along with Julia Kristeva and Luce Irigaray, as a leading French feminist. Her theoretical work is shaped by her strong political commitments. She desires to understand the politics of language, so as to discover and participate in the kinds of alteration necessary to make language and life more inclusive. In particular Cixous wants to redress the traditional absence of women's voices in literature and scholarship. She also uses the metaphors of sexual difference and motherhood to develop a theory of language which emphasizes the relation of similarity between text and world. She does this to such an extent that it has led some scholars to criticize her for being essentialist, that is, as arguing that female bodies (world) uniquely produce feminine discourse (text). But her thesis is a much more subtle and open-ended one than this.

Cixous was born in Oran, Algeria in 1937. She has taught at many different universities in France, including the Sorbonne and University of Paris VIII. She is a literary critic, a writer of fiction, plays and poetry – having published more than thirty such works – and a philosopher of language. Her published work translated into English includes, *Coming to Writing and Other Essays* (1991), *Inside* (1969), *The Exile of Joyce or The Art of Replacement* (her first critical book, 1968), *Portrait of Dora* (1976), *The Newly Born Woman (1975)* and *Reading with Clarice Lispector* (1990). Her influences include mythology (in particular Greek), literary sources (Marina Tsvetaeva, Ingeborg Bachmann, Franz Kafka and Clarice Lispector), philosophy (in particular **Hegel** and **Heidegger**) and psychoanalysis (in particular **Freud** and Lacan).

The themes that Cixous explores throughout the variety of her works remain constant and are interrelated: reading, writing, difference, self-other and love. Cixous starts from the position that language structures invariably create meanings and that the latter are essentially dichotomous and hierarchical, involving inclusion (privilege) and exclusion (marginalization). In an attempt to redress this language of value, Cixous argues for a process of learning how to 'unknow' the known, as it has come to be codified in language. Such a process enlists language in a poetics of *attention*, for this alone gives birth to the other *as other* (genuinely independent, different, etc.). Attention is a fidelity to what exists that involves returning to the same thing again and again in an effort to see it in its truth; it is to see the other as unfamiliar whilst simultaneously accepting the strange in oneself. To attend to the other is to take pleasure in, and ultimately celebrate, what is essentially outside of, resistant to, but received by the self. Such a language of intermingling and exchange is contrary to more traditional self-other politics, articulated in **Rousseau**'s and Hegel's philosophies, **Sartre**'s existentialism and Freudian psychoanalysis.

Cixous retains a broadly psychoanalytic framework, but in the spirit of romanticism. She argues that the paradoxical task of the individual in life is analogous to, if not the same as, the paradoxical task of the artist. The artist's project is undeniably creative, but with a view to faithfully rendering what she experiences as the reality of her subject matter – good art reveals this. Similarly with the individual: her existence is undeniably creative in the sense that she is avidly reading life for meaning (writing it) but with an almost desperate commitment that it capture the truth. Cixous represents this by way of the infant's gaze upon the mother's face, intently deciphering it as the signature of all life – a reading relationship that we then replicate in other contexts of life. As with bad art and the infant, human beings more often than not fail in their ability to read the world – what they see as the world is a projection.

As reading is the site of our failure to do justice to ourselves and the other, it is also the site of change and hope. By way of rereading and ultimately non-reading, any experience has the potential to be a rediscovery and recreation of oneself in one's re-encounter with the (m)other. It is possible for living and writing to be other than a projection. Truth in this context is not a term of constancy or stasis, but one of movement, as it relates to the constantly self-displacing individual/author. On Cixous' theory, to desire truth is to accept motion, have the courage to be afraid and embrace patience.

Suggested reading

Cixous, H. 1994. *Three Steps on the Ladder of Writing*. New York: Columbia University Press.
Cixous, H. 1992. *Coming to Writing and Other Essays*. Cambridge, Mass.: Harvard University Press.
Sellers, S. 1994 (ed.). *The Hélène Cixous Reader*. London: Routledge.

R. G. Collingwood
1889–1943   **Charles Booth**

Robin George Collingwood wrote on the philosophy of art, metaphysics, political philosophy, the philosophy of nature and, perhaps most famously, on the philosophy of history. Despite this seeming eclecticism, certain unifying themes can be discerned, ones which represent issues of enduring philosophical importance, fully justifying the recent renewal of critical attention that belies Collingwood's reputation as a neglected and marginal thinker.

Collingwood, the son of John Ruskin's secretary and biographer, was raised and educated within a milieu in which the aesthetic imagination was perceived as a paramount human experience. He was elected to a fellowship at Oxford in 1912, and apart from military service in Admiralty Intelligence from 1914 to 1918, he spent the remainder of his professional life at Oxford, being appointed Waynflete Professor of Metaphysical Philosophy in 1935. He was a professional archaeologist as well as a philosopher.

One important theme in Collingwood's work was the role of philosophy in uncovering how we structure our experience of reality. Specifically, Collingwood was concerned with the presuppositions through and with which we experience the world; and with the ways in which different concepts and categories govern or inform different kinds of experience – theoretical, moral, aesthetic – so that we are able to make potentially contradictory judgements concerning truth, goodness and beauty.

Collingwood argued that behind every perception, proposition or action lies a presupposition, behind every presupposition another presupposition, until one reaches bedrock in the form of an 'absolute presupposition'. He explicitly distinguished between an absolute presupposition and the relative presuppositions that both flow from it and are underpinned by it; and between presuppositions and linguistic entities such as theories and statements.

Absolute presuppositions are not verifiable by experience, nor can they be undermined by experience – rather they are the means through which experience is judged. Although absolute presuppositions may change, such changes are not a matter of fashion, choice or conscious thought; rather, they entail 'the abandonment of all [our] most firmly established habits and standards for thought and action.' Stephen Toulmin argues that Collingwood here anticipated much of what was significant about the work of **Kuhn** on scientific paradigms. Others, similarly, have argued that Collingwood's emphasis on complex contextual structures prefigured the use and meanings of words and sentences in language games proposed by **Wittgenstein** in his later work.

This framework informed both Collingwood's philosophy of history and his philosophy of art, as well as his metaphysics. Collingwood argued that the past does not exist entirely independent of the present, but that it lives on in the present, and that historical events, actions and processes may therefore be re-enacted (or reconstructed) through a disciplined logic of 'question and answer'. Investigation seeks to recreate the presuppositions of agents in re-enacting, not only the thoughts and actions of those agents, but the questions to which those actions were intended as a solution. If we merely interpret action according to *our* presuppositions, we are not carrying out accurate, effective or useful history.

Collingwood argued for precisely the same methodology in his account of art criticism and appreciation. The production of a work of art is an act of imaginative creation: appreciation of that work of art is an imaginative reconstruction of the act, and of the problems, questions, thoughts and emotions that inspired it. In these respects, Collingwood was concerned with elucidating history philosophically, and philosophy historically: a project which he called effecting a *rapprochement* between philosophy and history.

Underpinning this position was his credo that historical knowledge was self-knowledge, and that although philosophy generates principles through which a life might be lived, these are not rules to be slavishly followed. Collingwood made clear that a reliance on rules and theories derived from natural science, divorced from the context in which they were to be applied, is what bankrupted modernism. He suggested that in guiding moral and political actions, individual actors should instead rely on the ability to apply insight, derived from an understanding and application of artistic, religious, scientific, historical *and* philosophical principles.

His emphasis on context and on the unverifiability of absolute presuppositions left Collingwood with a difficulty in his late political philosophy. Writing against the background of totalitarianism rampant in Europe, Collingwood was concerned to depict a liberal civilization at threat from both without and within. Within his metaphysical project, however, the presuppositions of liberalism could no more be said to be 'true' than those of opposing political systems. Thus, his defence of liberalism was distinguished, in some senses, by a retreat from the even-handedness implied by his metaphysics, in that his defence of civility in liberal politics was explicitly informed both by his Christian religious beliefs and by his sense of imminent crisis confronting the liberal polity. Liberal humanism does not preclude a radical stance. In the closing words of his autobiography, he remarked, 'I know that all my life I have been engaged unawares in a political struggle, fighting against these things in the dark. Henceforth I shall fight in the daylight.'

Suggested reading

Collingwood, R. G. 1978 [1939]. *An Autobiography*. Oxford: Oxford University Press.
Collingwood, R. G. 1994 [1946]. *The Idea of History*. Oxford: Oxford University Press.
Johnson, P. 1998. *R. G. Collingwood: An Introduction*. Notre Dame, Indiana: St Augustine's Press.

Auguste Comte
1798–1857   **William Lawhead**

The French philosopher Auguste Comte is often neglected in histories of philosophy. Nevertheless, his influence over nineteenth-century thought and his foreshadowing of later intellectual movements assure him a place in the history of thought.

Comte's central task was to develop a scientifically based philosophy that would be free of all speculation and anchored firmly in positive knowledge. For this reason, he called his philosophy positivism. The only claims the positivist would embrace are those that scientists have empirically verified. As he put it, 'No proposition that is not finally reducible to the enunciation of a fact, particular or general, can offer any real and intelligible meaning.' His goal was to take the accomplishments of the sciences and apply them to the improvement of the social, political, and moral spheres of human existence.

Comte advanced a theory concerning the development of human history, which he called the 'Law of Three Stages'. The first stage of human intellectual development was the theological stage. Comte said that this stage represented humanity in its infancy, for just as a child attributes intentions and personality to his toy animals, so people at this stage assumed that the cosmos is governed by the actions of personal gods. The second stage of human history is the metaphysical stage, or the stage of humanity's adolescence. Here, events were explained in terms of impersonal and hidden causes, using abstract notions such as forces, essences, or faculties. The third, and final stage, is that of positivism. At this stage, humanity will have achieved adulthood, for now the world will be viewed scientifically.

To assist in carrying out his dream of putting human knowledge on a solid scientific foundation, Comte arranged the sciences in a logical order. At the foundation he placed mathematics. Though it is the most abstract science, it provides the principles for all the other more concrete sciences. At the apex of the sciences, he placed a new science, which he called sociology. In Comte's vision, sociology would unify the sciences by putting them in the service of humanity and its needs. For Comte, however, this meant replacing democracy with a centrally-run government controlled by scientific experts.

Comte recognized the power of religious ideals to serve as the mortar in constructing a coherent community. Consequently, he proposed a scientifically respectable religion which would have all the emotional appeal and motivating force of Christianity without its theological and metaphysical baggage. He called his new, secular religion, the 'Religion of Humanity', which was first set out in his *System of Positive Politics* (1851–1854). For example, in place of the notion of God, he proposed that the Supreme Being for the positivist should be Humanity. Furthermore, he reformed the calendar so that the significant dates no longer marked religious events but instead honoured the great intellects in human history. Major figures such as Gutenberg, Shakespeare and **Descartes** were used to name the months of the year.

Positivism and its humanistic ideals enjoyed a fair amount of influence over thinkers in the nineteenth century. Positivist societies sprang up in England and France to venerate and seek inspiration from the great minds in history. Positivism was even popular as far away as Latin America. Not only were churches established in Brazil, but the positivists put Comte's ideas to work in carrying out revolutionary political reform. To this day, the Brazilian flag carries the motto *Ordem e Progreso* (Order and Progress), the key phrase in all of Comte's writings.

Comte's attempt to limit science to a narrow empirical methodology encouraged those who wanted to sever science from any sort of metaphysical base. Furthermore, Comte, along with **Hegel** and **Marx**, contributed to the spirit of the nineteenth century with his claims that concepts should be studied in terms of their historical development and that historical progress follows a logical pattern.

By the end of the nineteenth century, the influence of Comte's social theory was eclipsed by the unashamedly metaphysical materialism of the Marxists. Still, the spirit of positivism took on a life of its own and lived on beyond Comte's explicit doctrines. His dream of making the study of humanity into a rigorous science has continued to be the goal for many in disciplines such as economics, psychology, and sociology. Comte's methodological spirit became an important force in the twentieth century and beyond among those who think that we should stick to what can be empirically verified (in the most narrow sense of those words) and that we should repudiate any metaphysical claims that go beyond sense experience.

Suggested reading

Comte, A. 1988. *Introduction to Positive Philosophy.* Indiana: Hackett.
Lenzer, G. 1998 (ed.). *Auguste Comte and Positivism: The Essential Writings.* New Jersey: Transaction.
Pickering, M. 1993. *Auguste Comte: An Intellectual Biography*, vol. 1. Cambridge: Cambridge University Press.

Charles Darwin

1809–1882   Simon Eassom

Charles Darwin must rank as one the greatest scientists in history. Alongside Copernicus, Galileo, and Newton he changed the world. But, despite being praised and vilified in his lifetime, his ideas were not new, and many of the ideas still associated with him are wrongly attributed. Probably the majority of people who know precisely who Darwin is, do not know exactly what he said.

The founder of evolutionary biology, who did not even use the word 'evolution' when he first explained his theory, started out in medicine, but was repelled by the sight of surgery without anaesthesia. He joined the crew of the *Beagle* in 1831 as a do-it-all scientist (botanist, zoologist, geologist, palaeontologist and anthropologist), and returned after five years at sea with the data he needed to begin the work for which he is best known: *The Origin of the Species by Means of Natural Selection.* It was thirteen years from the return of the *Beagle* in 1836 to the book's publication in 1859. In those years Darwin read and studied Adam Smith's *Wealth of Nations* and Thomas Malthus's *Essay on the Principles of Population;* reflected on the evolutionary theories of his own grandfather, Erasmus Darwin; and considered the possibility of an idea that had been around since first mooted by **Aristotle** and Lucretius over two thousand years before: species had *not* been created whole and perfect by God at the genesis of life on earth and thus come through the intervening period unchanged. This could not possibly be true. All around him, Darwin saw constant modification and adaptation. He saw what we now call 'evolution'. But what was needed – what Darwin provided that was new, unique, and truly earth-shattering – was a theory that explained the facts he had observed everywhere from field trips in Wales to the Galapagos Islands.

There already existed well-established, quite revolutionary and controversial ideas about population growth and decline, survival and strength, ancestry and heredity. Darwin brilliantly drew upon the best, most plausible of them and established the first supportable, empirically verifiable theory of Malthusian ideas 'applied to the whole animal and vegetable kingdoms'. The theory, laid out with incredible attention to detail and considerable evidence in the *Origin,* establishes three fundamental premises:

1. All organisms produce more offspring than can possibly survive.
2. There is significant variation amongst offspring; they are not all carbon copies of one immutable type.
3. At least some of the variation found in the offspring gets passed on to the next generation and to generations beyond.

Darwin combined these ideas and observations to put forward a startling hypothesis: if many offspring die out, and if there is significant variation amongst offspring, then those offspring most advantageously suited to their changing local environment will tend to survive.

The significant aspect of Darwin's theory that combines these premises is the notion of heredity: because variation is passed on to future generations, the offspring of surviving members of a species will resemble their parents more than they resemble the parents of the less successful members. Over a period of time, any species will change to reflect the cumulative effect of these variations.

In spite of Darwin's confidence in his theory, he was reluctant to express his 'dangerous idea' publicly. Quite by chance, he had received a letter from Alfred Wallace in the early 1840s putting forward exactly the same theory of 'descent with modification', but Darwin had the all-important evidence and with Wallace's encouragement the two men jointly presented their findings to a scholarly audience in July 1858. When the *Origin* was published the following year, all 1,200 copies sold out the first day.

The application of Darwin's ideas to humans had already occurred before the publication of *The Descent of Man* in 1871. Meanwhile, Darwin's theory had begun to take on a life of its own. Herbert Spencer had coined the phrase 'survival of the fittest' in 1862 and 'Darwinism' had already been utilized as an epithet for varied claims about the natural progression of humankind towards a more perfectible being. Surprisingly, the reaction of the religious fundamentalists to Darwin's suggestion that humans are related to chimpanzees was more muted than the furore that followed publication of the *Origin*. In any case, Darwin now had many defenders. In particular, his ideas were taken up and championed by his 'bulldog', Thomas Huxley, about whom the apocryphal comment by Bishop Wilberforce was made: 'I would like to ask Professor Huxley whether he is descended from an ape on his grandfather's side or grandmother's side?'

Whilst Darwin kept out of such controversies, it was clear where his sympathies lay, as well as his beliefs. *The Expression of the Emotions in Man and Animals,* published a year later in 1872, sold 5,000 copies within two months. For anybody who has taken on board Darwin's message, it has not been possible since to deny the connection between human beings and other animals.

Suggested reading
Darwin, C. (1982) [1859]. *The Origin of Species*. Harmondsworth: Penguin.
Darwin, C. (1992) [1871]. *The Descent of Man*. New York: Princeton University Press.
Darwin, C. (2002) [1872]. *The Expression of the Emotions in Man and Animals*. Oxford. Oxford University Press.

Donald Davidson
1917–2003   Christopher Norris

Donald Davidson was an American philosopher who developed some distinctive ideas about language, truth, and interpretation as well as contributing to debates in the philosophy of mind.

Probably his single most influential essay is 'On the Very Idea of a Conceptual Scheme' (1974), where he takes issue with the kinds of thinking that would relativise truth to this or that language, paradigm or conceptual scheme. On the contrary, he argues, truth – or the attitude of holding-true – is both logically and methodologically prior to any understanding we can gain with regard to other people's meanings, intentions or beliefs. Relativists go wrong by laying too much stress on differences of meaning (semantics) between languages and by ignoring those conceptually basic features of structure (syntax) and logic which every language must possess if it is to meet the most basic communicative needs.

Where the various forms of relativism advocated by B. L. Whorf, **W. V. O. Quine** and **Thomas Kuhn** break down is on the simple fact that these writers are able to convey quite a vivid sense of the difference between various languages, modes of understanding, scientific paradigms etc., despite their explicit commitment to the thesis that we cannot get a hold on any language or 'conceptual scheme' that differs from our own in certain crucial respects. That is to say, we should have no sense of the problems involved in translating from one language to another if their relativist claims held good. But certain underlying regularities identified by Davidson cut across such otherwise unbridgeable differences of cultural-linguistic grasp.

Thus relativists 'have the matter backwards', according to Davidson, when they take linguistic or cultural convention to determine what standardly counts as 'truth' by the lights of this or that 'language-game' or communally warranted 'form of life'. What they fail to acknowledge is the straightforward point that such issues could never arise except in so far as we *do* have a grasp of the criteria for adequate translation, i.e. for preserving standards of truth across and despite such differences.

For Davidson, then, truth is a logically basic concept which alone makes it possible to comprehend how speakers of diverse languages – or scientists working within different paradigms – can nonetheless achieve a fair working grasp of the problems that impede their mutual understanding or the conflicts of theoretical allegiance between them. If this weren't the case, translators would be wholly at a loss for standards of adequate (sense-preserving) translation and historians of science likewise stuck for any adequate criterion of what should count as a measure of progress from one Kuhnian paradigm to the next.

A problem with Davidson's approach is that he seeks to resolve these issues on the basis of a Tarskian theory of truth, according to which a proposition (statement) such as 'Snow is white' is true if and only if snow is white. This provides a purely formal definition of truth. Thus he has tended to vacillate, when pressed, between a version of the argument on which 'truth' comes out with substantive implications about the objectivity of truth and a version quite acceptable to those – like **Richard Rorty** – who maintain that 'truth' is just the compliment we pay to certain propositions or attitudes that are useful or valuable.

There is a kindred ambiguity about Davidson's chief contribution to philosophy of mind, namely his idea of 'anomalous monism'. He goes along with the hard-line physicalists, who claim that mental events are just brain events, in so far as he accepts that every mental event must be caused by – or is dependent upon – some particular physical brain-state.

That is, Davidson acknowledges the force of arguments against dualism – the view that mind and body are distinct substances – which hold it to be simply inconceivable that mental goings-on might belong to a realm unaffected by the laws of biology, chemistry, and physics. To this extent, his monism – his belief that mind and brain involve only one substance, not two – might seem to tally with the arguments of 'eliminative materialists' like **Paul Churchland** who regard all talk of thoughts, beliefs, attitudes, feelings etc., as the remnant of an old 'folk-psychological' vocabulary which we can and should abandon once informed of the latest scientific findings.

Yet Davidson's is an *anomalous* monist position in so far as it counts such talk perfectly acceptable when we bring those goings-on under a different description, i.e. one concerned with values such as truth, reason, logical consistency, or rightness in judgement. It is 'anomalous' in the sense of allowing this departure from the otherwise implacably law-governed order of physical causation.

Thus Davidson's approach to philosophy of mind connects with the arguments developed in his truth-based theory of meaning and interpretation. In both cases, there is room for doubt as to whether the proposed Davidsonian solution amounts to much more than an ingenious means of avoiding any head-on confrontation with the issues.

Suggested reading
Davidson, D. 1980. *Essays on Actions and Events.* Oxford: Oxford University Press.
Davidson, D. 1984. *Inquiries into Truth and Interpretation.* Oxford: Oxford University Press.
Davidson, D. 2001. *Subjective, Intersubjective, Objective.* Oxford: Oxford University Press.

Gilles Deleuze
1925–1995   **Matthew Ray**

Gilles Deleuze, like **Jacques Derrida**, is a recent French philosopher and historian of philosophy whose name is associated with such movements

as post-structuralism, post-modernism and deconstruction. Yet the association, in Deleuze's case, is almost wholly accidental: Deleuze has often
expressed confusion over the whole notion of post-modernism; has
sometimes implicitly attacked deconstruction; and is so far from being
concerned with the structuralist and post-structuralist problematic of
language that he has sought to undercut much of its mysterious force by
returning to the English philosopher J. L. Austin's famous analysis of
language as being one amongst many acts. Yet Deleuze and Derrida do,
at least, have this much in common: being modern Parisian philosophers, the history of philosophy that they engage with includes **Marx**,
Nietzsche and **Freud** as much as it does **Plato**, **Descartes** and **Kant**.

Derrida suggests that since language is a public medium, knowledge
of our self cannot, strictly speaking, be direct and unmediated. Deleuze
however disagrees, and in his book *A Thousand Plateaus* (1980), written
with the radical psychoanalyst Félix Guattari, he bypasses this preoccupation with language by approaching the topic by means of an analysis
of speech acts. According to the theory first systematized by Austin in
the 1960s, language does not comprise propositions devoid of social
context, but rather it comprises actions. Therefore, linguistic communication is not, as has generally been supposed, primarily the
communication of information, it is rather the production and perform-
ance of a speech act. For example, an order shouted from a sergeant to
a private is an action with certain determinate results in the physical,
social and political world. All other examples of language can also be
interpreted this way. This demystification of language allows Deleuze to
return to a direct, empirical intuition of the self, absolutely unmediated
by language, and thus he is not concerned to derive the essence of the
unconscious from or through its linguistic effects, as in both deconstruction and Lacanian psychoanalysis.

This anti-Lacanian intuition of the self as raw pre-personal desire is
most elaborately constructed in his unorthodox two-volume collaboration with Guattari: *Capitalism and Schizophrenia* (comprising
Anti-Oedipus (1977) and *A Thousand Plateaus*). The argumentative
structure of this work is difficult to discern and it is couched in a
technical vocabulary which goes largely unexplained. Nevertheless, we
can, at least, say that it is a critique of psychoanalysis which suggests
that psychoanalysis must be replaced with what Deleuze and Guattari

call, some would say irresponsibly, 'schizoanalysis'. It is not that we are to become like schizophrenics. Indeed, the schizophrenics inside psychiatric hospitals, Deleuze and Guattari believe, are not mentally ill, but have simply taken a wrong turn to the degree that they have allowed themselves to be defined as a clinical entity within the Freudian Oedipal framework. It is rather that those schizophrenics who assume other identities and multiple personalities have found an engaging truth about the unconscious: that contrary to the orthodoxy of psychoanalysis, it is cosmically unconcerned with our attachments to our mother and father and to personalities generally. Hence the title of the first volume: *Anti-Oedipus*. Other works by Deleuze supplement this anti-psychiatry with more specifically philosophical arguments: in *Difference and Repetition* (1968), for example, we are treated to an argument for the existence of non-conceptual experience (sub-representative experience, as it were) of difference, which obviously feeds into his model of immediate non-conceptual and non-verbal experience of desire.

Finally, in addition to his programme of tearing down the fetishization of language and liberating our schizophrenic desire, Deleuze is also a historian of philosophy and a lot of his work consists in commentaries on the texts of major philosophers like **Hume**, Kant, **Leibniz**, **Spinoza**, **Bergson** and Nietzsche. These works characteristically involve an enthusiastic digression upon one or other of the primary author's themes that imbues it with a status and emphasis that it did not originally seem to possess; a method which has often led critics to believe, not unfairly, that the work in question tells us more about Deleuze than it does about the subject of the commentary. His book on Nietzsche, *Nietzsche and Philosophy* (1962), is a case in point, revolutionizing Nietzsche studies with its extraordinary emphasis on the importance of the difference between active and reactive forces in Nietzsche.

Deleuze died in 1995, but the influence of his works has endured: both the work of the early Lyotard and that of the early to middle Derrida (particularly in the seminal essay Différance, which quotes *Nietzsche and Philosophy*) have clearly been written under a more or less lengthy Deleuzean shadow.

Suggested reading
Deleuze, G. 1983 [1962]. *Nietzsche and Philosophy*. London: Continuum.
Deleuze, G. & Guattari, F. 2002 [1980]. *A Thousand Plateaus*. London: Continuum.
Bogue, R. 1989. *Deleuze and Guattari*. London: Routledge.

Daniel Dennett

1942–   Guy Douglas and Stewart Saunders

Daniel C. Dennett presents a way to understand the human mind. He seeks to clarify what a mind is, what consciousness is, and what mental states like beliefs, desires and thoughts are.

Dennett earned his fame in philosophical circles for his approach to the problem of intentionality. When philosophers say the mind exhibits intentionality they are referring to the fact that mental states can be *about* something. When we think, we tend to think about objects in the world, and this thinking leads us to rational action and effective inter-action with the world. Dennett suggests that intentionality is not so much an intrinsic feature of agents (thinkers), rather, it is more a way of looking at agents. In the title of one of his books, Dennett refers to the seeing of agents as intentional beings as taking *The Intentional Stance* (1987).

Dennett asks us to consider the various ways we can look at an object with the goal of predicting and understanding what it is going to do. The most accurate, but in many cases the least practical, is taking the physical stance. For this we would apply the principles of the physical sciences to the object. A more practical approach, especially if the object is an artefact, is to take the design stance. When we do this we assume that the object will behave as it is designed to behave. For instance, we assume that the alarm will go off at the right time because it has been designed to do so by its human creator. Finally, there is the intentional stance: here we assume that the object has a mind and has goals or desires and that it will tend to operate in order realize its goals (according to its understanding of the world, or what could be called its beliefs).

So is intentionality really there, or is it only a useful fiction? Dennett's answer is that in taking the intentional stance one is perceiving a certain complex pattern exhibited by the agent. And this pattern is as real as any pattern. One should not assume, however, that the nature of this pattern is in any way reflected in the internal constitution of the agent. This is the basis of Dennett's criticism of intentional realists (like Jerry Fodor) who hold that intentionality is supported by internal mechanisms that reflect the structure of beliefs and desires.

In *Darwin's Dangerous Idea* (1995) and *Kinds of Minds* (1996), Dennett has focused on the idea that the intentionality characteristic of humans and other animals is a result of evolutionary processes. In this way Dennett hopes to account for the origin of the 'patterns of intentionality' within a framework that is consonant with natural science. This move is controversial, as many theorists believe that natural selection by itself cannot explain all features of an organism, arguing that often features are accidental by-products of evolutionary processes.

In *Consciousness Explained* (1991), Dennett aims to dispel the myth that there is a central theatre, literally or metaphorically inside the head, where the 'stream of consciousness' is viewed. While he admits that no theorist actually defends this view, it is his belief that a residual alliance to this way of thinking about the mind instils confusion in many of the current approaches to the topic of consciousness.

A more plausible candidate, he argues, is the Multiple Drafts Model. The central claim of the Multiple Drafts Model is that there is no one place where consciousness happens. Our mental states are processed in parallel in the brain, and there is no place where the signals have to reach in order to be conscious. Instead, all the mental activity in the brain is accomplished as a result of parallel processes of elaboration and interpretation of sensory inputs. Information is therefore under continuous editorial revision as it enters the nervous system. There is no canonical stream of consciousness to refer to in making a decision as to what we are actually conscious of, and when we first become conscious of it.

A possible weak point in Dennett's account is the claim that the phenomenal aspect of our experience – how experience seems to us – is a complex of judgements and dispositions. Many philosophers see the central question of consciousness as explaining the seemingly ineffable subjective quality of our experience, or 'qualia'. Dennett claims that there are no such things as qualia; the quality of conscious experience is a result of micro-judgements made by various parts of our brain. For Dennett there is no reality to the subjective quality of our experience over an above the fact that there seems to be that subjective quality.

A noticeable aspect of Daniel C. Dennett's work is his desire to make serious philosophy accessible to the general reader. He is a member of a regrettably small number of contemporary philosophers who are able to do philosophy in public, and do it well. This is in some ways related to his distinctive use of examples, metaphors and what he calls 'intuition pumps', which are analogies designed to prime the reader's intuitions in such as way as to make his arguments vivid and plausible.

Suggested reading
Dennett, Daniel C. 1987. *The Intentional Stance*. Cambridge, Mass.: Bradford Books/MIT Press.
Dennett, Daniel C. 1991. *Consciousness Explained*. London: Allen Lane.
Dennett, Daniel C. 1995. *Darwin's Dangerous Idea: Evolution and the Meanings of Life*. New York: Simon & Schuster.

Jacques Derrida
1930–   **Robert Eaglestone**

Jacques Derrida is one of the most significant and hard to categorize of contemporary philosophers. Deconstruction, the movement that he began, perhaps inadvertently, is contentious, receiving as much disdain as admiration. Born in 1930 in El-Biar in Algeria, Derrida was educated in France. In an interview he said that 'I am Jew from Algeria, from a certain type of community, in which belonging to Judaism was problematic, belonging to Algeria was problematic, belonging to France was problematic. So all this predisposed me to non-belonging'. This non-belonging, which is neither in nor out, characterizes all his work. His philosophical orientation comes from the phenomenological tradition of **Husserl**, **Heidegger** and **Levinas**, and from those he calls the 'masters of suspicion': **Marx**, **Nietzsche** and **Freud**. Although he is often assumed to be part of the 'linguistic turn' in contemporary thought, and does have some affinities with it, he rose to prominence in 1967 when, in a series of papers and books, he 'deconstructed' the presuppositions that underlay precisely this turn.

Derrida's philosophical work aims at what he called in *Of Grammatology* (1967) the 'exorbitant'. By this he does not mean 'grossly expensive', but rather an older sense of the word which derives from the Latin root, *exitorbitare*, meaning 'to go out of the wheel track'. The exorbitant is that which is outside the orbit, the orb (eye) or, more prosaically, the wheel rut of western philosophy. His interest lies in what lies outside systems of thought which claim to explain everything, what they claim to explain but cannot. Although his work has never rejected coherence (a 'system' in a 'minimal sense of the word'), deconstruction is 'not only a search for, but itself a consequence of, the fact that the system is impossible'. To look for the 'exorbitant' in a philosophical text means seeing it in a new way, questioning its framework and making new connections. These moments where the 'exorbitant' appears he calls 'traces'. For example, he might ask what sort of non-philosophical ideas lie outside the 'wheel rut' of a book like this one: what or who is excluded and why? What is the very idea of a short introduction to great thinkers saying 'between the lines' about, perhaps, the canon of great philosophers? Is there, perhaps, some common logic to the very process of introducing philosophers in 800 or so words that betrays their thought? (And isn't 'betray' in that sentence interesting? It means seemingly opposite things: both 'to represent incorrectly' and 'to reveal truly an inner thought', as a Freudian slip betrays a desire. What might it mean about a philosopher if their work could be 'betrayed' in a book like this?)

In order to prevent his thought becoming a system, and to stress the activity of reading and doing philosophy, and how it varies from philosophical text to philosophical text, Derrida constantly renames and develops his terms in different contexts. This is why Derrida claims that deconstruction is not a method: it is different in every case. It also means that unless you are familiar with the text Derrida is discussing, his work can be quite obscure. Derrida is one of the most demanding reads because to read him properly, you usually have to read something else carefully first.

His work is not a rejection of philosophy, but what he calls an attempt to find 'a non-philosophical site from which to question philosophy', and since western philosophical language permeates all western culture (especially when, for example, it engages with non-western cultures), this process of turning the tools of reason onto reason itself is quite complex. A 'non-philosophical site' cannot simply be chosen, since we are already enmeshed in western thought. It has to be uncovered by a sort of philosophical unweaving: and this is exactly the process of deconstruction.

However, if Derrida's work is not a method and does not offer a philosophical position, it is motivated by a consistent series of concerns about ethics, about identity and belonging, about politics and community, and about aesthetics, a consistency he says that 'others may find downright monotonous'. Some commentators have suggested that his work in the 1960s and 1970s was concerned principally with language, and in the 1980s and 1990s has turned to more ethical and political concerns. However, as early as *Of Grammatology*, Derrida points out that the very reason for undertaking this deconstructive attempt is ethical, aiming to uncover the (male, white, European, Christian) exclusivity of western thought. Later, he argued that 'Deconstruction is justice'.

Suggested reading
Derrida. J. 1976. *Writing and Difference*. London: Routledge.
Derrida, J. & Ferraris, M. 2001. *A Taste for the Secret*. Oxford: Polity.
Royle, N. 2003. *Jacques Derrida*. London: Routledge.

René Descartes
1596–1650   Jonathan Walmsley

Descartes set out to destroy Aristotelean philosophy. He was entranced by the certainty that mathematics conferred upon its conclusions. Kepler and Galileo, moreover, had shown that mathematics had application to the natural world. **Aristotle**'s philosophy placed no emphasis upon irrefutable certainty and relied upon consensus as a basis for knowledge. Nor did Aristotelean natural philosophy lend itself to mathematicization. It was Descartes' aim to underpin his knowledge of the world with unshakeable foundations by importing the certainty of mathematics into the physical and metaphysical spheres.

This was no simple task – where was the purity of mathematics in the chaos of experience? To find the wanted certainty, Descartes had to remove any hint of doubt from the premises upon which he would build his new knowledge. It was his methodology at this point that set him apart from his predecessors. He chose not to rely upon popular opinion, or the writings of the ancients. He even questioned his own perceptions, opinions and knowledge.

Rather than review each of his opinions individually, Descartes examined the foundation on which they were all based – perceptual experience. If this foundation was found wanting, the structure built upon it should be dismissed. Descartes recognized that his perceptual faculties misled him through illusion and hallucination. In dreams he had experiences which were not real. Perception produced only dubitable beliefs.

But the possibility of doubt was difficult to maintain against the vigour of sensation. To counter this weakness, Descartes supposed there was a powerful evil demon whose vocation it was to deceive us. Such a mighty creature would be well equipped to feed sensations of all sorts. The world would seem to you as it does now, but there would be nothing correspondent to any of your perceptions. The scepticism engendered by this creature would cast doubt on all beliefs derived from sensation. All that remained after this epistemic cleansing would be certain.

But what was left? Certainly not the objects around me, nor even my body. Knowledge of these was based on sensation and sensation could not guarantee certainty. What then could be known? Must I doubt the existence of everything? Might I doubt that I exist? It is here that the doubt comes to an end. I cannot doubt that I exist – for, Descartes maintains, in this very act of doubting I am existing. 'I think', declared Descartes, 'therefore I am.' But what is the 'I' that exists? It is not some material thing – it is possible to doubt that all material things exist, but not that 'I' do. 'I' am a thinking thing and a thing, moreover, that certainly exists. This was Descartes' Archimedean point, from which he would move the world.

Yet in comparison to our former knowledge, this point seems hopelessly small. Where previously we had the richness of the entire world in which to believe, now we only have one small set of disembodied thoughts and memories. How can we move from this minute point of thought to the pageant of experience? Our knowledge of the world had to be constructed of the most solid of certainties. Descartes thought that such material could be found in God. If God truly existed, the things that we clearly and distinctly perceive must surely exist, as God is benevolent and would not allow us to be deceived. A demonstration of the necessary existence of God is thus crucial to Descartes' plan. It is consequently unfortunate that the arguments that Descartes advanced to prove the existence of God were all flawed.

Descartes did destroy Aristotle, but his own programme was a failure. Yet it was not his success that was important, it was the radical nature of his strategy and the way in which he attempted to execute it. His emphasis upon mathematical certainty and universal law had a profound effect upon science. This soon found profitable expression in Newton's hands. Descartes' individualism defined modernism in philosophy. But the sceptical spectre of the evil demon still haunts modern philosophical work – it is a possession that no one has yet managed to exorcise, except by neglecting to consider it in the first instance. Descartes was the making of science and the downfall of philosophy.

Suggested reading
Cottingham, J., Stoothoff, R., Murdoch, D., Kenny, A. 1988 (eds). *Descartes: Selected Philosophical Writings*. Cambridge: Cambridge University Press.
Williams, B. 1990. *Descartes: The Project of Pure Enquiry*. London: Penguin.
Garber, D. 1992. *Descartes' Metaphysical Physics*. Chicago: University of Chicago Press.

John Dewey
1859–1952   Jack Ritchie

To appreciate all aspects of the thought of John Dewey, who was a philosopher, educationalist and social campaigner, we need to understand his theory of inquiry or what he sometimes called his logic. Unlike **Peirce**, from whom Dewey takes many of his ideas, this theory of inquiry encompasses morals and politics as well as science.

Inquiry begins when we encounter a problem of some kind. When things go smoothly there is a seamless interaction between ourselves and the world. This is the normal course of experience. However, sometimes what we expect to happen does not. The results of an experiment are not what we predicted; a piece of legislation does not have the desired effect; our hammer breaks or something similar. The first task of inquiry is to isolate what has gone wrong and then to attempt to reconfigure our ideas and tools to help us cope with the problem. This practice is social. To ensure we get the best answer possible we must consult widely within our community in order to eliminate errors and oversights due to our own idiosyncrasies and biases. Finally, we return with our new beliefs and tools to experiment to see how things go and to improve and modify where necessary. However, even after this is done the beliefs that we have arrived at will be pro-visional for two reasons: first, because we are fallible; and second, because the contexts in which the problems initially arose are continually evolving and being changed by our solutions.

Dewey was tempted to call the beliefs that we come to at the end of our inquiries 'truths', but fearing this would just cause confusion opted instead for the term 'warranted assertions'. Although there is no end point to our inquiry, we can be said to make progress by coping better with a wider range of experience. The more I know about something, the deeper its meaning for me and the more possibilities there are in my interactions with it. For example, the greater the theoretical knowledge a scientist has of an electron, the more she will be able to interact with and manipulate electrons; and equally the more she can manipulate an electron, the more she will know about it.

Dewey claims that this picture of inquiry dissolves old problems of knowledge. Beliefs and desires are not representations of an external world, but tools, like hammers, which help us interact with the world. It makes no sense therefore to ask how we can be certain that our beliefs represent things as they really are. Moreover, according to Dewey, the division between the subject of experience (i.e. ourselves) and the experienced object, a division which lies behind many sceptical questions, is not our primary experience, it is rather the result of the first stage of analysis when we realize something has gone wrong. Experience in its original, unproblematic sense forms a unity.

To be successful, inquirers have to respond intelligently and imaginatively to new situations. This has a direct bearing on the way we think
of education. Just as knowledge is not the passive acquiring of bits of
experience, education should not be the passive activity of learning
isolated facts. Proper learning is training the mind to cope with new
experiences better and more imaginatively. The ideal educational system
must stimulate children with new experiences and cultivate the imaginative and varied responses required for inquiry. Dewey had the chance to
apply some of these ideas in the Laboratory School he established at
Chicago University.

Dewey's theory of inquiry also has political consequences. A society
progresses when it solves its problems. Inquiry is at its best when it is
social, when it involves as many minds as possible and when it is willing
to experiment and to adapt in the light of the new contexts and difficulties which it encounters. According to Dewey, the system of government
which ensures both this participation and experimentation is democracy.

The philosopher, as well as describing this process of inquiry, is also an
inquirer seeking solutions to problems. What is special about the
philosopher is that she has the opportunity and training to stand furthest
back from the details of society to question some of its fundamental
values; and it is the role of the philosopher to be always questioning.
However, even she cannot view things entirely from the outside and thus
her proclamations must be treated also as provisional and fallible.

Dewey remained philosophically and politically active right up until his
death in 1952. By that time the pragmatism which he had spent his
career articulating was on the wane. Philosophy departments became
largely dominated by the more technical analytical style which continues
to dominate today. However, the last twenty years have seen renewed
interest in Dewey's ideas among many philosophers, including such
philosophical heavyweights as **Hilary Putnam** and **Richard Rorty**, and
indeed there is much to learn from this humane and optimistic voice
which sees the problems of philosophy as the problems of society.

Suggested reading
Dewey, J. 1997 [1916]. *Democracy and Education*. New York: Free Press.
Dewey, J. 1977 [1925]. *Experience and Nature*. Chicago: Open Court.
Dewey, J. 1980 [1934]. *Art as Experience*. New York: G. P. Putnam's Sons.

Wilhelm Dilthey

1833–1911   Marc A. Hight

Despite being hailed by the famed Spanish philosopher Ortega y Gasset as 'the most important thinker of the second half of the nineteenth century,' Wilhelm Dilthey remains an obscure figure to the Anglo-American world. This while notables like **Heidegger** and **Husserl** openly recognize their debt to the breadth and depth of Dilthey's thought.

Dilthey is best known for his defence of the distinction between the human sciences (*Geisteswissenschaften*) and the natural sciences; a distinction his positivist-minded contemporaries were intent on denying. Yet this defence is best understood as a part of his lifelong goal to provide a secure foundation for the human sciences. These include disciplines like history, psychology, economics and sociology. Dilthey asked what history and psychology and the other human sciences require in order to be done at all. That is, what is required to understand humanity? The individual human sciences are portrayed by Dilthey as interrelated and to some degree inseparable parts of a distinctive way of knowing.

Both a professional philosopher and a practising historian (he acquired some fame for his intellectual biography of Schleiermacher), Dilthey believed that historical reflection was essential to understanding humanity. He also believed that philosophy only has value when serving a practical end. Humans are constantly wrestling with pain, irrational upsets, and questions about meaning in the world. We all have what Dilthey calls a 'metaphysical impulse' to find a coherent picture of reality (a *Weltanschauung* or worldview) which addresses these concerns. Religion is one response to this impulse. When the response is governed by critical reflection, we call it 'philosophy'. Philosophy thus serves an important role: to produce rules for action and empower those who use it by increasing self-awareness. Various religions and philosophies generate worldviews which seek to account for the world as we experience it.

Alas, these worldviews frequently conflict. Although Dilthey argues that widely-held views must have some element of truth, he claims that each particular view is historically determined and essentially relative. This claim, which has popularly become known as historicism, pushes Dilthey towards relativism about the nature of the world and what we can know about it. Yet Dilthey resists complete relativism, asserting that core ways of thinking (like basic logic) are independently true regardless of historical context. This move allows us to study humanity in its temporal forms and learn from the worldviews we encounter.

What then separates the human sciences from the natural? Dilthey indicates that the human sciences share one vital feature: they are essentially about the life of the mind. This includes not only the capacity for abstract thought, but also what is produced by this activity: things like language, religion, law, even the fruits of ingenuity and technology such as tools and machines. Dilthey collectively calls these consequences the 'objective mind'.

What is unique about the life of the mind is that it essentially makes reference to purposiveness and to judgements of value in a manner that is conventional and historically conditioned. When a natural scientist asserts a law of nature, no assumptions about context or intention are made. The claim is true or false independently of where and when it is made. But claims about humans are relative to the purposes of those involved, the interests and values of those making the claim, and the context surrounding both the subject and the object of the inquiry. As Dilthey summarizes the difference, natural science provides explanations whereas the human sciences produce understandings.

What provides the subject matter for social scientists is what Dilthey named 'life expressions'. The physical events that constitute human activity (whether the utterance of a word, a facial expression, or the act of leaving a room) carry both meaning and intention that reveal the human mind. We do not know about our humanity from mere intro-spection – such information is too limited to constitute science. The most revealing life expressions are the objective mind. The task of the human scientist is thus to study the consequences of the activities of the mind. By recognizing the limits imposed by historical context and interpreting them appropriately (Dilthey helped develop contemporary hermeneutics – the study of interpretation), we can hope to achieve genuine and useful knowledge about ourselves and humanity generally.

Dilthey was one of the first philosophers to argue persuasively that the methods of positivistic natural science should not be applied to the study of humankind. Instead, he sought to ground our knowledge of humanity on its own separate yet reliable foundation.

Suggested reading

Makkreel, R. and Rodi, F. 1992 (eds). *An Introduction to the Human Sciences: Selected Works of William Dilthey*. Princeton: Princeton University Press.

Makkreel, R. 1992. *Dilthey: Philosopher of the Human Studies*. Princeton: Princeton University Press.

Makkreel, R. 1997 (ed.). *Wilhelm Dilthey: Selected Works: Poetry and Experience*. Princeton: Princeton University Press.

Albert Einstein

1879–1955   Irving Krakow

Albert Einstein is famous as the creator of the special and general theories of relativity, and as a co-founder of quantum theory, the two major revolutions in twentieth-century physics. Einstein contributed to statistical physics and the theory of radiation, but this work is not well-known to the public. For many years, Einstein argued with Niels Bohr and his followers about problems with causality and probability which arise in quantum theory. Today, it is recognized that Einstein mistakenly rejected Bohr's views. During the last thirty years of his life, Einstein tried unsuccessfully to unite gravity and electromagnetism in a single theory, a project discussed in his paper on general relativity in 1916. Einstein's contributions to physical theory make him one of the very few giants in the history of physics.

Einstein was born on 14 March 1879, in Ulm, Germany, to Jewish parents. He was quite religious until the age of 12, but his readings in popular science convinced him the stories in the Bible were flawed. For Einstein, a stubbornly independent thinker, schools were too rigid, and examinations too arbitrary. He learned mathematics from his uncle and through self-study. A music lover all his life, Einstein was a good violinist, and played chamber music with his friends to relax. His left-leaning political views, fuelled by his concern for social justice, led to a large FBI file comprising letters from his critics. In 1939, he and Leo Szilard sent a letter to President Franklin Roosevelt about work in nuclear physics which could lead to the creation of a powerful explosive device, and Roosevelt took the letter seriously. Einstein's action led directly to

American atomic research. He was offered the presidency of Israel in 1952, an honour he sadly turned down. Einstein, never a good family man, was married twice, first to Mileva Maric, a fellow student at the polytechnic, in 1903. They had two sons, Hans Albert and Eduard, but were divorced in 1919. Einstein then married his cousin Elsa, a childhood companion, who cared for him during a long illness.

In 1905, while working as a patent examiner in Zurich, Einstein's creativity exploded. He wrote six extraordinary papers. In March, his enormously influential paper on the photoelectric effect introduced the concept of light as both particle and wave, and led to his receiving the Nobel Prize. In April, he completed his doctoral thesis on determining the size of molecules. In May, in a paper on Brownian motion, he showed how molecules can cause the movement of small particles dispersed in a liquid.

In June, his first paper on special relativity was published. He postulated that the velocity of light was constant in empty space – later verified in studies of the motion of double stars – and that nothing can travel faster than light. He also showed that time 'slows down' on a moving object, an effect which was experimentally verified. A short paper appeared in September, in which Einstein wrote, 'We are led to the more general conclusion that the mass of a body is a measure of its energy content.' This sentence is in effect the famous equation, $E = MC^2$. Finally, a second paper on Brownian motion appeared in December.

Einstein's theory of general relativity appeared in 1916. It introduced the concept of four-dimensional space-time, and showed how gravity could be conceived as the 'curvature' of space-time created by the presence of matter. Einstein insisted that the curvature of space-time must be distinguished from everything else that exists, such as electro-magnetic fields and atomic particles. This vital, but problematic, distinction plagues us today in the unsuccessful efforts to combine general relativity and quantum mechanics into a single theory.

Einstein's first paper on the behaviour of light in a gravitational field appeared in 1911. He predicted that the sun's gravitational field, acting like an optical lens, would carry the light of a star located behind the sun around to the front of the sun so it could be observed. This prediction was verified, with great fanfare, by a famous expedition to observe an eclipse in 1919.

Einstein is still famous today although he died in 1955. All talk about the size of the universe, black holes, worm-holes, and time travel are based on his general relativity. We can't exaggerate how much Einstein's scientific work and personal charisma influenced the popular interest in science today. We will always remember Albert Einstein as a great scientist, and as a very human person.

Suggested reading

Frank, P. 2002 [1953]. *Einstein: His Life and Times*. Cambridge, Mass.: Da Capo Press.

Levenson, T. 2004. *Einstein in Berlin*. London: Bantam Books.

Pais, A. 1984. *Subtle is the Lord: the Science and Life of Albert Einstein*. Oxford: Oxford University Press.

Desiderius Erasmus

c. 1467–1536   **Alex Voorhoeve**

In the summer of 1514, Desiderius Erasmus was beginning to establish his name as the leading humanist scholar of his age, when he was recalled to his monastery in his native Holland. Orphaned at the age of seven, Erasmus had been pressured into monastic life by his guardians, and had only escaped in his mid-twenties. He refused to return, as the idea filled him with dread. 'Whenever I consider it, the jealousy and lack of learning of the priests come to mind,' he wrote to his prior. 'Those cold, useless conversations! I am not fit for that life, as I have a horror of ceremony and a love of freedom. The study of humane letters alone attracts my spirit.'

These 'humane letters' were the literature of classical antiquity. The study and dissemination of these works was the aim of the Renaissance humanists. They opposed the established study of Aristotelian philosophy and science, and scholastic speculative metaphysics. Instead, they focused on the practical arts of social life: rhetoric, grammar, history, poetry, and moral philosophy. Reflecting the needs of an increasingly urban and literate society, the humanists were preoccupied with the place and potential of the individual in this world. In classical antiquity they found a culture which appeared to have answers to the questions they faced regarding the individual's relation to the community. To the humanists, the stylistic training of the ancients, as well as their discourses on citizenship, offered a course in civic virtue. Their principal ideal was the eloquent, informed and moral person who could be a persuasive civilizing presence in Christian society. Erasmus was the embodiment of this ideal.

Orthodox theologians accused humanists of exposing the young to 'heathen, lascivious authors'. Erasmus dealt with this objection in his first important work *Antibarbari* (*Against the Barbarians*, 1520). He argued that though the Fall had darkened the human intellect and undermined human potential for virtue, it had not eradicated them altogether. Consequently, not all knowledge was laid down in the New Testament. Excellent classical authors had achieved the highest form of secular wisdom, and the aim should be to use the best of classical and Christian teaching to restore man to his prelapsarian nature. Erasmus's life was devoted to this aim through, among others, his popular collection of classical sayings, the *Adagia* (1500), and his great theological work, the first Greek printing of the New Testament, with his new Latin translation and annotations.

Erasmus also aimed to educate people by revealing their weaknesses. He exposed the contrast between the behaviour of society's leaders and their professed standards of behaviour in his best-known work, *In Praise of Folly* (1509), in which Folly lauds herself as the source of human happiness. For without madness 'what man or woman would offer their necks to the halter of matrimony?' And what of the philosophers and teachers, 'the most disaster-stricken of people, who stand dishevelled in their classrooms, wasting away because of their labours, deafened by their students' shouting', who wouldn't last another day without their illusions of grand learning? Folly also mercilessly exposes the delusions of warring princes, and pompous cardinals and popes.

These works inspired many leaders of the Reformation. Erasmus's scepticism about individual powers of reason, however, led him to distance himself from their conception of a wholly personal relationship with God. The frail judgement of the individual, he believed, needed support from the judgement of others in the community represented by the Church. This disagreement found expression in his exchange with

Luther on free will. Luther had argued that individuals were incapable of choosing the right life freely, being wholly dependent on divine grace. Erasmus contended that the subject was too complicated, and the Bible too difficult to interpret on the topic. He therefore recommended that one suspend judgement while accepting the traditional church view, that humans were capable of choosing the path to salvation with the help of grace. Luther answered that Erasmus could remain a sceptic if he wished, but should be aware that Judgement Day was coming and that 'The Holy Ghost is not a sceptic'.

Erasmus's stress on the need for a cosmopolitan community of discourse, along with a vivid awareness of the horrors of war, led him to fiercely oppose armed conflict. His moving *Dulce Bellum Inexpertis* (*War is Sweet to the Inexperienced*, 1515) still inspires pacifists.

To present-day believers, Erasmus offers an example of how faith can be combined with a sceptical and cosmopolitan outlook. And to those 'disaster-stricken' scholars, his writing represents an inspiring faith in the humanizing power of the humanities.

Suggested reading

Erasmus, D. 1993 [1509] *In Praise of Folly*. Harmondsworth: Penguin.
Augustijn, C. 1996. *Erasmus: His Life, Works and Influence*. Toronto: University of Toronto Press.
Rummel, E. 1991. *The Erasmus Reader*. Toronto: University of Toronto Press.

Michel Foucault

1926–1984 **Jeremy Stangroom**

Michel Foucault trod a new path for French philosophy in the second half of the twentieth century. Drawing on the disciplines of history, psychology, sociology and philosophy, he was interested in the way in which power and knowledge interact to produce the human subject (the self). Foucault sought to show how the human subject is constituted, as a knowing, knowable and self-knowing being, in relations of power and discourse. His pursuit of the human subject involved rethinking the concept of power, and investigating the links between power and knowledge.

According to Foucault, in contemporary western society, there are three 'modes of objectification' which transform human beings into subjects, and taken together these form the central focus of his work. These are: 'dividing practices'; 'scientific classification'; and 'subjectification'.

'Dividing practices' serve to objectify people by dividing them from others by means of such distinctions as the normal and the abnormal, the permitted and the forbidden. Through dividing practices, people are categorized, for example, as madmen, prisoners, or mental patients. These categories provide individuals with identities by which they will be recognized both by themselves and by others. Hence in *Madness and Civilization* (1961), Foucault detailed the way in which 'madness' became recognized as a specific and real category of human behaviour, one which legitimized the confinement of people in institutions.

The mode of 'scientific classification' objectifies the human subject by means of the discourses and practices of the human and social sciences. For example, it is possible to break down 'mental illness' into the myriad categories of the American Psychiatric Association's *Diagnostic and Statistical Manual of Mental Disorders*. And in *The Birth of the Clinic* (1963), Foucault shows how the development of the human sciences in the nineteenth century saw the human body increasingly being treated as an 'object' – as it is in the discourses and practices of modern medicine.

'Subjectification' differs from the preceding modes of objectification in that it concerns the way in which humans are actively involved in constituting *themselves* as subjects. This theme runs through Foucault's three-volume *The History of Sexuality* (1976, 1984, 1984), where he describes how the wish to understand oneself prompts confession of our innermost thoughts, feelings and desires both to ourselves and to others. This involves us in networks of power relations with authority figures – for example, doctors and psychiatrists – who claim to be able to interpret our confessions and reveal their truth. According to Foucault, through the expansion of this process of confession, individuals become objects of knowledge both to themselves and to others, and objects, moreover, who have learned how to change themselves. He argues that this process is a fundamental aspect of the expanding technologies for the control and discipline of bodies and populations.

The general process of the objectification of the human subject is rooted in historical developments in the nature of power, and in corresponding developments in the fields of human and scientific knowledge. Foucault uses the term 'power/knowledge' to describe this conjunction of power and knowledge. Rather than stressing coercion, repression and prohibition, he wants to demonstrate how power *produces* both the human subject and the knowledge which may be gained of him. This idea reaches its fullest expression in his notion of 'bio-power'.

In the course of the seventeenth century, Foucault noted, state power came to intrude on every aspect of people's lives. Then with the emergence of industrial capitalism there was a shift away from the use of physical force as a form of negative power, towards new, more effective technologies of power, which were productive and sought to foster human life. The state began to pay increasing attention to the growth and health of its population. Foucault argued that a new regime of 'bio-power' had taken hold, one which focused on the management and administration of the human species or population and the control or 'discipline' of the human body.

In *Discipline and Punish* (1975), Foucault used **Jeremy Bentham**'s plan for a type of prison called the panopticon as a paradigmatic example of disciplinary technology. The architecture of the panopticon is such that the power apparatus operates effectively whether or not there is a guardian present. The prisoner has no way of knowing whether he is being watched so he must behave as if surveillance were constant and unending. Since the prisoner never knows when he is being observed, he becomes his own guardian. For Foucault, the panopticon brings together power, knowledge, the control of the body and the control of space into an integrated disciplinary technology. The parallels with wider society are clear. Society exerts its greatest power to the extent that it produces individual human subjects who police themselves in terms of the discourses and practices of sexual, moral, physical and psychological normality.

Suggested reading

Foucault, M. 1991 [1975]. *Discipline and Punish: The Birth of the Prison*. Harmondsworth: Penguin.
Couzens Hoy, D. 1986 (ed.). *Foucault: A Critical Reader*. Oxford: Blackwell.
Rabinow, P. 1991 (ed.). *The Foucault Reader*. Harmondsworth: Penguin.

Gottlob Frege

1848–1925   **Peter Herissone-Kelly**

Without doubt, Gottlob Frege deserves to be counted amongst the most important and influential philosophers and logicians of the past two centuries. In his early *Begriffsschrift* (*Concept Script*, 1879), he single-handedly took the first major leaps forward in formal logic since **Aristotle**, inventing the propositional and predicate calculi (even though the unwieldy notation he used for their expression was soon understandably abandoned by others).

He also made, in *Grundlagen der Arithmetik* (*Foundations of Arithmetic*, 1884), a valiant and ambitious attempt to prove the thesis of logicism in mathematics: the belief that the whole of mathematics can (contra **Kant** and others) be shown to be a branch of logic. This involved providing a definition of number in terms of the logical notion of a class, or set. Fascinating as his attempt was, it was ultimately proved by **Bertrand Russell** to be doomed to failure, relying as it did on an axiom that entailed the existence of the set of all sets that are not members of themselves. What has come to be known as Russell's Paradox shows that such a set is an impossible item. That is, clearly the set is either a member of itself, or it is not. If it is a member of itself, then it is not a member of itself, and if it is not a member of itself, then it is a member of itself.

However, it is chiefly in connection with the sense/reference distinction in the philosophy of language that Frege's name is known to modern-day students of philosophy. The introduction of this distinction in the seminal paper 'Über Sinn und Bedeutung' ('On Sense and Reference', 1892) is motivated by a puzzle about the nature of true identity statements of the form 'a = b'. To see what this puzzle is, consider the following two sentences:

(1) Hesperus is Hesperus
(2) Hesperus is Phosphorus

Since the names 'Hesperus' and 'Phosphorus' both refer to the same object (the planet Venus), both (1) and (2) are true. And yet whilst (1) is clearly trivially true, (2) is not: it had to be empirically discovered by astronomers to be true. Thus, (1) and (2) differ in informational content.

Yet the puzzle is that since Hesperus is Phosphorus, we could be forgiven for supposing that (1) and (2) should be alike in meaning, and hence should both convey precisely the same information.

Frege's solution is that whilst the names 'Hesperus' and 'Phosphorus' share a reference, they nonetheless differ in sense. The reference of an expression E is characterized by Frege as the extralinguistic item which E picks out (in our example, Venus); the sense of E, on the other hand, is explained – not completely unmysteriously – to be E's reference's 'mode of presentation'. He further portrays E's sense as that aspect of its meaning that determines, or fixes, what E's reference is; in other words, the sense of E is what needs to be grasped if we are to understand what object E picks out.

Crucially, it is quite possible, and indeed frequently occurs, that two expressions E1 and E2 might offer a different mode of presentation of one and the same object, or (which is perhaps to say the same thing) that the reference of E1 might be determined in a different way to that of E2. And just this is the case, so Frege argues, in our Hesperus/Phosphorus example. As a result of the disparity in sense between 'Hesperus' and 'Phosphorus', it is possible to know that Hesperus is Hesperus (since Hesperus has the same sense in both its occurrences in (1)), yet simultaneously not to know that Hesperus is Phosphorus.

Frege takes great pains to point out that sense is most definitely not something subjective, perhaps akin to an idea awakened in us when we hear an expression. Since the sense of E must be grasped by anyone who is to know what E stands for, it clearly must be something publicly accessible, something thoroughly objective.

Although not widely recognized in his own lifetime, over the last century or so Frege's theory of sense and reference has provided an indispensable philosophical springboard for an immense amount of work on the nature of meaning and the relationship between the world and language. It is beyond question that, without Frege, the contemporary philosophical landscape would be very different – and much less featureful.

Suggested reading
Frege, G. 'On Sense and Reference'. 1892. in Moore, A. 1993 (ed.). *Meaning and Reference*. Oxford: Oxford University Press.
Dummett, M. 1973. *Frege: Philosophy of Language*. London: Duckworth.
Kenny, A. 2000. *Frege: An Introduction to the Founder of Modern Analytic Philosophy*. Oxford: Blackwell.

Sigmund Freud

1856–1939   Jack Furlong

Confessing to his biographer, Ernest Jones, that he had read very little philosophy, Sigmund Freud remarked that 'As a young man, I felt a strong attraction toward speculation and ruthlessly checked it.' Philosophy, according to Freud, 'clings to the illusion that it can produce a complete and coherent picture of the universe.' If any human enterprise is able to give us such a picture, thought Freud, only science could do so, and so he strenuously allied himself and his programme with science. Ironically, most theorists today ridicule Freud's claim to scientific objectivity, while the 'speculative' aspect of his writing, not so ruthlessly checked as it turned out, continues to exercise philosophers.

Freud contended that his creation – psychoanalysis – marked the last of three scientific revolutions against human vanity. First, Copernicus showed that the earth was not the centre of the universe; Darwin then cast humans as merely one more species of animal. Subsequently, psychoanalysis undermined the final illusion – one closely associated with philosophy – that reason governs passion. Freud contended to the contrary that at every moment of our lives we are driven by unconscious desires which we cannot access owing to internal structures and mechanisms that protect us from facing raw 'untamed passions'. Underneath our conscious lives a struggle ensues between indiscriminate, mostly sexual, desires (the Freudian 'id') and the 'censor' of those desires (the 'superego'), both juggling for control of the ego or the self. In other words, conscious life, the realm of philosophy, reflects merely the surface of the mental; most of our thinking lives – feelings, motivations, thoughts – are not formed by *us* (as egos) but rather by the dynamic processes of the unconscious. Psychoanalysis, Freud teaches, aims to interpret messages the unconscious sends us through dreams, slips of the tongue, symptoms, jokes – routes not patrolled by the superego – in order to achieve insight into our inner lives. What the psychoanalyst uncovers will not comfort (sexual desire for our mothers, death wishes etc.). However, knowing the unconscious roots of our selves can ultimately restore the control and order we thought we had enjoyed originally. In this respect, Freud is no revolutionary.

Philosophers have participated vigorously in the unmasking of Freudian pretensions to scientific and moral authority. Yet many have found inspiration in parts of Freud's vision.

Philosophers of mind, reading Freud, have focused mainly, though not exclusively, on how unconscious processes undermine the traditional understanding of the self as an autonomous, rational, agent. For Freud, reasons we give for our actions are self-deceiving, since the ego, the rational self, is not in control of its own motives. Whether they applaud or lament Freud's demolition of the conscious, autonomous self, most philosophers working in this area reject the dynamic nature of the unconscious: it is one thing to show how we might view ourselves as constituted largely by blind, unconscious processes; it is quite another to claim that that such 'primary processes', as Freud calls them, actively shape, displace, condense ideas and images, as if a homunculus or 'little self' is pulling the strings of the larger, conscious, one.

A different kind of engagement with Freud began in the 1920s when the fledgling Institute for Social Research – later known as the Frankfurt School and then the school of Critical Theory – sought to use psychoanalytic concepts to soften the economic determinism of orthodox Marxism in order to develop a more nuanced critique of bourgeois culture. Thinkers such as Max Horkheimer, **Theodor Adorno**, Erich Fromm and Herbert Marcuse explored ways in which unconscious desires are structured by economic necessities and vice versa – including the socio-economic structuring of psychoanalysis itself, which they accuse of supporting the status quo. Today the current generation of critical theorists, notably **Jürgen Habermas**, continue to incorporate Freudian concepts into their analyses of bourgeois society.

A third employment of Freud in contemporary philosophy was inaugurated by philosopher/psychoanalyst **Jacques Lacan**, who explored the relation of language to unconscious desire. The unconscious, he is famous for saying, 'is structured like a language', and, hence, our desires cannot take shape except through that medium. Language structures the self, melding words and desires unconsciously, creating the 'symbolic order'. Because this order is built out of unconscious desires, it supports law – the authority of the father – since, according to Freud, our conscious lives begin with a love/hate relationship with the father. Feminist philosophers have exploited Lacan's approach to Freud as a way of detecting and unseating patriarchal elements in his thought. Luce Irigaray, for instance, calls for a 'women's way' of writing which would subvert the accepted order and liberate women from the oppression of the symbolic. Most recently, the so-called 'Slovenian School' of Slavoj Žižek has cast Lacanian/Freudian analysis more widely into the area of culture criticism.

All told, philosophers have exploited that very 'speculative' aspect of Freud's writing which he sought to repress, discovering ever more promising possibilities for his thought.

Suggested reading
Freud, S. 1991 [1917]. *Introductory Lectures on Psychoanalysis*. Harmondsworth: Penguin.
Gay, P. 1995 (ed.). *The Freud Reader*. New York: Norton.
Storr, A. 2001. *Freud: A Very Short Introduction*. Oxford: Oxford University Press.

Hans-Georg Gadamer
1900–2002   **Chris Lawn**

Since Descartes, modern philosophy has regarded correct method as a route to absolute certainty. Armed with a rational procedure, human thought becomes equal to natural science in replacing the dark forces of tradition with objective truth. The work of Hans-Georg Gadamer, especially *Truth and Method* (1960), contests this optimistic account of modernity. Gadamer starts by re-valuing the idea of tradition – from which Enlightenment thought distanced itself – claiming that 'tradition' and 'reason' cannot be so easily teased apart. For Gadamer, tradition cannot be an object of 'pure' rational enquiry. The idea that we can step outside our own cultural reference points to embrace timeless truth is a demonstrable fiction of modernist thought.

Gadamer relates his idea of 'tradition' to a reworked notion of 'prejudice', which he understands as pre-judice or pre-judgement, in other words as that which makes *any* kind of discrimination possible. A prejudice is not a distorting form of thought that must be shaken off before we see the world aright. For Gadamer prejudices are present in all understanding. Against Enlightenment claims that reason, detached from historical and cultural perspective, gives a test for truth, Gadamer claims that we are irredeemably embedded in language and culture – and that the escape to unclouded certainty via rational method is a chimera.

How does Gadamer substantiate the assertion that forms of under-standing are always prejudicial and that we cannot make strictly objective claims about the world? Here is where we find his singular con-tribution to contemporary thought. Understanding is invariably 'hermeneutical', he claims. The term derives from hermeneutics – theory of interpretation. Historically, hermeneutics was the art of correctly reading and interpreting ancient texts, notably the Bible. In Gadamer's hands hermeneutics becomes a more general procedure for understand-ing itself, which he terms 'philosophical hermeneutics' and characterizes in terms of a 'hermeneutical circle'. The idea of the circle refers to the constantly turning movement between one part of a text and its total meaning. In making sense of a fragment of the text one is always simul-taneously interpreting the whole. Gadamer justifies extending the role of hermeneutics, making it a necessary characteristic of any attempt to understand the world, by referring back to the history of hermeneutics and early attempts to codify interpretative practice.

Hermeneutics is also a submerged strand running through the history of philosophy. **Aristotle**'s account of *phronesis* or 'practical wisdom' is a case in point. In becoming moral we are habituated into a moral tradition, Aristotle asserts, but the moral agent is always confronted with situations that go beyond the regularities of habit. This oscillation between habit and novelty is similar to the dynamic of the hermeneutical circle.

Gadamer's principal authority for his claims is his teacher **Martin Heidegger**. In *Being and Time* Heidegger shows how interpretation of the world is impossible without pre-understanding. Against **Descartes** he shows that understanding is not worked out in the privacy of consciousness but through our being in the world. But if all understanding is interpretation, it is still guided by what Gadamer calls a 'fusion of horizons'. A text, or any thing or event within the world we interpret, has its own 'horizon of meaning'. Interpretation is sited within the mutual horizon of the interpreter and the thing to be interpreted.

The modernist thought that understanding depends on a detachment from tradition, effected by rational method, is undermined when viewed from the hermeneutical perspective. For Gadamer, truth is not method but simply what happens in dialogue. Acts of interpretation are dialogical, a ceaseless conversation that is, within tradition. The interpreter projects provisional meanings but these are disturbed and re-defined when the interpreter's own prejudices are questioned by the horizon of the text or the partner in dialogue. Ultimately, Gadamer claims, meanings can never be complete.

Another consequence of Gadamer's 'fusion of horizons' is a re-defined relationship to the past. If all understanding is dialogue, it is as much a conversation with the past as with the future. So the past is not 'another country' but a continuous effect in the present as contemporary language and that of antiquity work together within a common tradition. Here again the idea of methodological detachment is, for Gadamer, a non-starter. We cannot find an Archimedean point outside culture and language in our pursuit of truth, as our prejudices, the conditions of understanding, are part of what we seek to make comprehensible.

Gadamer's questioning of rational method rejects the view that reason stands behind language. Cultural products (including art) and the natural world are not objects for rational investigation but voices within the fabric of an interminable conversation.

Suggested reading

Gadamer, H-G. 1989 [1960]. *Truth and Method*. London: Sheed and Ward.
Gadamer, H-G. 2001. *Gadamer in Conversation: Reflections and Commentary*. New Haven: Yale University Press.
Grondin, J. 2003. *The Philosophy of Gadamer*. Chesham: Acumen.

Mahatma Gandhi

1869–1948   **Douglas Allen**

Mohandas Karamchand Gandhi, better known as Mahatma ('Great Soul/Self'), is arguably the most admired human being of the twentieth century. Not an academic philosopher, Gandhi was never concerned with abstract philosophical analysis. When asked his philosophy, he typically responded, 'My life is my message.' And yet one could make a strong case that Gandhi is more philosophically interesting and significant than most professional philosophers.

Gandhi, like Socrates, was a gadfly, and he was often an embarrassment and an irritant, even to his friends and allies. He challenges unacknowledged assumptions and uncritically accepted positions and allows us to envision different ways of seeing things. He explodes myths and arrogant provincialism and challenges power positions that pretend to be based on sound knowledge and morality.

Best known as a proponent of nonviolence (*ahimsa*), Gandhi challenges our analyses of violence and non-violence. Violence and non-violence, for Gandhi, include overt physical acts, but they include so much more.

As with **Kant** and many other philosophers, Gandhi focuses much of his attention on motives and intentions. Violence is often equated with hatred, and non-violence with love. However, Gandhi goes beyond most philosophical analyses by focusing on the violence of the status quo: economic violence, cultural violence, psychological violence, linguistic violence, and so forth. For Gandhi, if I am accumulating wealth and power, and my neighbour is in great need, and I do nothing to help alleviate the suffering of the other, then I contribute to and am complicit in the violence of the status quo.

Unlike most philosophers, Gandhi, like **Levinas**, emphasizes the primacy of morality. Gandhi has little sympathy for detached theories of knowledge that are not grounded in morality, or for theology and metaphysics which pretend to transcend morality.

In his approach to morality in general and violence in particular, Gandhi is well known for his emphasis on the integral, mutually reinforcing relationship between means and ends. One cannot use impure or immoral means to achieve worthy goals. This is the major reason he rejects utilitarianism. Although there may be short-term desired results, violent immoral means inevitably lead to defective ends. We fuel and become trapped in endless escalating cycles of violence and mutual destruction.

Gandhi's approach expresses an activist philosophy, which he often relates to the action-oriented philosophy of karma yoga in the *Bhagavad-Gita*: Act to fulfil your ethical duties with an attitude of non-attachment to the results of your actions. In this way, Gandhi experimented with ways to intervene non-violently to weaken endless cycles of violence and mutual destruction and allow us to realize ethical goals.

Although Gandhi's emphasis on intentions and duties often allows us to relate him to Kant, he is not really a Kantian. First, Gandhi describes himself as a 'pragmatic idealist'. He focuses on results. When he acted with good intentions and according to moral duty, but did not succeed in resisting hegemonic British imperialism, alleviating poverty and suffering, or overcoming caste prejudice and oppression, he evaluated his position as a 'failed experiment in truth'.

Second, Gandhi opposes any abstract, formalistic, universal, decontexualized approach which is then applied to particular situations. Gandhi contextualizes his analysis and is always experimenting with an open-ended truth reflecting imperfect understanding.

In this regard, Gandhi presents views that are relevant to recent philosophical developments regarding pragmatism, phenomenology and hermeneutics, relativism, anti-essentialism, and postmodernism. How do we deal with the inadequate dichotomy of universal, absolute essentialism versus particular, relative anti-essentialism? Gandhi, avoiding a kind of facile relativism, embraces absolute universals, such as non-violence, truth and the unity of all life. But Gandhi also maintains that as particular, relative, embodied human beings, none of us fully comprehends the absolute. The unity is always a unity with particular differences. The absolute may serve as a regulative ideal, but at most we have 'glimpses' of a truth that is always relative.

Therefore, we should be tolerant of the other, who has truths that we do not have, and we should realize that the movement toward greater truth is an action-oriented, co-operative, mutually reinforcing effort. This philosophical approach to truth necessarily involves dialogue, recognition of integral self-other relations, and embracing an open-ended process that resists the domination of false attempts at philosophical, religious, cultural, economic, or political closure.

Suggested reading

Gandhi, M. 1982. *An Autobiography, Or, The Story of My Experiments with Truth*. Harmondsworth: Penguin.

Iyer, R. 1993 (ed.). *The Essential Writings of Mahatma Gandhi*. Oxford: Oxford University Press.

Johnson, R. 2004 (ed.). *Gandhi's Experiments with Truth: Essential Writings by and about Mahatma Gandhi*. Lanham, Maryland: Lexington Books.

Kurt Gödel

1906–1978   **Christopher Norris**

Kurt Gödel was a Czech-born, Vienna-trained and US-domiciled logician and mathematician whose thinking is widely held to have transformed the conceptual bases of both disciplines. His doctoral thesis was devoted to proving the 'completeness' of logic, i.e., that there exists a sound and valid formal system wherein all logical truths have a well-defined place. (This thesis is limited to what is technically known as first-order logic.)

However, by far his best-known achievement was his proof of the incompleteness of any mathematical or logical system sufficiently complex to generate the truths of elementary arithmetic. That is to say, if such a system is logically consistent then it must contain at least one unprovable axiom, while any proof-procedure for this or that axiom will entail some result that is logically inconsistent with other axioms. Thus one is faced with the choice between proof and logical consistency, or with the prospect that even such basic truths as those set out by Peano for arithmetic must be regarded as incapable of rigorous proof.

In fact Gödel produced two separate theorems to this effect, the second more powerful (and hence more deeply disturbing for philosophy of mathematics) in so far as it established the logical impossibility that *any* fully axiomatized formal system could meet both of the classical requirements for proof and logical consistency. In short, *tertium non datur*: there was no third way or alternative approach that would reconcile the claims for completeness (i.e. truth under logical closure) and provability as regards each and every axiom of the system in question. From which it followed that something must be wrong with systems – like that developed in **Whitehead** and **Russell**'s *Principia Mathematica* – which purported to place the entirety of mathematics on a firmly logical basis.

This result – arrived at (ironically enough) through a formalized proof procedure – had all the more impact for emerging when mathematics seemed set upon the course predicted by David Hilbert just a few decades earlier: that it would soon resolve all the main outstanding problems with respect to its conceptual and logical foundations. At about the same time, Russell hit upon a kindred difficulty with his own earlier project, one that famously involved certain paradoxes about set theory. These had to do with self-referential instances like 'the set of all sets that are not members of themselves', or – as in Russell's more homely example – the barber in a certain town who shaves every man who doesn't shave himself. (In which case: who shaves the barber?)

Russell's solution to this – his 'theory of types' – was really just a stopgap remedy that sought to defuse such paradoxes by introducing a stipulative rule which scarcely resolved the deeper conceptual problem. Along with Gödel's incompleteness-proof this marked the end of that confident phase in philosophy of mathematics which followed the striking advances in set theory achieved during the late nineteenth and early twentieth centuries.

There is still widespread debate as to just what philosophical consequences should be drawn from Gödel's disconcerting result. Some commentators – 'postmodern' cultural theorists among them – are apt to treat it (along with quantum physics, Einsteinian relativity, chaos theory, and other such hybrid topoi) as marking the closure of science as an enterprise governed by the classical 'modernist' values of reason, objectivity and truth. However, nothing could be further from Gödel's Platonist outlook, convinced as he was that mathematical objects (numbers, sets, classes, etc.) exist quite apart from our knowledge of them and hence determine the truth-value – that is, the objective truth or falsehood – of any statements we might make concerning them. This applied even to certain undecidable theorems such as Cantor's continuum conjecture (the topic of a paper where Gödel's mathematical realism found its most forceful expression) or Goldbach's so-far exceptionless yet formally unproven hypothesis that every even number is the sum of two primes.

Thus Gödel was a Platonist about mathematics although one who believed – what many find incomprehensible – that at least in some cases we can and do have knowledge of such truths through a faculty of direct intuitive grasp that transcends the limits of empirical knowledge or formal-deductive reasoning.

Hence the claim (advanced by Roger Penrose and others) that Gödel's incompleteness theorem has far-reaching implications for cognitive psychology and philosophy of mind. For if indeed it is the case that we can know certain truths which by very definition exceed the utmost limit of formal, algorithmic, or computational proof, then of course this would entail that the human mind has powers of comprehension beyond anything specifiable in such terms. From which one may deduce that its workings cannot be explained – as advocates of 'strong' Artificial Intelligence would argue – by analogy with those of even the most powerful machine-run software program. That is to say, Gödel's incompleteness proof (his ability to produce it and ours to grasp the truth of it) offers good reason to suppose that human intelligence outruns the limits of effective computability.

Suggested reading

Gödel, K. 1962. *On Formally Undecidable Propositions of Principia Mathematica and related systems*. Edinburgh: Oliver & Boyd.

Nagel, E. and Newman, J. R. 1959 (eds). *Gödel's Proof*. London: Routledge & Kegan Paul.

Shanker, S. 1988 (ed). *Gödel's Theorem in Focus*. London: Routledge.

Jürgen Habermas

1929–   **James Gordon Finlayson**

Jürgen Habermas is arguably the most important and influential social theorist of the post-1945 world. Since the 1960s he has made notable contributions to Marxist theory, social philosophy, ethics, legal and political philosophy and he has recently written on biotechnology and on terrorism. He is probably best known for his first major work, *Theory of Communicative Action* (1982), for having developed the programme of 'discourse ethics' and for his major work on law and democracy, *Between Facts and Norms* (1992).

In *Theory of Communicative Action*, Habermas develops his social theory by giving it a 'linguistic-pragmatic' turn. Habermas begins from the assumption that the meaning of an utterance is inherently public and 'intersubjective': in other words, the product of the communicative interaction of language users. Habermas claims that there is a necessary connection between the validity of utterances and 'reaching-under-standing' (*Verständigung*), such that if there is reason to assert that something is true, then everyone ought to be able to accept it in an ideally prosecuted discourse. An ideally prosecuted discourse is one where every participant is sincere, no one is prevented from participation and everyone reasons correctly such that the better argument always wins. What makes utterances valid, therefore, is not some feature internal to them, but the underlying consensus-bringing norm of correctness, of which the two most important forms are truth and rightness.

Habermas draws a distinction between two types of action: communicative action, where the agents base their actions on (and coordinate their interactions by) their mutual recognition of validity-claims; and instrumental/strategic action, where the co-ordination of actions is linked to the their successful completion. Habermas argues that instrumental and strategic actions are (conceptually and in reality) always parasitic on communicative action. Hence instrumental and strategic actions alone cannot form a stable system of social action.

Habermas's conceptual distinction between communicative action and instrumental action is paralleled by his distinction between lifeworld and system in his social ontology: his description of the nature of social being. The lifeworld concerns the lived experience of the context of everyday life in which interactions between individuals are coordinated through speech and validity-claims. Systems are real patterns of instrumental action instantiated by money (the capitalist economy) and power (the administrative state).

This social ontology enables Habermas to offer an evaluative diagnosis of the pathologies of contemporary forms of life. The problem with modern society is not that it is too fully rationalized, as Weber and the Frankfurt School argued, but that systems of instrumental action (the capitalist economy and the state) have 'colonized' the lifeworld and dried up the natural reservoir of communicative action. Hence capitalist societies give rise to institutions, policies and laws which cannot find reasoned public agreement.

The programme of discourse ethics is thus a normative ethics cantilevered out of Habermas's communication theory. Discourse is the name for the rule-governed game of argumentation that agents enter into whenever they are required to back up the validity claims of their utterances by good reasons. In modern societies discourse is the unique default mechanism for settling conflicts of interest in the lifeworld. Habermas claims that on the basis of a rational reconstruction of the rules of discourse, and given certain assumptions about the nature of modern societies and about what it means to justify a moral norm, he can derive the moral principle he calls (U). A recent formulation of (U) states that: 'A norm is valid if and only if the foreseeable consequences and side effects of its general observance for the interests and value-orientations of each individual could be freely accepted jointly by all concerned.'

Habermas's political theory builds on his discourse ethics. Basically he argues for a version of liberal democracy which does justice to the ideals of inclusiveness, equality and universal solidarity that are implicit in the pragmatic presuppositions of discourse. The legitimacy of democratic laws and institutions rests on a complex of moral, ethical and pragmatic criteria; they must be consistent with morality, with a community's conception of the good, and practically enforceable.

Whether Habermas's social, moral and political theories form a consistent and coherent theory is a moot point. Habermas is unwilling to give up the central assumptions of his communication theory and tends to make everything fit in with it, rather as Microsoft once made all their software backwards – compatible with DOS. However, each branch of his theory has appeal in its own right, independent of the other branches. Habermas is a synthesizer, but he also a creative and original thinker, with a distinctive voice, seeking novel and practical solutions to real problems.

Suggested reading

Habermas, J. 1989 [1982]. *Theory of Communicative Action*. Oxford: Polity Press.
Habermas, J. 1996 [1992]. *Between Facts and Norms*. Oxford: Polity Press.
Finlayson, G. J. 2004. *Habermas: A Very Short Introduction*. Oxford: Oxford University Press.

F. A. Hayek

1899–1992   Orlan Lee

In 1974, the Nobel Committee awarded the prize for economics to Gunnar Myrdal and F. A. Hayek: not, as hitherto, for 'pure economics', but rather, 'for their penetrating analysis of the interdependence of economic, social and institutional phenomena'.

Friedrich August von Hayek – F. A. Hayek in his Anglo-American émigré career – was a descendant and interpreter of the 'Austrian school' of economics. Throughout most of his career he was loved and hated for only one early, popular, but polemical piece, *The Road to Serfdom* (1944). This essay on the dangers of economic decline and loss of social and political freedom which result from undue reliance on the doctrines of central planning, is widely regarded as one of the most influential books of the century. If read in context, it is an attack on the dictatorial systems of Soviet Russia and Nazi Germany, which both made use of social planning. J. M. Keynes, a moderate planner, agreed that such dangers existed, but argued that, in a free society, economists like Hayek and himself would be able to prevent them. But Keynes dismissed Hayek's more serious reviews because 'I don't believe that any more.'

Hayek was influential in the early 1930s, but lost ground to Keynes as the latter's theory for recovery from the great depression and for paying for the Second World War became dominant. The sudden widespread interest in Hayek's work is a very recent phenomenon. In the 1980s, the Reagan administration in the US and the Thatcher government in Britain openly avowed the ideas of Milton Friedman and Hayek for combating the inflationary policies of the 1970s. But Hayek was not really 'mainstream' until later still. Only in the 1990s did one find Hayek societies springing up all around the world, even at the London School of Economics – which would have been unthinkable for most of the twentieth century – and in China, the last major society officially committed to Marxist communism.

Hayek studied in post First World War Vienna. He became the Director of the Austrian Institute for Business Cycle Research in 1927. And he took part in the intellectual movement known as the Vienna Circle. His work on business cycles and *Prices and Production* caught the attention of Lionel Robbins, and in 1931 Hayek was invited to come to the London School of Economics.

In London, Hayek was prominent among leading British and émigré scholars. In 1947, he organized the Mt. Pelerin conference of intellectuals concerned about ideas affecting the reconstruction of Europe. The University of Chicago was another meeting place of émigré and social and economic thinkers in those years, and in 1951 Hayek was invited to move there.

Social thought and scientific reasoning had become the academic focus of Hayek's scholarship. Hayek stressed that the central question of economics was not allocation of resources, but how best to use knowledge of the economic process. For Hayek, the appearance of economic 'order' in society derived only from the market-driven reasoning of economic man. Practical experience of many individuals with respect to opportunities perceived contributes to a 'spontaneous order', the product of individual market-based action, not the product of overall design.

The 'scientism' of those who uncritically match the methodologies of the social sciences with those of the natural sciences has led, he contended, to unwarranted claims for certainty in the social sciences (*The Counter-Revolution of Science*, 1952). Like **Popper**, Hayek believed that if unwarranted claims for scientific validity go unchallenged, it will ultimately justify efforts at more intrusive government.

Ideally, the laws of society, like the laws of economics, should be seen only as practical, historical means of meeting social needs. In *The Constitution of Liberty* (1960), Hayek traced the historical emergence of the concept of political liberty – based upon limited government – in the Anglo-American tradition to which he had become a devoted adherent.

In 1962, Hayek returned to Europe to the University of Freiburg, the centre of liberal economic thought in Germany. Hayek distinguished between two theories of liberalism, the individualistic and the 'constructivist'. The one sees liberty as the result of limitations on the power of government, while the other is bent on creating new rights along with greater central power. The latter theory relies on the belief that planned social action can create what the former theory attributes only to often unconscious historical development.

Suggested reading

Hayek, F. A. 2001 [1944]. *The Road to Serfdom*. London: Routledge.
Hayek, F. A. 1976 [1960]. *The Constitution of Liberty*. London: Routledge.
Hayek, F. A. 1973. *Rules and Order Vol. 1: Of Law, Legislation, and Liberty*. Chicago: University of Chicago Press.

Georg Hegel

1770–1831   **Jeff Mason**

Unlike many philosophers, G. W. F. Hegel took change seriously. He saw that even the most enduring forms of life can end. Human being is historical and developmental. Our thinking strives to reach an adequate idea of reality and will never rest until it does. This need forces thought to a better understanding of its object. Hegel's great idea is that we can see a way beyond sensuous immediacy to increasingly adequate conceptions of reality. Finally, we arrive at a conception of reality as the unfolding of the human spirit, conceived as a unity of substance and subject.

We start with an idea we take to be true, find it contradicted in thought or by external reality, and must think again. Thinking again involves negativity. Philosophy questions and analyses old certainties and finds them one-sided and insufficient. Someone comes up with a better idea. The process is repeated many times. Slowly perceptive consciousness becomes self-conscious, then rational, and finally returns home to itself as spirit aware of itself as existing in and for itself. This is the famous Hegelian dialectic that starts with a thesis, generates an antithesis, and concludes by a leap to a new synthesis which overcomes the failings of the opposing views, while preserving what is true in them. Through it our understanding becomes ever more comprehensive, inclusive and systematic.

Consider two examples from his amazing *Phenomenology of Spirit* (1807). In one, we, who already understand the process, observe a human being, ignorant of reality as reason or spirit, who meets another conscious being like itself. The presence of this 'Other' makes the individual aware of itself in a new way, in fear and pride. The Other threatens to rob it of its independence as a self-conscious being, or, what seems to be the same thing, its life. They fight to the death in the mistaken belief that they cannot maintain their independence in mutual recognition.

Sadly, the exhilaration of victory does not last. The death of the Other merely produces a corpse. The victor learns to let the vanquished live on as slaves. In this act, consciousness splits itself in two. The master does not recognize itself in the slave, nor the slave in the master. Yet the advance in consciousness eventually belongs to the slaves, not to the masters, who remain mired in their obstinate pride. The slaves learn to co-operate. By transforming the world through work, they transform themselves. Finally, they have only to realize their own power and truth, achieved through work, and they will advance to a more adequate idea of the human spirit than that of the master.

In the other example, Hegel saw the unifying power of reason sweeping away customs and forms of daily life, overturning monarchy, religion and superstition and, in short, all the straws by which we mortals try to stay afloat in life. Reason demanded a clean break with the past. If the people do not wish to be free, then they must be forced to be free. Hegel connects the Enlightenment with the terror of the French revolution. This event showed him that there can be no clean break with the past. The trick is to mediate fairly between all the contesting interests of individuals and groups. The outcome is uncertain.

Hegel despaired over the question of how to ameliorate the inequalities produced by a capitalist mode of production. He saw a postponement of the problem in the European colonization of the rest of the world, circa 1830, but also that, eventually, it would bring a truly global market. In such conditions, the difficult task is to avoid injustice and the creation of a large alienated underclass that produces social unrest.

For Hegel, history is the imagining and the realization of freedom in the realm of 'objective mind', that is, in the mores, institutions and customs of people. It took a long time for the idea of freedom to appear in the world, and it will take a lot longer to become established everywhere. However, once propounded, the principle of freedom is undeniable. The gap between our idea of freedom and political reality can motivate us to change the world and make it fit for the life of free citizens. Any other response is to move backwards, but that, too, is possible.

Hegel did not predict the future so much as draw out a meaning from the past. We live through, with him, the formative moments of the western tradition, and in so doing begin to grasp the world conceptually. Spirit ends up in the *Phenomenology* aware of itself as an infinite Idea, or Absolute Being, first in art, then in religion and, finally, in philosophy. Hegel wants to retrieve spirit from its alienated forms and, by reliving its history, preserve and surpass what has gone before. He intimates that, through conceptual thought, the knower will finally come to posses an idea that is adequate to its object, and the knower and the known will be one.

Suggested reading

Hegel, G. 1979 [1807]. *Phenomenology of Spirit*. Oxford: Oxford University Press.
Weiss, F. 1974 (ed.). *Hegel: Essential Writings*. London: Harper and Row.
Singer, P. 2001. *Hegel: A Very Short Introduction*. Oxford: Oxford University Press.

Martin Heidegger

1889–1976   **Iain Thomson**

Martin Heidegger is widely considered to be one of the most original and important philosophers of the twentieth century and, thanks to his (failed) attempt to assume philosophical leadership of the century's most execrable political movement (Nazism) and his later critique of the history of metaphysics from Anaximander to **Nietzsche** as inherently nihilistic, he is also certainly the most controversial.

He was born in Messkirch, Germany, on the outskirts of the Black Forest. Like Nietzsche, he came from a devoutly religious lower middle-class family. From very early on, the young Martin's intellectual gifts marked him out for a career in the priesthood and, although he eventually abandoned this path, the education it afforded him proved a firm foundation for his remarkable intellectual trajectory.

Heidegger published his early *magnum opus*, the brilliant but unfinished *Being and Time*, in 1927. In this book, he develops and deploys a method called 'phenomenological testimony' in order to interpret 'ontologically' – that is, in terms of what they reveal about the structural characteristics definitive of human existence – our ordinary everyday ('ontic') experience of phenomena such as guilt and anxiety. For example, Heidegger argues that our ordinary feelings of guilt bear phenomenological witness to the fact that as we make the choices which determine who we are, we are always actualizing one possible self at the expense of many others.

Using the same methodology, Heidegger argues that our ontic feelings of anxiety testify to the 'groundlessness' of human existence, revealing an ineradicable insecurity which Heidegger connects to the fact that our existential trajectories – the life-projects, roles, and identities which define who we are – have 'always already' been shaped by a past which we can never get behind and head off into a future in which these self-defining projects will always be incomplete, cut short by a death we can neither avoid nor control. In Heidegger's famous phrase we exist as a 'thrown project': thrown out of a past we cannot get behind, we project ourselves into a future we can never get beyond. 'Existence' *is* this standing-out into time, a temporal suspension between natality and mortality.

Heidegger divides this temporal suspension into its three 'existential structures': affectivity, telling and understanding. These existentials are three in number because they characterize the way in which the past, present and future allow things to show themselves to us. Thus the past filters the way things matter to us through our moods. In the present, things are made manifest through our use of language to articulate the meaning of our situation. Finally, the horizon of the future shapes the way things show up for us, in that the projects which define us extend into the indefinite future, thus running ultimately up against death, the final horizon which our projects can neither occupy nor secure.

Heidegger's analysis of the three temporal 'ecstases' – past, present and future – privileges futurity, then, because it is this running out toward and rebounding back from death which underlies the self-awareness distinguishing the 'world-constituting' existence of human 'Da-sein' from both the 'world-poor' awareness of the animal immersed in perceptual immediacy and from a 'worldless' entity – like a chair – which has no awareness at all.

Thus the big 'fundamental ontological' pay-off of *Being and Time* is Heidegger's claim that the three 'existentials' map onto the three 'ecstases,' and in their unity constitute the temporal structure according to which we make existence intelligible. In other words, Heidegger's 'existential analysis' yields a picture in which 'intelligibility' is grounded in time.

More precisely, Being is grounded in the temporal structure of those beings ('Da-sein') who have an understanding of Being. With this famous reconceptualization of the self not as a subject, consciousness, or ego but as a 'Dasein', Heidegger takes the German word for 'existence' (*Dasein*) and interprets it in terms of its basic semantic elements – 'there' (*Da*) + 'Being' (*Sein*) – in order to illustrate his claim that existence is fundamentally a 'being-there', that is, a temporally-structured making intelligible of the place in which we find ourselves.

In the second division of *Being and Time*, Heidegger argues that once we have used 'phenomenological testimony' to become aware of the ontological structures conditioning our 'existence', an 'authentic' life lived in ontic-ontological accord becomes possible. Heidegger claims that in decisive instants of resolution, we can envision ways of integrating our new-found existential knowledge into the projects which constitute our lives, thereby appropriating 'existence' so as to make it our own. Such 'authenticity' thus characterizes an existence in which an individual's life projects are brought into harmony with the existential structures which condition them, transforming that individual's guilty and anxious repression of their essential finitude and groundlessness into a reverence for the possible.

Heidegger was an extremely prolific writer and one should recognize that his work did not come to a stop with *Being and Time*. He continued to develop, extend, and in some places revolutionize his own thinking for another half century.

Suggested reading

Heidegger, M. 1978 [1927]. *Being and Time*. Oxford: Blackwell.
Dreyfus, H. L. 1991. *Being-in-the-World: A Commentary on Heidegger's Being and Time, Division I*. Cambridge: MIT Press.
Wrathall, M. and Dreyfus, H. L. 2004 (eds). *Blackwell Companion to Heidegger*. Oxford: Blackwell.

Thomas Hobbes

1588–1679 **Simon Eassom**

When Thomas Hobbes died in 1679 at the age of 91 his reputation as an atheist in religion and an absolutist in politics not only rendered him highly disreputable but also served to shunt his political ideas into relative obscurity for the next three hundred years. He was undoubtedly ahead of his time and his contribution to political philosophy has only been fully recognized more recently in the huge range of scholarship devoted to his most enduring work, *Leviathan* (1651).

At first, the impact Hobbes might make in the world of philosophy was not at all certain and it appeared his life would be spent in the conventional way for a graduate of the time, as a tutor to the sons of aristocracy. But by chance he gained service with William Cavendish, soon to be Earl of Devonshire. Hobbes spent the next twenty years as much Cavendish's friend and personal secretary as tutor, and the apprenticeship served him well. Most important, it introduced Hobbes to the scientific circle of England and France.

During this time Hobbes served as secretary to **Francis Bacon** – it is through Hobbes we know the apocryphal story of how Bacon caught his fatal cold, going out into the winter snow to stuff a dead chicken and prove the preservative power of freezing.

If Hobbes had achieved the acclaim he desired in his lifetime it would have been as a scientist. He achieved a modicum of success and a degree of notoriety, in part through his regular and frequent debates with leading members of the Royal Society and most notably through the open animosity between him and the French philosopher and mathematician **René Descartes**. Hobbes developed a radical theory of light and optics in the 1630s: he was probably the first person to suggest that colour is a creation of the brain and does not reside in the object. When Descartes published his own theory of vision in one of the appendices to his *Discourse On Method* (1637), the mutual distrust and jealousy grew. Yet Hobbes and Descartes were actually closely matched in their philosophies. Both were enamoured with mathematics and Euclidean geometry, the power and perfection of logical deduction, and their belief that mathematics begets physics and that both can explain the entire nature of reality. The significant difference between them was that Hobbes was a committed materialist on matters of psychology and the mind.

Between 1641 and 1658 Hobbes published the three parts of *The Elements of Philosophy*, a clear early attempt at a unity of science. *De Corpore* (1655) combined his views on scientific method, language and logic and formed the first part of his trilogy. *De Homine* followed in 1658. But ironically it was the third part *De Cive* – actually written first in 1640 – that gained Hobbes his reputation as a political theorist. In it Hobbes rejected the traditional view of **Plato** and **Aristotle** that political life is natural to human beings. By denying any innate desire of humans to be governed, the goal of political philosophy ceases to be the search for a theory of government but instead becomes a justification for accepting or needing government and a determination of what kind of government best fits humans' natural desires. *De Cive* served to situate political philosophy firmly within Hobbes' materialist conception of the world through its requirement for politics to be predicated on a scientific explanation of the nature of human beings.

But it was not until 1651 and the publication of *Leviathan* that Hobbes developed these ideas into a full and detailed political treatise.

He initiated what has become known as social contract theory. He argued the case for the state and a contract between the individuals in a society and the state. Significantly, the state is obligated to protect certain natural rights of citizens, act as arbiter in disputes, and generally enforce the mutually agreed-upon contract. If it fails to do this, the right to govern is forfeit. The basis for Hobbes' contract is twofold: first, humans are selfish and need their egoism restrained in order to act morally; and second, the establishment of a commonwealth is purely for the mutual benefit of its citizens.

The most controversial final stage of his argument is that the commonwealth is best served by a state with absolute powers, able to enforce the contract if necessary. Paradoxically, at a time of civil war and after the execution of Charles I, Hobbes defended the principle of absolute rule with a clear indication that a monarch could best serve the interests of citizens of a commonwealth as an impartial referee. His consummate skill was in arguing his case in a way that was palatable to republicans and royalists alike – a fact that no doubt kept him alive for 28 more years.

Suggested reading

Hobbes, T. 1981 [1651]. *Leviathan*. Harmondsworth: Penguin.

Sorrell, T. 1996. *The Cambridge Companion to Hobbes*. Cambridge: Cambridge University Press.

Hampton, J. 1988. *Hobbes and the Social Contract Tradition*. Cambridge: Cambridge University Press.

David Hume

1711–1776   Peter S. Fosl

When David Home (as his name was spelled then) entered the University of Edinburgh in 1723–25, his family expected him to pursue a career in the law. Hume, however, soon turned his attention to philosophy.

After a brief and disastrous experiment with the world of business in Bristol, Hume travelled to France where he would compose his monumental *Treatise of Human Nature* (1739–40). In Hume's somewhat misleading description, the text 'fell dead-born from the press, without reaching such distinction, as even to excite a murmur among the zealots'.

In Book I of the *Treatise*, Hume advanced the startling notion that 'All the sciences have a relation, greater or less, to human nature; and that however wide any of them may seem to run from it, they still return back by one passage or another.' Contrary to **Locke**, then, for whom philosophy was understood as the under-labourer of natural science, Hume maintains that the science of humanity is logically prior to any other science.

Unlike **Descartes**, Malebranche and **Berkeley**, Hume wished to root philosophy in human experience and do so in a way that both acknowledged the limits of reason and eschewed metaphysical posits such as 'spirit' or 'God'. 'When we see, that we have arrived at the utmost extent of human reason, we sit down contented; tho' we be perfectly satisfied in the main of our ignorance, and perceive that we can give no reason for our most general and most refined principles, beside our experience of their reality.'

Hume wished to produce a secular philosophy in the tradition of Newton, Shaftesbury, Mandeville, Hutcheson and Butler. As a sceptic, however, Hume never lost sight of the fact that nature itself is only grasped through human life and experience, and it remained for him doubtful as to whether human experience is actually able to yield knowledge.

The third book of Hume's *Treatise*, 'Of Morals', was published in 1740. Rather than appealing to a divine basis for morality, Hume instead looked only to humanity's animal capacity for 'sympathy' and upon the universalizing 'moral sentiment'. **Adam Smith** would follow a similar line of thought in his *Theory of the Moral Sentiments* (1759). It is a strategy that militates against Christian and rationalistic efforts, including those of Descartes and Locke, to deploy reason or revelation in the establishment of moral norms.

Hume's moral theory also rejects the egoistic naturalism developed by Hobbes and Mandeville, which explains apparently altruistic acts as really expressions of self-interest. Hume accepted the naturalistic, sentimental basis for morality developed by the egoists but sought to mitigate, if not wholly undermine, it by maintaining that the natural capacity for sympathy extends human concern beyond the immediate self. In many such instances, concern for one's own feelings of pleasure and pain converge with universal regard for others.

In 1752 Hume published the *Political Discourses*. This text, together with his other popular essays, would catapult Hume into the intellectual limelight. In 1754 Hume began publishing his *History of England*, a series of volumes which would secure his standing in Europe. Across the Atlantic Hume's work was influential with many, including Benjamin Franklin, Alexander Hamilton, and quite possibly James Madison.

Hume was, however, less well received among the religious. He was denied several academic posts, and the General Assembly of the Church of Scotland considered formally prosecuting Hume in 1755 and 1756. Hume suppressed many of his writings out of concern for reprisals, including his posthumous *Dialogues concerning Natural Religion* (1779), a text that advances perhaps the most powerful arguments ever launched against natural theology and the argument from design.

In 1763 Hume assumed the position of private secretary to the British ambassador to France, a post which brought him into contact with many important French intellectuals, including d'Alembert, Buffon, Diderot, Turgot, Helvétius, and d'Holbach. The Scotsman found himself, however, at times disaffected among the *philosophes*, discovering his sceptical reserve to be as inconsistent with their dogmatic atheism and deism as it had been with dogmatic Christianity in Britain.

In the latter part of 1765, Hume helped **Rousseau** to flee Switzerland and France, where he had been prosecuted for sedition and impiety, for the protection of England. Rousseau, however, came to believe that Hume was in league with his enemies and broke off all connection with him.

Hume died at approximately four o'clock in the afternoon on 25 August 1776 in Edinburgh. As his death approached, crowds gathered to see whether or not he would embrace Christianity in his last moments. James Boswell recounts that Hume 'said he never had entertained any belief in Religion since he began to read Locke and Clarke . . . He then said flatly that the Morality of every Religion was bad, and, I really thought, was not jocular when he said "that when he heard a man was religious, he concluded he was a rascal, though he had known some instances of very good men being religious".'

Suggested reading

Hume, D. 2000. [1739/40]. *A Treatise of Human Nature*. Oxford: Oxford
   University Press.
Hume, D. 1990 [1779] *Dialogues concerning Natural Religion*. Harmondsworth:
   Penguin.
Ayer, A. J. 2000. *Hume: A very short introduction*. Oxford: Oxford University Press.

Edmund Husserl

1859–1938   **Laura Duhan Kaplan**

Edmund Husserl is considered the founder of phenomenology, that is,
the philosophical study of human consciousness. He developed a
particular method for studying his own consciousness, and used his
findings to help answer traditional philosophical questions. His method
was taken up enthusiastically by philosophers, psychologists, and sociologists throughout the twentieth century.

One might think at first that Husserl's method was highly subjective.
After all, in his study of his own consciousness he was both researcher
and subject. But paradoxically, his aim was to develop an objective
foundation for all of human knowledge. As he wrote in *Crisis of the
European Sciences* (1936), he was frustrated with the prejudiced way
philosophers and psychologists conduct their research. They start out, he
complained, already 'knowing' what kinds of observations count as
evidence for their conclusions. Yet they have no clear understanding of
the relationship between observation, evidence and conclusions. Only a
fresh, unprejudiced look at the workings of human consciousness can
give them that clarity.

Husserl viewed his phenomenological method as an improvement on
the work of **René Descartes** in his *Meditations on First Philosophy*.
Descartes wanted to find a principle that could guarantee the certainty
of human knowledge. He proceeded by purposely doubting all of his
faculties, hoping he would find something he could not doubt. 'I sense
the world,' he thought to himself, 'but I cannot conclude that my perceptions are true. I apply mathematical formulas, but I cannot conclude
that they describe the real world. I hold religious beliefs, but I cannot

assume that they describe ultimate reality.' Descartes found he could not doubt the 'I' making these assertions. From this one certainty, Descartes deduced many others.

Husserl wrote in his own book *Cartesian Meditations* (1931) that he was extremely impressed with Descartes' method of doubt. However, he thought Descartes did not spend enough time using it. Instead of learning how his consciousness works, Descartes jumped too quickly to find certainty. In the end, Descartes only reaffirmed all the old prejudices about the organization of knowledge. Husserl hoped to do better.

Husserl developed a toolkit of concepts to make the practice of doubt productive. Most important is the practice he named 'phenomenological reduction'. 'Phenomena', as defined by **Immanuel Kant**, are appearances in consciousness, that is, perceptions, thoughts, and images, rather than things in themselves. When Husserl practised the phenomenological reduction, he reduced everything in consciousness to the status of appearances. He contrasted the phenomenological reduction with the 'natural attitude', that is, our everyday mode of thinking. In the natural attitude we view our thoughts as windows onto the world. For example, we might say to ourselves, 'I see a tree limb in the road; I'd better not hit it.' 'I feel sick; is there something wrong with my body?' In the phenomenological reduction, we view the same thoughts as events in consciousness: 'I *see* a tree limb; I *plan* to avoid it; I *feel* sick; I *hope* to be well.' Using phenomenological observation followed by reflection, Husserl developed additional concepts with which to organize and describe the events of consciousness.

Husserl believed that the observation of pure consciousness could clarify the relationships between philosophical theories and the evidence for them. Thus it would yield new answers to important philosophical questions. In *Ideas* (1913) he presents some of his answers. For example, he considers the great metaphysical question of the distinction between the mental and the material. What makes them so different that philosophers have often found them to be two irreducible categories? Under phenomenological reduction they appear in consciousness as two distinct types of objects. Material objects appear as a series of perspectives, that is, different views from different sides, all of which are referred to a single object of consciousness. Each mental object, however, appears to be given whole all at once, and related in time to other mental objects.

Husserl never completed his work of systematically articulating the relationships between observation, evidence and conclusions. Yet every step along the way, he discovered features of consciousness that he found enormously exciting. His passion and intellectual depth can sometimes be hard to see, however, because his writing style is downright turgid. Sadly, most of the popular criticisms of his work come from readers daunted by the technical vocabulary. Instead of engaging with Husserl's work, they argue that the phenomenological reduction is impossible or that Husserl failed because he never reached his goal. But the viability and success of Husserl's method are attested to by his influence. The leading continental philosophers of the twentieth century, **Martin Heidegger** and **Emmanuel Levinas**, were avid students of Husserl, applying his conceptual toolkit in original ways. Humanistic psychologists credited Husserl with teaching them to emphasize consciousness, and critical sociologists credited him with helping them recognize political distortions of knowledge.

Suggested reading
Husserl, E. 1977 [1931]. *Cartesian Meditations*. Dordrecht: Kluwer.
Husserl, E. 1990 [1913]. *Ideas Pertaining to a Pure Phenomenology and to a Phenomenological Philosophy*. Dordrecht: Kluwer.
Kohak , E. 1978. *Idea and Experience: Edmund Husserl's Project of Phenomenology in 'Ideas I'*. Chicago: University of Chicago Press.

Luce Irigaray
1932–   **Alison Stone**

Luce Irigaray, born in Belgium but working mainly in France, is one of the most influential, original and controversial writers in feminist philosophy today. Ironically, she hesitates to identify herself as a feminist – preferring to speak of 'women's liberation' – but this is because her feminism takes an unusual form, not because she rejects feminism as such. Irigaray believes that feminism should aim to create a society and culture which recognize, cultivate and accentuate the differences between the sexes, rather than encouraging sexual equality. Irigaray's 'sexual difference feminism' reflects her conviction that western culture subordinates women by denying and refusing to recognize their distinctiveness – an ethical failing that her philosophy aspires to put right. Irigarayan feminism poses an important challenge to mainstream understandings of feminism as a movement for equality.

Irigaray's philosophical position has three central, closely interwoven strands: her critique of western culture and philosophy; her positive rein- terpretation of feminine identity; and her political analysis and proposals for legal-political transformation.

Irigaray's earlier writings criticize western culture as 'masculinist': pervaded by a hierarchical sexual symbolism that construes femininity as merely the lack or opposite of masculinity – its inferior counterpart. Irigaray traces how this symbolism recurs across the history of philosophy from **Plato** onwards, decisively shaping culture's broader masculinist bias. Her primary interest is not in philosophers' explicit pronouncements concerning men and women, but rather in implicit textual patterns of imagery, metaphor and association. Through this imagery, Irigaray argues, philosophical texts tacitly allocate hierarchical gender connota- tions to ostensibly gender-neutral items – such as mind and body, which are aligned with masculinity and femininity respectively. Irigaray's critical method thus involves close textual interpretation (drawing, partly, on her trainings in linguistics and psychoanalysis). Although her studies have greatly influenced feminist approaches to the history of philosophy, most feminist historians of philosophy remain wary of the large-scale general- izations about western culture which Irigaray extrapolates from her readings of particular texts. Indeed, she has been repeatedly criticized for neglecting historical and cultural variations within the philosophical tradition.

Irigaray's critique of masculinism underpins her positive project of reinterpreting femininity as an independent identity, different from masculinity but of equal value. This project occupies her writings from 1984 onwards. Irigaray intends these often poetic and visionary texts to contribute to – perhaps even initiate – the constitution of a 'sexuate' culture in which women, as well as men, can articulate their distinctive identity in positive terms. Irigaray has no wish to replace traditional masculinism with a culture exclusively oriented around femininity. Instead, she explores how a previously unattainable level of dialogue and interrelation might become possible *between* the sexes once they acquire the cultural resources to be genuinely different. Unfortunately, her explorations of this theme tend to degenerate into a mythologization of heterosexuality. More promising is her claim that a sexuate culture would facilitate improved relationships between mothers and daughters. The established, negative, picture of femininity tends (so Irigaray believes) to equate femininity with maternity, itself understood as the function of passively sheltering the active male seed. This picture obliges all women to identify as mothers, engendering widespread competitiveness and hostility between daughters and mothers. In contrast, if femininity were reconceived as a genuinely independent identity, then maternity, too, could be seen as independent and creative, and, moreover, as only one possible form of feminine activity. This would remove the sources of mother–daughter animosity, enabling what Irigaray calls a 'female sociality'.

Since the mid–1980s, Irigaray's attention has increasingly turned to politics. She criticizes western political institutions for failing to recognize women as legal subjects or citizens in their own right. Accompanying her criticisms are positive proposals for legislative reforms recognizing women and men as sexually specific types of citizen, with differentiated sets of legal and political rights and obligations (for instance, Irigaray suggests a special feminine right to 'virginity'). Her readers have been somewhat unenthusiastic about her proposed legal reforms, arguing that they contradict her positive cultural project: if enacted, these reforms would impose a fixed and homogeneous content upon femininity, which ought – as a positive, non-hierarchical identity – to remain open-ended, amenable to ongoing redefinition and rearticulation.

Irigaray's concerns with feminine identity, mother–daughter relationships and the need for a sexuate culture and society diverge considerably from what might be considered classic philosophical preoccupations with truth, meaning, reality, or the good. Yet Irigaray carefully articulates her position as a transformation of those traditional preoccupations. Far from being anti-philosophical, her work is feminist *philosophy* – or, equally, philosophical feminism. Her writings brilliantly illustrate how feminist concerns for political transformation can revitalize philosophical enquiry and redirect traditional metaphysical and ethical debates along new and fruitful paths.

Suggested reading
Irigaray, L. 1993. *Je, Tu, Nous: Toward a Culture of Difference*. London: Routledge.
Whitford, M. 1991 (ed.). *The Irigaray Reader*. Oxford: Blackwell.
Whitford, M. 1991. *Luce Irigaray: Philosophy in the Feminine*. London: Routledge.

William James
1842–1910   Jack Ritchie

William James was eclectic in both his philosophy and life. He was born in New York but educated in Europe. He studied first to become a painter before switching to medicine – which he qualified in but never practised – and then to psychology. He battled to reconcile the rise of science (to which he was a contributor, setting up the first psychology lab in the United States) with a religious and existential sensibility. Some sense can be woven out of the many strands of James's thought by focusing on three ideas which feature in various ways in his thought: the continuity of experience, voluntarism and his later pragmatist theory of truth.

James's first significant and perhaps greatest work, *The Problems of Psychology* (1890), contains the first of these ideas. Instead of thinking of experience as a series of discrete ideas and impressions, as the British empiricists had, James claims that in reality each moment of experience blends one into the other in a stream of consciousness; and that this consciousness has a certain rhythm, 'flights and perchings' as he puts it. This was an idea which was to influence **Husserl** and other phenomenologists.

The first intriguing suggestion of a kind of voluntarism appears in an article called 'The Will to Believe' (1897). James claimed that in certain situations the act of deciding to believe something can help bring about the truth of the belief. For example, imagine I need to cross a ravine and that the only way I can do it is by jumping across. I may be uncertain whether I will succeed in jumping across, but both jumping and not-jumping are 'live' options for me – it makes sense for me to do one or the other. Now the decision needs to be made – I either jump or I do not – it is 'momentous' as James puts it. James claims that before I could successfully jump across the ravine I must believe that I can, hence the belief that p helps to make it true that p. So you have a right to believe in such cases even without sufficient evidence one way or the other. James thought that this could provide a justification for a belief in God, given that one's possible salvation depends on faith.

James first claimed to be a pragmatist in a lecture in 1898. He endorsed **Peirce**'s view that the meaning of a term is exhausted by the bearing it would have on our practice. Notoriously James used this pragmatist principle to define truth as what it is useful to believe or what has 'cash-value'. (Peirce was so horrified by James's account of pragmatism that he was moved to rename his own views pragmaticism.) James thought pragmatism provided a useful way of debunking certain kinds of meta-physics, and also another way of justifying certain religious beliefs. Just as certain scientific beliefs are useful for, say, prediction and control and thus true by James's definition, so too do our religious beliefs have a certain cash-value, responding to other needs and thus they may also be called true. **Russell** famously (and probably justifiably) condemned this theory of truth when he said: 'ironclads and Maxim guns must be the ultimate arbiters of . . . truth' if James's definition was deemed acceptable. Even those sympathetic to James's views, like **Dewey**, were moved to replace the word 'truth', with 'warranted assertibility'.

These strands of James's thought came together in his later work. The continuity of experience is turned into the metaphysical doctrine that all reality is pure (and continuous) experience. When we talk of mind and matter, we are in effect talking about different ways of relating elements of this pure experience. Clearly this idea has affinities with Russell's neutral monism (as he acknowledged) and **Davidson**'s Anomalous Monism. It also transcended and transformed the voluntarism of 'The Will to Believe' and combined it with his pragmatism. We pick out the various patterns from experience depending on our interests and in a sense make them true. We can see the influence of this Jamesian idea in Nelson Goodman's talk of world-making.

James's philosophy is lively, readable, suggestive and influential. However, if the philosophical ideal is rigorous and detailed argument, then James falls well short. But if we are equally enthralled by imagination and vivid phrase-making, then reading James will offer rich rewards.

Suggested reading

James, W. 2000. *'Pragmatism' and Other Writings.* Harmondsworth: Penguin.
James, W. 1955 [1890]. *The Principles of Psychology* (two volumes). New York: Dover Publications.
Bird, G. 1986. *William James (Arguments of the Philosophers).* London: Routledge.

Immanuel Kant

1724–1804   **Peter Herissone-Kelly**

Immanuel Kant is widely acknowledged by philosophers of all persuasions to have been one of the greatest thinkers of all time. He is also notorious for being one of the most difficult to understand. The complexity of his prose, however, is not due to any wilful obscurantism. In reading Kant, one is aware of a thinker struggling to clothe in language ideas of the very highest level of complexity and profundity.

Kant's unique contribution to western thought is his 'Critical Philosophy', as set out in the *Critique of Pure Reason* (1781). Kant introduced the distinction between 'analytic' and 'synthetic' judgements. The standard example of an analytic judgement is 'All bachelors are unmarried'. Here, the 'predicate' ('are unmarried') simply 'unpacks' the conceptual content of the subject ('bachelors'). A distinguishing feature of such propositions is that they tell us nothing about the way the world is, but simply clarify what is involved in our concepts. Hence an analytic judgement is one in which 'the predicate B belongs to the subject A, as something which is (covertly) contained in this concept A'.

In the case of synthetic judgements, by contrast, Kant tells us that the predicate 'lies outside the [subject] concept'. An example might be 'All humans are under twenty feet tall'. Whilst this proposition is no doubt true, it is nonetheless certainly not a feature of the concept 'human' that anything falling within it is under twenty feet tall. Thus we are given a substantial piece of information about the world rather than our concepts.

Analytic truths are a priori: that is, knowable independently of any particular experience. I do not have to carry out a survey of bachelors to find out that they are all unmarried. Synthetic truths, in contrast, appear to be a posteriori – they require verification through experience. For example, 'All humans are under twenty feet tall' could never be known a priori. Kant held, however, that there exists a special class of propositions that are both informative and knowable independently of this or that experience: they are synthetic a priori. The truths of mathematics (perhaps most significantly those of geometry), he maintained, fall into this class, as do certain other propositions, such as 'Every event has a cause'.

There is nothing about the concept of 7+5 that dictates that it should be equal to 12, nor about the concept of a straight line that it should be the shortest distance between two points. And yet the propositions '7+5=12' and 'A straight line is the shortest distance between two points' are both knowable a priori. Similarly, it is not part of the concept of an event that it should have a cause, and yet we can know with absolute certainty, thinks Kant, that any event will be caused. But how can we know such truths a priori?

Kant's answer to this question is both radical and astonishing. Let us start with the case of geometry. There can only, thinks Kant, be one explanation of our a priori knowledge of the properties of space: the spatial properties of the world must be contributed by the knowing subject. That is, the world as it is in itself is not made up of objects arranged in space. Only the world as it appears to us is spatial, and this is precisely because space is nothing more than our way of representing the world to ourselves. In Kant's own terminology, space is nothing more than a 'form of intuition' [i.e. perception]. Kant employs a similar argument to conclude that time, too, is a mere form of intuition. Space and time are features of the phenomenal world – the world as it appears to us – only. The noumenal world – the world of things as they are in themselves – is aspatial and atemporal. Similarly, causal relations have a subjective origin, being, as it were, 'projected' into the world by the experiencing consciousness.

Kant's epistemology stands as a critique of both empiricism and rationalism. The empiricist view is wrong, since the mind is not a mere blank slate which passively receives knowledge of the world through the senses. The rationalist model of knowledge is just as mistaken, as reason alone can never give rise to knowledge, since knowledge demands both concepts and the raw data supplied by the senses. Thus speculative metaphysics – the attempt to achieve theoretical knowledge of non-empirical subjects such as the existence of God, freedom and immortality – inevitably fails.

But whilst Kant held that we have no theoretical knowledge of such things, he maintained that we can have a practical knowledge of them. Consider free will. When I think of my actions as constituents of the phenomenal world, I am obliged to regard them as produced by rigid deterministic laws. But when I consider those same actions as they are in the noumenal world I am not so obliged. I can have practical knowledge of that freedom, which I am required to postulate in order to account for my inescapable sense of myself as a responsible moral agent.

It seems to many that a choice has to be made between two apparently incompatible ways of looking at the world: the spiritual and ethical on the one hand, and the scientific on the other. If Kant is right, the dichotomy between these two ways of looking at the world is purely illusory. There is room in the world for both determinism and freedom, spirituality and science.

Suggested reading

Kant, I. 1963 [1781]. *Critique of Pure Reason*. London: Macmillan.
Kant, I. 1997 [1785]. *Groundwork of the Metaphysics of Morals*. Cambridge: Cambridge University Press.
Scruton, R. 2001. *Kant: A very short introduction*. Oxford: Oxford University Press.

Søren Kierkegaard

1813–1855   **Julian Baggini**

The biographies of most philosophers are usually considered largely irrelevant when explaining their work. But this position is hard to sustain in the case of Søren Kierkegaard, for whom life and work are inseparable.

Casting a long, dark shadow over Kierkegaard's life was his father, a man who, as Kierkegaard's journal recalls, 'as a small boy tending sheep on the Jutland Heath, suffering many ills, famished and exhausted, stood up on a hill and cursed God!' The curse and the guilt it induced haunted both father and son. Before Kierkegaard was twenty-one, no fewer than four of his siblings and his mother had died. It was as though God's retribution had fallen on the whole family.

As a young man, Kierkegaard tried to throw off this melancholy and he did indeed become known as quite a bon viveur in Copenhagen society. However, his journal revealed a darker, suicidal side. His unwillingness to do what was expected of him was demonstrated most dramatically in what was probably the most important event in his life: the breaking of his engagement to Regine Olsen. This decision caused a great deal of anguish, and flimsily disguised references to this event can be found in many of his works, notably *Either/or* (1843) and *Repetition* (1843). His explanation of the decision was that married life was incompatible with his vocation as a writer. As if to prove the point, over the ten years from 1843 Kierkegaard produced more than two dozen works. One can hardly imagine how he had time to eat, let alone fulfil any conjugal duties.

That there is a connection between Kierkegaard's life history and the production of books with titles like *Fear and Trembling* (1843) and *The Sickness Unto Death* (1849) is obvious. Thankfully, as well as being a depressive, Kierkegaard was also a thinker worthy of the accolade 'genius'. His ideas are often presented obliquely, through pseudonymous authors with different points of view. This is no mere literary affectation, but essential to the message Kierkegaard was trying to get across. Medium and message were perfectly fused, for one of Kierkegaard's key ideas was that a philosophy or way of life has to be understood and criticized from within, since there is no neutral perspective from which we can judge them.

At the core of his work is the rejection of systematized, logical thought as an adequate guide to life and meaning. His chief target here was **Hegel**, whose philosophical system was seen by many in the mid-nineteenth century as able to explain virtually everything. Hegel thought that wherever there appeared to be a contradiction – a thesis and antithesis – it would be possible to reach rational harmony by means of a synthesis between the two. What is irrational in the original two positions is thus eliminated and what is rational is preserved. But Kierkegaard argued that the 'movement' in the synthesis is not explained. If the synthesis is fully contained in the thesis and antithesis, then the synthesis is no real progression at all. If, on the other hand, there is something novel in the synthesis, then the movement is not strictly rational, as something new must have been introduced that was not contained in the original pairing.

Kierkegaard's point is that no matter how rigorous your logical system, there will always be gaps. As these gaps are logical gaps, it is futile to try to bridge them with logic. Instead, they can only be breached by a leap of faith. What characterizes a leap of faith is the absolute uncertainty that underlies it. Faith takes us beyond that which can be demonstrated. That is why a leap of faith is undertaken in 'fear and trembling'.

That provided, for Kierkegaard at least, a justification for the religious life. This was Kierkegaard's third sphere of existence. The first was what he called the aesthetic, which was a life dedicated to or trapped in the instant. The second was the ethical, where one tries to live in accordance with eternal values. For Kierkegaard, both are incomplete, in terms of rationality and of satisfying human needs. Only Christianity, which para-doxically combined the temporal and the infinite in the God-man Jesus Christ, bridges this gap. But because it is paradoxical, embracing Chris-tianity requires leaving rationality behind and taking a bold leap of faith.

The existentialist movement was the natural heir to Kierkegaard's thought. Philosophers like **Sartre** and **Nietzsche** also emphasized the limits of logic and the centrality of personal choice. But as critics have complained, once this stance is taken, anything seems justified. What seems to matter is not what you choose, but that you choose it freely.

Kierkegaard's complex, poetic work rewards careful reading. But perhaps at its core, the moral of Kierkegaard's philosophy can be

summed up in the single sentence of Kierkegaard scholar Michael
Collins: 'Human existence requires real "passion" as well as thought.'

Suggested reading
Kierkegaard, S. 1989 [1843]. *Fear and Trembling*. Harmondsworth: Penguin.
Chamberlain, J. and Ree, J. 2001 (eds). *The Kierkegaard Reader*. Oxford:
   Blackwell.
Hannay, A. 1991. *Kierkegaard (The arguments of the philosophers)*. London:
   Routledge.

Saul Kripke
1940–   **Christopher Norris**

Saul Kripke is an American philosopher whose work on modal or
'possible worlds' logic has exerted great influence during the last quarter
of the twentieth century. This is due mainly to his novel ideas about
naming, necessity and natural kinds.

On his account, the reference of proper names like 'Aristotle' or
natural-kind terms such as 'gold' and 'water' is fixed by an inaugural act
of designation and thereafter holds firm despite and across any
subsequent changes in our knowledge concerning them. Thus it is a
necessary truth that Aristotle was just that individual whose identity was
fixed at the moment of conception and who was named 'Aristotle'. And
it is likewise a necessary truth that gold and water are just the kinds of
substance that have been correctly picked out as 'gold' and 'water' for
as long as those names have been in use.

Kripke rejects the hitherto standard 'descriptivist' theory of sense and
reference proposed by **Frege** and **Russell**. On this view we refer to
'Aristotle' by way of a certain associated cluster of descriptions, such as
'student of Plato', 'tutor of Alexander', 'author of the *Metaphysics*, the
Prior Logic, the *Nicomachean Ethics* and so on. Those descriptions will
have changed with the passage of time and with each new scholarly
addition to or subtraction from the stock of available knowledge.
Likewise, people have attached different senses to 'water' and 'gold' in
keeping with their current best state of information. They may have

started out with fairly vague ideas of what characterized the stuff in question: thus 'water' was a 'transparent, tasteless, odourless liquid that falls as rain, boils and freezes at certain temperatures, fills up lakes, has useful cleansing properties', and so forth. Nowadays we specify 'water' more exactly by its molecular constitution (H_2O) and 'gold' by its possessing the unique atomic number 79.

However, the descriptivist theory gives rise to certain counter-intuitive or downright absurd conclusions. For if reference is ultimately fixed via a range of descriptive attributes then it follows that, with every change or advance in our knowledge, we shall have to issue statements such as 'gold is not gold', 'water is not water', or 'Aristotle was not Aristotle'. (Suppose we discovered that he hadn't, in fact, been Plato's student, Alexander's teacher, and the author of all those works.) Hence Kripke's alternative proposal: that reference-fixing occurs through an inaugural 'baptism' or act of designation – 'this is gold', 'that stuff is water', 'we name this child Aristotle' – and henceforth remains unaffected by shifts in the currency of knowledge or belief.

Kripke takes the argument to possess important implications with regard to philosophy of mind. Those who advocate some version of central state materialism (the thesis that mind and brain are identical) do so most often on the understanding that this is a contingent truth, one to be discovered only through a process of a posteriori enquiry (observation, experiment, neurophysiological investigation) into the way things stand with respect to carbon-based sentient life-forms such as ourselves.

However, according to Kripke, there is no making sense of this idea since the claim, if true, is necessarily so in virtue of the strict identity between mind and brain. To this extent it is on all fours with other identity-statements such as 'water = H_2O', 'heat = mean kinetic energy of molecules', or 'lightning = atmospheric electrical discharge'. In which case the thesis comes to look less persuasive in so far as we can readily conceive of mind-states or modes of phenomenal experience that are altogether similar to ours even though realized in some different (perhaps silicon-based) life-form. This aspect of Kripke's argument has not gone unchallenged but it does convey something of the range of issues opened up by his deployment of modal logic in diverse contexts of debate.

Meanwhile the curious reader might like to track down a copy of Rebecca Goldstein's novel *The Mind-Body Problem*. Here we meet a character named Saul Kripke who has nothing whatever (so far as we can tell) in common with the real-world Kripke, and another, differently named, character whose interests, life-history, philosophical convictions, and so forth, just happen to approximate Kripke's own in various striking respects. One way of interpreting Goldstein's brilliant *roman à thèse* is as a fictive demonstration of what other philosophers have argued – that is, the need to devise some synthesis of the 'old' (descriptivist) and 'new' (Kripkean) theories of reference so as to accommodate certain kinds of problem or borderline case. Another is to take it as exploring the rich possibilities for fictive treatment of Kripke's various counterfactual 'worlds' and their degrees of divergence from or convergence with the world that we actually inhabit.

At any rate there is no doubting the extent to which Kripke has set new terms for the discussion of issues in logic, metaphysics and philosophy of language.

Suggested reading
Kripke, S. 1980. *Naming and Necessity*. Oxford: Blackwell.
Goldstein, R. 1993. *The Mind-Body Problem*. New York: Penguin.
Schwartz, S. 1977 (ed). *Naming, Necessity and Natural Kinds*. Ithaca, NY: Cornell
    University Press.

Thomas Kuhn
1922–1996   **Frank Pajares**

Of the five books and countless articles he published, Kuhn's most renowned work is *The Structure of Scientific Revolutions* (1962), which he wrote while a graduate student in theoretical physics at Harvard. It has sold some one million copies in 16 languages and is required reading in courses dealing with education, history, psychology, research and, of course, history and philosophy of science.

Throughout thirteen succinct but thought-provoking chapters, Kuhn argued that science is not a steady, cumulative acquisition of knowledge. Instead, science is 'a series of peaceful interludes punctuated by intellectually violent revolutions', which he described as 'the tradition-shattering complements to the tradition-bound activity of normal science'. After such revolutions, 'one conceptual world view is replaced by another'.

Although critics chided him for his imprecise use of the term, Kuhn was responsible for popularizing the term 'paradigm', which he described as essentially a collection of beliefs shared by scientists, a set of agreements about how problems are to be understood. According to Kuhn, paradigms are essential to scientific inquiry, for 'no natural history can be interpreted in the absence of at least some implicit body of inter-twined theoretical and methodological belief that permits selection, evaluation, and criticism'. Indeed, a paradigm guides the research efforts of scientific communities, and it is this criterion that most clearly identifies a field as a science.

A fundamental theme of Kuhn's argument is that the typical develop-mental pattern of a mature science is the successive transition from one paradigm to another through a process of revolution. When a paradigm shift takes place, 'a scientist's world is qualitatively transformed [and] quantitatively enriched by fundamental novelties of either fact or theory'.

Kuhn also maintained that, contrary to popular conception, typical scientists are not objective and independent thinkers. Rather, they are conservative individuals who accept what they have been taught and apply their knowledge to solving the problems that their theories dictate. Most are, in essence, puzzle-solvers who aim to discover what they already know in advance.

During periods of normal science, the primary task of scientists is to bring the accepted theory and fact into closer agreement. As a consequence, scientists tend to ignore research findings that might threaten the existing paradigm and trigger the development of a new and competing paradigm. For example, Ptolemy popularized the notion that the sun revolves around the earth, and this view was defended for centuries even in the face of conflicting evidence. In the pursuit of science, Kuhn observed, 'novelty emerges only with difficulty, manifested by resistance, against a background provided by expecta-tion'.

And yet, young scientists who are not so deeply indoctrinated into accepted theories, a Newton, Lavoisier, or **Einstein**, can manage to sweep an old paradigm away. Such scientific revolutions come only after long periods of tradition-bound normal science, for 'frameworks must be lived with and explored before they can be broken'. However, crisis is always implicit in research because every problem that normal science sees as a puzzle can be seen, from another perspective, as a counter-instance and thus as a source of crisis.

All crises are resolved in one of three ways. Normal science can prove capable of handing the crisis-provoking problem, in which case all returns to 'normal'. Alternatively, the problem resists and is labelled, but it is perceived as resulting from the field's failure to possess the necessary tools with which to solve it, and so scientists set it aside for a future generation with more developed tools. In a few cases, a new candidate for a paradigm emerges and a battle over its acceptance ensues – these are the paradigm wars.

Kuhn argued that a scientific revolution is a noncumulative developmental episode in which an older paradigm is replaced in whole or in part by an incompatible new one. The new paradigm cannot build on the preceding one, it can only supplant it. Revolutions close with total victory for one of the two opposing camps.

In the face of these arguments, how and why does science progress, and what is the nature of its progress? Kuhn argued that normal science progresses because members of a mature scientific community work from a single paradigm or from a closely related set and because different scientific communities seldom investigate the same problems. The result of successful creative work addressing the problems posed by the paradigm is progress. In fact, it is only during periods of normal science that progress seems both obvious and assured.

As to whether progress consists in science discovering ultimate truths, Kuhn observed that 'we may have to relinquish the notion, explicit or implicit, that changes of paradigm carry scientists and those who learn from them closer and closer to the truth.' Instead, the developmental process of science is one of evolution from primitive beginnings through successive stages that are characterized by an increasingly detailed and refined understanding of nature. Kuhn argued that this is not a process of evolution *toward* anything, and he questioned whether it really helps to imagine that there is one, full, objective, true account of nature. He likened his conception of the evolution of scientific ideas to **Darwin**'s conception of the evolution of organisms.

Suggested reading

Kuhn, T. 1962. *The Structure of Scientific Revolutions*. Chicago: University of Chicago Press.

Kuhn, T. 1977. *The Essential Tension: Selected Studies in Scientific Tradition and Change*. Chicago: University of Chicago Press.

Kuhn, T., Conant, J. and Haugeland, J. (eds). 2002. *The Road Since Structure: Philosophical essays, 1970–1993, with an autobiographical interview*. Chicago: University of Chicago Press.

Jacques Lacan

1901–1981 **Jack Furlong**

At least since Descartes in the seventeenth century, thinkers in the West had found it possible to doubt the existence of God, the nature of morality, or even the efficacy of science. But the belief that they themselves constitute unique, indivisible and autonomous persons did not come under sustained attack until **Nietzsche** and **Freud** in the late nineteenth and early twentieth centuries. Jacques-Marie-Emile Lacan in the late twentieth strove to eradicate it completely. Lacan called his own decades-long project a 'return to Freud' and at the end of his life, he exclaimed to French psychoanalysts, 'It is up to you to be Lacanians if you wish; I am Freudian.'

Though he studied first medicine, then psychiatry, Lacan's influences are hardly orthodox Freudian. Like many French intellectuals who would become famous in the post-war period, Lacan also closely read **Hegel**'s *Phenomenology of Spirit*. Moreover, he melded Hegel and Freud with structuralist anthropology and linguistics, game theory and topology into a forbiddingly complex body of work. Added to the difficulty such sources present, Lacan scholars often point to shifts in his long career at which he abandons heretofore important concepts and reconceives others. Further, his writing style suffers from an almost purposeful obscurity. Such factors prevent either easy or complete summary of Lacan's thinking.

Like Freud, Lacan focuses on the development of selfhood from the womb. Before we are born, the womb provides us unreflexive, uneventful well-being: the 'pleasure principle' reigns. Leaving the womb causes a rift between the feeling/demanding aspect of the organism and its biological drives, which strive to return it to the original happy state of quietude. We are born then with 'a hole in the self' even before a self can be fully formed. From our beginnings, we are never going to be able to be whole, autonomous selves, for we will always be 'decentred' owing to our unfulfillable desires, our essential 'lack'. Worse, as infants, we don't really know what to desire; we must learn how to satisfy our needs through others. Desire, says Lacan, is always desire of the Other's desire; that is, we desire *x* only because we see an Other desiring *x*. The most important Other is, of course, our mother. We soon learn to desire what our mother desires not only because we know no better but because doing so attracts our mother's attention. In effect, we try to become a phallus – the major love object – for our mother. The 'father', however, thwarts our attempts, causing, both for boys and girls, 'castration' and Lacan's version of the Freudian Oedipus complex. Though painful, this intrusion of the 'father' helps us order our desires according to the same law that controls our mother's desires – the Law (or, as Lacan often says, the 'name') of the Father.

'Castration' then is the moment at which we become human beings, for the Law makes us '*parle-être*' or speaking beings. Language from then on structures our desires: language comprises the Symbolic Order. We figuratively must 'be told' what we feel and think through the big Other, the arbitrarily and socially-constructed matrix of words, which is the active functioning of the Symbolic Order.

It is now relatively clear how Lacan might criticize the dominant western tradition which upholds the belief that language aids us in becoming thinking, autonomous persons. The major assumption of this Cartesian picture of subjectivity and language is precisely what Lacan intends to undermine, namely, that *we use language* to create ourselves. Lacan maintains that *language uses us* to create at most a social fantasy of unitary selfhood.

Even our unconscious lives are 'structured like a language'. The unconscious often 'speaks' for repressed desires in slips of the tongue, jokes and other 'parapraxes' that are 'symptoms' of our split selves. Words, however, are constantly in flux and hence do not make good tools for representing or explaining our feelings or motives to ourselves.

We are often faced with 'little bits of the Real', impossible events which cannot be 'nailed down' and therefore keep returning under different descriptions. Traumas, for instance, refuse symbolization and hence keep coming back to us as 'impossible kernels' of the Real. This last move of Lacan's – a version of Freud's 'return of the repressed' – forecloses any last comfort we might get from relying on language to make us whole.

Virtually all postwar European philosophical movements – deconstruction, Foucaultian genealogy, versions of French feminism, left Heideggerianism, Althusserian structuralism and, most recently, Slovenian psychoanalytic culture critique (most prominently Slavoj Žižek's) – have assimilated the Lacanian demolition of the unitary self. Even Anglo-American pragmatic and radical feminists have found it necessary to distance themselves explicitly from what they see as dangerous patriarchal tendencies in his approach. As a result, Lacan's critique of autonomy continues to maintain a significant presence decades after the master's death.

Suggested reading

Lacan, J. 2001 [1967]. *Ecrits*. London: Routledge.

Lacan, J. 1997. *The Four Fundamental Concepts of Psychoanalysis (The Seminars of Jacques Lacan, Book 11)*. New York: W. W. Norton.

Žižek, S. 1992 (ed.). *Everything You Always Wanted to Know about Lacan (but were Afraid to Ask Hitchcock)*. London: Verso.

Gottfried Leibniz

1646–1716 **Peter Cave**

'That which is not truly one entity is not truly one entity.' From the pen of Gottfried Wilhelm Leibniz, such an elusive observation is no surprise. And although it sounds platitudinous, it is at his metaphysical heart.

Leibniz was born into an academic Leipzig family. In young adulthood, declining a law professorship, he chose diplomacy's practical world, working for barons and dukes – hoping to travel and contact other thinkers. Leibniz was invigorated by discoveries, be they courtesy of

Leeuwenhoek's new microscopes, showing the world teeming with life, or **Plato**'s reasoning to abstract entities, or even eastern mysticisms: witness his paper's title, 'A Specimen of Discoveries about Marvellous Secrets of a General Nature'. Rejecting monkish erudition which lacks experience and activity, he devised computing machines (they worked), constructed a windmill for the Harz silver-mines (it didn't) and invented the differential calculus (independently of Newton). Possessing kaleido-scopic interests, he founded the Berlin Academy, sought to reconcile Catholicism and Protestantism – the French and Germans – and encouraged Russia's Peter the Great to trade with China.

Leibniz introduced much of today's philosophical diet – possible worlds, the identity of indiscernibles and the rejection of absolute space/time. He grappled with probability, sought sentences' logical form beneath misleading surface grammar and related meaning to truth. Famously, he conceived reality as consisting of monads (unities). This is where the seemingly uninteresting aphorism 'what is not truly one entity is not truly one entity' comes into play. A real entity, a substance, needs unity; it must be determinate. Indeed, indeterminacy is what characterizes fictions: Sherlock Holmes smoked, but there is no answer about his heart size or preference in socks. Nothing extended in space – cornflakes, the sun, your brain – has the unity required of a monad, since all such items are divisible without end. Hence monads – reality – cannot be extended.

What then is an example of a monad? Leibniz turns to one's self, the soul, the mind. I am real and, from within, I experience unity: I cannot make sense of my self dividing. I am a monad, a rational soul; what makes me *me* are these strivings and perceptions. Metaphorically, monads possess different perspectives on the universe, as if viewing a town from different vantage points.

Of course, if monads are just mirrors mirroring other mirrors, all might rise in a puff of reflected nothings. So these monadic perceptions need some content, they need to be perceptions of something real; but reality remains, obscurely, just monads. What of the items around us – shoes, shampoos and seashores? Although monads, lacking extension, cannot compose material items, these items have some reality. Leibniz grounds them in bare monads, soul-like unities, yet ones lacking the self-awareness of rational souls. They are well-founded phenomena, existing independently of our perceptions.

Descartes' mind-body interaction problem is now a problem of the relationship between my mind and the bare monads constituting my body. Monads are 'windowless': it is nonsense to think of qualities or particles nipping over from monad to monad. If this is what is meant by causality, then there is no such thing. There are regularities – harmony – between monads, pre-established by God. There is also an internal causality, an unfolding, within each monad, whereby I, a rational soul, give rise to my monadic states. I set about raising my arm, causing my subsequent arm-raising perceptions; and, courtesy of pre-established harmony, appropriate changes occur in the relevant bare monads.

Leibniz is also known for his 'principle of sufficient reason', which is the claim that there must be a sufficient reason for why everything is as it is. There must be something now about, say, Winthrop that makes it true that he is 2,873 miles away from yawning crocodiles, living 2,402 years after Socrates' death, eating Gorgonzola – and soon to be on a low cholesterol diet. He is related to everything past, present and future. Leibniz curiously would conclude that, within Winthrop, there are marks of everything past, present and future. Thankfully, Leibniz adds that only God knows them all.

If everything is as it is for a reason, where does that leave free will? Room remains for contingency and free will because God freely chose between an infinity of possible worlds. In some possible worlds, there are counterparts of Winthrop acting in ways different from the actual Winthrop. These possible Winthrops mysteriously account for the actual Winthrop's freedom.

In many ways, Leibniz is modern. In contrast to Descartes, he rejects discontinuities between man, animals and the environment; monads come with differing degrees of awareness, including unconscious perceptions. He would have lapped up genetic explanations, delighted in modern logical techniques and wallowed in today's numerous journals and conferences. Leibniz was prolific – 'an academy in himself' said Frederick the Great – yet he produced no *magnum opus*. His ideas – and they developed – are found in a voluminous correspondence and essays, engaging contemporaries such as **Spinoza**, Arnaud and **Locke**.

His last years were stuck in Hanover, a backwater, reluctantly labouring on a history of the House of Brunswick. With the Newtonians whispering against him, Leibniz failed to persuade George I to appoint him Historiographer Royal and bring him to London's intellectual buzz. Leibniz died lonely and disenchanted. Only his secretary attended his funeral. His grave was unmarked.

Suggested reading

Leibniz, G. W. 1998. *Philosophical Texts*. Oxford: Oxford University Press.
Jolley, N. 1995 (ed.). *The Cambridge Companion to Leibniz*. Cambridge: Cambridge University Press.
Macdonald Ross, G. 1984. *Leibniz*. Oxford: Oxford University Press.

Emmanuel Levinas

1906–1995   **Lawrence R. Harvey**

Levinas was born in Kovno, Lithuania, in January 1906. Having completed his secondary education in the Ukraine, he attended the University of Strasbourg where he studied philosophy in conjunction with subjects such as psychology and sociology. In the late 1920s he travelled to Freiburg, Germany, where he studied under **Husserl** and **Heidegger**. In 1930 Levinas was granted French citizenship. In the same year his doctoral thesis was published in Paris. It was this publication that first introduced **Sartre** to phenomenology. The outbreak of World War II saw Levinas drafted into the French army. He served as an interpreter until his capture in June 1940. Despite being a Lithuanian Jew by birth, he was interned in a military prison camp where he endured forced labour. As an officer in the French army he was spared the fate that befell his immediate family – most of whom were murdered by the Nazis.

Unsurprisingly, the memory of the Nazi horror dominates much of Levinas's work. Although sometimes nuanced and labyrinthine, Levinas's philosophy is clearly governed by a deep-seated pacifism. In fact, it is one of Levinas's central contentions that western philosophy is wedded to a counter-ethical process of conflict. It is this radical idea that underpins Levinas's first *magnum opus, Totality and Infinity* (1961). This treatise opens with a discussion of war – an all-encompassing as well as literal term for conflict. Levinas states that it is the western preoccupation with the truth that generates this conflict. In short, if one is able to apprehend the truth, one is essentially self-sufficient or 'total'. For Levinas, this reassuring sense of totality is disastrous for it harbours an underlying antagonism towards others who are liable to challenge one's authority.

Levinas traces this conception of totality back to the teachings of **Socrates** and **Plato**. According to classical authority, the self is literally self-contained – it is able to contain the truth. For Levinas, this spirit of autonomy was perpetuated in the work of philosophers as diverse as **Plotinus, Berkeley** and **Hegel**. In addition, Levinas also detected a return to this spirit of self-sufficiency in the phenomenological work of his former tutors, Husserl and Heidegger.

In an attempt to evade this tide of thought, Levinas turned his attention to the constitution of subjectivity. For Levinas, far from being self-sufficient or total, the self (the subject) can only exist through reference to the non-self. In short, self-knowledge presupposes the existence of a power infinitely greater than oneself. Echoing the famous Cartesian cosmological argument, Levinas thus suggests that the subject is indebted to the idea of infinity. In direct opposition to contemporary continental thought, Levinas thus reinstates the subject – a subject that encounters itself through the mediation of an-Other. According to Levinas's intricate argument, such an encounter precedes the disastrous desire for truth.

Crucially, Levinas argues that the encounter between the self and the Other is always passive. In slightly different terms, one welcomes the Other as the measure of one's own being. It would seem to follow that one's subjectivity depends upon a non-aggressive or non-violent interface. Given its passive nature, Levinas concludes that this interface is a proto-ethical moment that precedes all other ethical discourse. In this way Levinas undercuts traditional ethical debate.

Levinas's work can lack analytic clarity. He does not define key terms such as the Other beyond a series of vague associations and analogies. But to a greater extent, this lack of clarity is necessary because Levinas is trying to transcend what he regarded as the fetters of western thought. Nevertheless, in 1964 Jacques Derrida published an essay in which he explored the extent to which Levinasian thought was still bound to the western tradition. Levinas's rejoinder was *Otherwise than Being* (1974) – a complex reconfiguration of his earlier work, composed in the light of poststructural concerns.

Today, Levinas's ethical thought is frequently discussed in relation to diverse academic fields beyond the traditional boundaries of philosophy. Disparate fields such as sociology, literary theory, historiography and anthropology have all benefited from the priority Levinas accorded to 'the Other'. This ubiquity stands as testimony to both Levinas's profundity and growing contemporary relevance.

Suggested reading
Levinas, E. 1969 [1961]. *Totality and Infinity*. Pittsburgh: Duquesne University Press.
Davis, C. 1996. *Levinas: An Introduction*. Oxford: Polity.
Hand, S. 1986 (ed.). *The Levinas Reader*. Oxford: Blackwell.

David Lewis
1941–2001   Michael LaBossiere

David Lewis is probably best known among philosophers for making grand metaphysics and systematic theory building fashionable again.

Lewis entered college with the intention of receiving a degree in chemistry. Fortunately for philosophy, he visited Oxford and attended **Gilbert Ryle**'s lectures. This set him on a path that led to his completing his PhD at Harvard under **Willard van Orman Quine**.

With such an auspicious background, it is no surprise that Lewis made numerous and significant contributions to the philosophical world. One of his first major works was a revision of his doctoral thesis, which was published as *Convention: A Philosophical Study* (1969). This work opened up new territory in the philosophy of language.

In addition to his work in language, Lewis also made contributions in the area of philosophy of mind. Going beyond Ryle's behaviourism, Lewis argued in favour of identity theory, which is the view that mental states are numerically identical to neurological states.

Although Lewis later moved away from the original identity theory, he remained committed to refuting traditional dualism – the view that the essentially non-physical mind interacted with the physical body. Lewis contributed to the development of functionalism – the view that mental states are to be defined in terms of inputs (from the environment or other mental states) and outputs (behaviour).

Though deservedly well known for his earlier work in the philosophies of language and mind, Lewis is probably best known for his work in the metaphysics of modality (possibility and necessity). His work in this area began with the classic *Counterfactuals* (1973) and reached its culmination in the highly controversial *On The Plurality Of Worlds* (1986). At its heart, this book addressed the key question of the metaphysical grounding of possibility (that which could be, but need not be) and necessity (that which must be). Unlike previous philosophers, Lewis was not content to explicate possibility and necessity in terms of mere concepts. He argued for the existence of possible worlds, as real as our own world (the actual world), which serve to ground claims about possibility and necessity. For example, if it is true that JFK might not have been assassinated, then there is some possible world in which he made it safely out of Dallas and went on to finish his term. Of course, the JFK in that world is not the same JFK who died in our world – they are counterparts of each other. Unlike in some science fiction tales, we cannot journey to other possible worlds – they are isolated from each other in all ways but one: according to Lewis, we have 'doxastic' accessibility to these worlds (put roughly, we can know about them).

Not surprisingly, this extravagant metaphysics led to many incredulous stares which were followed by a raft of objections and interpretations. The acceptance of possible worlds as real entities, known as 'modal realism' or more aptly 'possible worlds realism', was found to have great philosophic power and was soon applied to semantics, linguistics, economics, game theory and many other areas.

Regardless of what one thinks of possible worlds, most philosophers credit Lewis with helping to make metaphysics, especially systematic metaphysics, respectable again. Through his many works, he is taken to have produced a unified thesis, which has been dubbed 'Humean supervenience'. On this view the world is a vast mosaic of tiny facts and, at any moment in time, what it is and what can be said about it supervenes (depends) on the patterns of these facts. The typical analogy is that the facts are like the dots in a newsprint picture or a pointillist painting. On this view, no specific event at a specific point determines events at other points. Rather it is the totality of occurrences that sets everything else.

Lewis noted that the problem of chance could short-circuit the thesis, but was unable to complete his solution to the problem.

Lewis's works were skilfully written and often included humorous content (his famous article on mad pain and Martian pain included a Martian who reacted to injury by inflating bladders in his feet) as well as references to science fiction (he lists Larry Niven among the works cited in *On the Plurality of Worlds*).

Personally, Lewis was best known for his modesty, generosity and a general inability to engage in small talk. Though he bore a more than passing resemblance to Kris Kringle, he was graced with the nickname 'Machine in the Ghost'.

Lewis formed ties with Australian philosophers Jack Smart and David Armstrong (best known for his theory of immanent universals) and became quite a fan of Australian football. Though reports on his singing voice vary, he is said to have been a very enthusiastic singer of Australian folk ballads.

Lewis' favourite hobby was his model train set. His basement, which he expanded, featured a rather impressive railway layout (developed, some say, with the same systemic methodology he used in philosophy).

Suggested reading
Lewis, D. 1986. *On the Plurality of Worlds*. Oxford: Blackwell.
Lewis, D. 1973. *Counterfactuals*. Oxford: Blackwell.
Preyer, G. and Siebelt, T. 2001 (eds.). *Reality and Humean Supervenience: Essays on the Philosophy of David Lewis*. New York: Rowman & Littlefield.

John Locke
1632–1704   Jonathan Walmsley

It is perhaps a measure of John Locke's greatness that nowadays his views seem prosaic commonplaces. The force of his arguments and the influence of his conclusions were so powerful as to become entwined in the warp and weft of western thinking. It was not always so. In his own time, Locke was a revolutionary.

Locke crammed an awful lot into one lifetime: Oxford don, physician, meteorologist, chemist, horticulturist, secretary, tutor, civil servant, political advisor, diplomat, theologian, exile and, once, an enemy of the state, implicated in a plot to assassinate the king. But he is best known as an epistemologist and political philosopher. One of the most crucial aspects of Locke's thought was his challenge to traditional political and religious authority. This finds its expression in two of his most influential works: the *Essay concerning Human Understanding* (1690) and the *Two Treatises of Government* (1690).

The *Essay* commenced with a lengthy diatribe against innatism. This was the view that there were certain innate principles imprinted upon the brain of every human as guides to both practical and ethical life. Although this now seems massively anachronistic (thanks largely to Locke's influence) these were manifest truths in the middle of the seventeenth century. Even **Descartes** resorted to innate ideas to bridge the gap from mind to world. It has been remarked that whilst Descartes was the first modern philosopher, Locke had the first modern mind. His rejection of innatism is a reflection of this fact. The doctrine had been used as a tool for the dogmatist to inculcate obedience. Locke's dismissal of this view paved the way for the legitimacy of individual intellectual integrity.

As Locke had vanquished dogmatism in epistemology, so he attacked it in politics. The first of the two *Treatises* was designed to show that the divine right of kings was nonsense. It had been maintained that kings had authority since they were direct descendants of Adam who, as owner of the earth, had sovereign power over it. Locke produced many criticisms of this, not least that it was implausible as a matter of fact. More importantly, however, he showed that ownership had nothing to do with sovereignty – the fact that I own some land does not give me a power of life or death over those standing on it.

In the place of these traditional views Locke put forward more measured alternatives. In the *Essay* he proposed to provide a map of the mind's faculties through introspection. It was his hope to set the limits of human knowledge, faith and opinion, so as to prevent fruitless disputes on topics the understanding was not fit to deal with. The most famous and influential of Locke's findings was that all knowledge was founded on and derived from experience. This thought found expression in

Locke's 'new way of Ideas'. There were two sources of ideas: sensation and reflection. It was these combined, compared and contrasted which provided the basis for all human knowledge. It was these also that fixed the boundaries of human thought and provided some of Locke's most controversial conclusions.

Locke held that simple ideas enter the mind single and unmixed; thus all complex ideas are products of the understanding's faculty of compounding. Consequently, complex ideas of objects were merely stuck-together simple ideas. But what of the substance of things? For Locke, our idea of substance is the something, we know not what, which we suppose to glue the causes of our ideas together. This, of course, was anathema to both the Aristotelean and Cartesian traditions which placed substance at the heart of their respective systems. For Locke, the idea was merely a peculiar place-holder with no correlate in our experience.

Locke's addition to the subject-matter of philosophy was the issue of personal identity. By rejecting a notion of contentful substance, Locke had to provide another criterion of personal identity over time, and did so in the form of psychological continuity, mainly of memory: I am the same as my younger self if I can recall the actions of this more youthful me. Although his solution fades in and out of fashion, the problem itself remains an enduring philosophical issue.

In the political arena Locke is seen as the founder of the modern liberal tradition, with its emphases on limited government by social contract and the right of the people to overthrow a ruler. Locke's arguments were directed against not only traditionalists, but also the extremism of **Hobbes**' *Leviathan*. The Lockean society with its emphasis upon consent and toleration is not only more realistic, but provides the model for modern democracy and, it has been argued, even supplies the blueprint for the American Constitution.

There is a very great deal more to John Locke. He wrote on many subjects and founded several new schools of thought. Nevertheless, it is as a philosopher that Locke will be remembered. A philosopher, moreover, who is once more beginning to regain the recognition he so much deserves.

Suggested reading
Locke, J. 1975 [1690]. *An Essay concerning Human Understanding.* Oxford:
    Oxford University Press.
Locke, J. 1960 [1690]. *Two Treatises of Government.* Cambridge: Cambridge
    University Press.
Chappell, V. 1994 (ed.). *The Cambridge Companion to Locke.* Cambridge:
    Cambridge University Press.

Niccolò Machiavelli

1469–1527   Peter Cave

Niccolò Machiavelli was primarily a diplomat and spin-doctor, committed
to enhancing the power of his native city republic, Florence. When the
Medici family ousted the republicans, Machiavelli was treated with
suspicion and eventually accused of plotting against the Medici.

In 1513, Machiavelli was tortured, and retired to a farm – an internal
exile. There he wrote *Il Principe* (*The Prince*, 1513) – a gift for the
powerful Medici. Machiavelli hoped that his exposition on how rulers
should secure power would re-ignite his political career, even if in
support of the princely dictators. *The Prince* failed in that, but brought
him posthumous fame – fame as the political philosopher best known
for (seemingly) being prepared to justify any means for political preserva-
tion. He later wrote the *Discourses* (1517), justifying republicanism,
and *The Art of War* (1520), arguing for a citizen militia rather than
mercenaries.

It was *The Prince*, though, which gave rise to the term 'machiavellian',
for there Machiavelli advocates the use of cunning, machinations and
ruthlessness – all apparently in the service of political success. It is this
which is much admired these days (often off the record) by spin-
doctoring politicians, salesmen, even academics ready to wield the
knife for advancement. Yet is this 'Mac the knife' stance all there is to
The Prince's philosophy? Is it merely a handbook on how princes – and,
by extension, other leaders – can gain and maintain power?

Certainly, it differs radically from previous works which would
recommend justice, honesty and compassion – man, as a reasoner – as

the best means of securing glory. In contrast, Machiavelli admires the cruelty of Cesare Borgia, advocates treachery, and argues that in the real world leaders need to be half rational man, half beast, possessing the fox's guile and the lion's brutality on the beastly side. Machiavelli's manly prowess – '*virtù*' – is very different from the virtues found in **Plato**, **Aristotle** and, indeed, Christianity.

Although such ruthlessness suggests Machiavelli is immoral, some say he is merely amoral. Machiavelli tells us not how things should be, but merely explains what to do if we seek certain ends. But this defence won't suffice, since taking what seems to be an amoral stance can itself be immoral. Merely to discuss how best to tie fireworks to cats to maximize pain is already to be in the realm of the immoral. So maybe *The Prince* simply is the work of an immoralist, with Machiavelli knowingly advocating actions which are wrong. Yet, although he explicitly writes that a prince needs to learn how *not* to be good, he may yet resist the immorality charge. To challenge conventional moral thinking is not thereby to be immoral; and contrary to popular image, *The Prince* is much concerned with which actions truly are right.

Philosophers who seek to justify actions primarily in terms of their consequences, or at least their likely or intended consequences, are (somewhat ambiguously) known as 'consequentialists'. Certainly Machiavelli has strong consequentialist streaks. But what are the consequences which Machiavelli values? He speaks of maintaining power, of glory and posthumous fame; but these are essentially intertwined with the state – that is, the citizens – flourishing. Machiavelli would not be satisfied with a prince securing illusory glory and fame in some virtual reality machine. He wants the real thing – and that requires the prince's citizens prospering. So the immorality charge will not stick with regard to his recommended ends.

How about the means? Even here, Machiavelli shows moral concern. He explicitly advocates maintaining traditional moral values as far as possible, using cruelty and deceit only when necessary for the common good. He also reminds us that moral virtue is not episodic. True kindness towards children is not to give them ice-creams whenever they demand; sometimes you say 'no' and upset them – but such episodes of seeming unkindness may be manifestations of continuing concern. Machiavelli argues similarly that seeming cruelties might be the actions of a compassionate leader, prepared not to shirk duties, acting for the greater good.

When dealing with family and friends, suggests Machiavelli, sticking to traditional moral rules can probably be relied upon, for family and friends are likely to reciprocate. In politics, adversaries cannot be relied upon; for this reason – and because Fortuna (chance) throws up the unexpected – princes need flexibility. Even then, he notes, things can still run out of your control. Machiavelli's recognition of political luck presages recent concern for moral luck. X is accepted as a typical driver who occasionally drives above the speed limits; Y, driving just the same, hits unlucky, kills a child – and gets imprisoned. Reflect on events outside our leaders' control. Would George W. Bush have been so popular, but for Mr Bin Laden? Margaret Thatcher but for the Argentinian war? Was not her inflexibility the cause of her eventual downfall?

When asked what shaped his political strategy, Harold Macmillan answered, 'Events, dear boy, events!' Machiavelli gives substance to this answer, saying much more than is conjured up by the term 'machiavellian'.

Suggested reading
Machiavelli, N. 1988 [1513]. *The Prince*. Cambridge: Cambridge University Press.
Machiavelli, N. 1971 [1517]. *The Discourses*. Harmondsworth: Penguin.
Skinner, Q. 2000. *Machiavelli: A very short introduction*. Oxford: Oxford University Press.

Alasdair MacIntyre
1929– Matthew Ray

Alasdair MacIntyre is one of the most innovative moral philosophers writing in untechnical English today. A prolific author, his early writings include influential articles on modern philosophy and philosophical theology as well as monographs on Marcuse and on the concept of the unconscious in the writings of **Freud**, together with a now standard text on moral thinking, *A Short History of Ethics* (1966). But it is for *After Virtue* (1981) and the various texts which followed in its wake – *Whose Justice, Which Rationality?* (1988), *Three Rival Versions of Moral Enquiry*

(1990) and more recently *Dependent Rational Animals* (1999) – that MacIntyre is probably most celebrated.

The main goal of *After Virtue* – a goal motivated in part by **Nietzsche**'s persuasive attack on morality, which essentially argued that many moral agents are duped into acting ethically – is to provide us with a good reason for acting morally today. He does so by introducing his notion of a 'practice'.

Practices, MacIntyre tells us, are found in some form or other across all human cultures and in a sense constitute goals for human desire. Thus, where utilitarians argue that happiness is the goal of humanity, MacIntyre argues that that honour belongs to practices. But what are practices? Very basically, they are co-operative human activities with a standard of excellence through which certain goods inherent in that form of activity are realized. Thus, for example, social activities like playing chess would count as practices because the good of playing chess well can only be achieved through engaging in that practice, a practice with a developed standard of excellence. Practices must also, MacIntyre adds, extend human powers to achieve excellence.

So the goods of a practice, we might say, are those goods which can only be achieved through participation in that specific practice and such goods must, moreover, have historically evolved standards of excellence internal to them. Virtue then becomes MacIntyre's name for those human capabilities that allow us to pursue practices and therefore aim for the goods internal to those practices. Resilience, for instance, allows us to pursue the good internal to the practice of sailing a ship. Similarly, diligence allows us to pursue the different good internal to the practice of playing in a string quartet and honesty allows us to pursue the good internal to, say, playing chess (we could, of course, cheat but only external goods could be achieved that way: a rather restricted and short-lived form of social prestige, perhaps).

All these practices, because they have historically developed standards of excellence, call for the virtue of accepting the judgement of a legitimate authority on our part: as novices or beginners, we have to accept the judgement of a past master as to what the good of chess, or of a particular kind of musicianship, consists in.

Thus practices, which we all engage in, require virtues, from which it follows that it is rational to foster them. Such, then, is the central line of argument in *After Virtue*, an argument which provides us with a rational reason for acting ethically, a rationale much needed in the post-Nietzschean world (MacIntyre is one of a small set of major Anglophone philosophers who take Nietzsche very seriously indeed). This line of argument, it is further worth mentioning, situates MacIntyre within a broad movement in moral philosophy called 'virtue ethics'.

It remains to be mentioned here that the major work *Whose Justice, Which Rationality?* argues that certain social traditions – such as the Christian religious tradition – embody conceptions of rational enquiry within them, so that what makes for a rational reason to act, for example, can only be answered by accepting the philosophical commitments of a given tradition in the first place. On this view, what justifies a theory is 'the rational superiority of that particular structure to all previous attempts within that particular tradition to formulate such theories and principles'. There is thus no conception of rationality to be found over and above any tradition, no possibility of an objective rationality outside – and therefore able to adjudicate between – all traditions. Both in his ethics – perhaps most particularly in his stress on the role of a legitimate authority – and in his thoughts upon rationality, therefore, MacIntyre can be seen to be a defender, but also an extender, of tradition.

We might then say that MacIntyre maintains that it is rational both to act virtuously and to accept the philosophical commitments of a given tradition; a position illuminated and supplemented in all his later writings.

Suggested reading
MacIntyre, A. 1981. *After Virtue*. Notre Dame, Indiana: University of Notre Dame Press.
MacIntyre, A. 1988. *Whose Justice, Which Rationality?* Notre Dame, Indiana: University of Notre Dame Press.
Knight, K. 1988 (ed.). *The MacIntyre Reader*. Notre Dame, Indiana: University of Notre Dame Press.

Karl Marx

1818–1883   **Sanghamitra Bandyopadhyay**

In Highgate Cemetery, London, the grave of Karl Marx is inscribed with a quote from one of his famous theses: 'The philosophers have only inter-preted the world; the point, however, is to change it.' While others shaped the course of philosophy, he shaped the history of the world. His rhetoric is powerful, his message is compelling, and his followers attract both wholehearted approval and widespread scorn.

So what makes Marx a philosopher? Of the numerous treatises on subjects ranging from anthropology to medicine, his main contribution as a philosopher, economic theorist and political scientist is a theory of the development of society. Marx belongs to a league of anti-philosophers, with **Nietzsche**, **Heidegger** and **Wittgenstein**, who were out to deflate the metaphysical pretensions of philosophy and discuss something more fundamental, such as power, being or, in Marx's case, the 'historical conditions of man'. He intended to fashion a practical philosophy with the means to transform the world.

For Marx, what was wrong with the German philosophy of his day was its assumption that nature and society were immutable. This was his starting point – to abort the assumption of an unchanging world, an assumption which would prove central to his ideas in the following years.

German philosophy had, however, made a great leap forward under Schelling, Fichte and **Hegel** in recovering the best of Greek philosophy – the *dialectic* or the art of argument. Marx fell under their influence – particularly Hegel's – during his years at Berlin University. Marx's funda-mental philosophical contribution, historical materialism, is the theory that economic, social and political life is in a process of transformation. As one social structure or institution assumes authority or eminence, another rises to challenge it. And with this challenge and conflict comes a new synthesis and a new power, these to be challenged in turn. An illustration of this process is the way in which the new industrialists of his day were challenging the then ruling landed classes. Marx envisaged that in his future these new industrialists, having reduced the power of the old landed aristocracy and having achieved a new synthesis (i.e. capitalism), would in turn be challenged by the workers whom they had amassed in their service. This idea of 'class struggle' takes centre stage in his work – different social classes exist in a state of mutual antagonism because of their conflicting material interests. If we ask why it is that social classes live in this state of permanent warfare, the answer for Marx has to do with the history of material production.

Marx's numerous theses, in particular the three volumes of *Das Kapital,* theorize why and how the demise of capitalism is inevitable. Marx did not doubt the productive achievements of the system of capitalism – to these he gave his strongest praise. But capitalism had fatal vulnerabilities, in particular the unequal distribution of power and income, and perhaps most importantly, the disposition of capitalism to economic depression and unemployment. Marx considered these vulnerabilities as central to the causes of the breakdown of capitalism and thus its eventual transition to a post-capitalist – that is communist – society as a historical inevitability.

But the Marxian system itself had obvious points of vulnerability, which he was aware of, one of which was the threat of reform, the possibility that the hardships of capitalism would be so cushioned as to not rouse the revolutionary anger of the workers. Nevertheless, Marx proposed reforms in the interest of the worker.

The closest to a programme proposed by Marx, in collaboration with Friedrich Engels, is found in the famous ten points of *The Communist Manifesto* (1848), the most celebrated, and most energetically denounced, political pamphlet of all time. It urged, along with much else, a progressive income tax, public ownership of railroads and communications, free education, abolition of child labour and jobs for all. Curiously, much of the industrial world in the twentieth century is in step with a lot of *The Communist Manifesto,* not, however, by revolutionary action but through parliamentary reform.

In essence, Marx's philosophy seeks to dismantle the major social contradictions which prevent us from living what he would see as a truly human life. In Marx's world, we are only free as individuals when, like artists, we can produce gratuitously, independent of material need. Freedom for Marx entails release from commercial labour – possible when society has achieved a certain economic surplus over material necessity. For in Marx's 'utopia', enjoying Bach or writing poetry are elements of our self-realization as much as building dams or

manufacturing cars. Till then, to quote **Sartre**, one cannot go beyond
Marxism, 'because we have not gone beyond the circumstances which
engendered it'.

Suggested reading
Engels, F., & Marx, K. 2002 [1848]. *The Communist Manifesto*. Harmondsworth:
    Penguin.
Marx, K. 1993 [1861]. *Capital: A Critique of Political Economy*. Harmondsworth:
    Penguin.
Singer, P. 2000. *Marx: A Very Short Introduction*. Oxford: Oxford Paperbacks.

Maurice Merleau-Ponty

1908–1961   **Mark Paterson**

Maurice Merleau-Ponty was not only a leading exponent of phenomenology in France, but also a literary critic who wrote extensively on
Marxism and aesthetic theory. He taught at élite institutions, notably he
was Professor of Child Psychology at the Sorbonne and later Professor of
Philosophy at the Collège de France.

Merleau-Ponty's most important works of philosophy were *The
Structure of Behaviour* (1942) and *Phenomenology of Perception* (1945).
Though greatly influenced by the work of **Edmund Husserl**, Merleau-
Ponty grounded his own theory in a deeply humanistic and poetic
analysis of perception and bodily behaviour. In *The Structure of
Behaviour* he used contemporary physiology and psychology to argue
for the primacy of perception. These ideas were developed further in his
most famous book, *Phenomenology of Perception*. Perception is key
because sensory stimuli cannot be considered alone; the organism as a
whole, including the bodily senses and memory, is the basis of his
phenomenology and he sees it as being the ground of experience. It is
through the different aspects of the organism, for example, that we get
a sense of space. The phenomenology of perception becomes a way to
analyse our primordial contact with the world prior to the impact of
conventional scientific knowledge or anything else.

While this sounds like a recipe for a deeply subjective interpretation of human engagement with the world, it is important to make two points. First, Merleau-Ponty made use of the available psychological and neuro-scientific literature of his time, and far from dismissing scientific evidence he used this research to advance his own ideas of the connections between phenomenological experience and the mechanisms of mind and perception. Thus he did not write in a bubble of his own philosoph-ical making, but produced a marvellously rich and poetic mixture, combining psychology, philosophy and literary theory. Secondly, one of the main projects throughout his philosophical life, from *The Structure of Behaviour* (1942) right through to *The Visible and the Invisible* (1964), was to elide that distinction in the history of western philosophy between the human subject and the non-human object, as enshrined in Cartesian dualism.

Along with **Sartre** he was one of the founding editors of the journal *Les Temps Modernes*, but they fell out and Merleau-Ponty resigned from the editorial board. Not only was he disappointed with Sartre's naïve politics, but also, philosophically, he questioned the privileging of the subject-object relationship in Sartre's version of phenomenology. In this questioning, he continually revisited territory that is problematic for the phenomenology of Husserl, **Heidegger** and Sartre, since each of these philosophers attempts to escape Cartesian dualism yet arguably each ends up perpetuating it. Merleau-Ponty's means of positing something between the subject and object world in *Phenomenology of Perception* is to foreground the importance of the body. Already latent in Husserl's 'aesthetic body' and Heidegger's distinction between ready-at-hand and ready-to-hand, Merleau-Ponty's concept of the 'lived body' is central in terms of establishing an embodied context for our knowing and experi-encing a world. Thus the body becomes a 'third term' between subject and object: 'My body is the fabric into which all objects are woven, and it is, at least in relation to the perceived world, the general instrument of my "comprehension",' he argues. The body is neither subject nor object, but is the basis of our experience of such things as space, time, language and memory. He concludes that there is no such thing as perception *per se*, only embodied perception, and hence the 'lived body'.

Yet just as he attempted to escape the dualism of mind and body, subject and object, through the body and lived experience, there remains a tension in his philosophy between consciousness and lived experience whereby 'otherness' or alterity is arguably not granted sufficient importance in his philosophy. This is a perennial problem for most phenomenology, and forms the basis of feminist critiques of the 'lived body', being universalized as white, male and without disability. This is the problem of elevating the lived experience of the body as the foundation for our perceiving, understanding and knowing a world.

Merleau-Ponty's unfinished final book *The Visible and the Invisible* extended his ideas of perception into semi-religious themes of flesh and transcendence. In part, his notion of 'flesh' was an augmentation of the 'lived body' of experience, accommodating the fact that both body and world are made of the same material, implicated or enfolded into each another. Our 'flesh' is made of the same flesh as the world, and it is because the flesh of our body is also the flesh of the world that we can know and understand the world.

Suggested reading

Merleau-Ponty, M. 1984 [1942]. *The Structure of Behaviour*. Pittsburgh: Duquesne University Press.

Merleau-Ponty, M. 1998 [1945]. *Phenomenology of Perception*. London: Routledge.

Dillon, M. C. 1991. *Merleau-Ponty's Ontology*. Evanston: Northwestern University Press.

John Stuart Mill

1806–1873   **Peter Holmes**

John Stuart Mill's *Autobiography* (1873) reveals his prodigious early capacity for learning, best shown by studying, under his father's tuition, ancient Greek from the age of three. His first set-text was Aesop's *Fables* and by the time he was 13 he was reading the first five dialogues of **Plato** – in the original. Mill's own comment on this is that it shows that what he achieved in terms of intellectual development, anyone else of average intelligence could also achieve, given the same high-powered education. Such a statement may have been false modesty, but there is some evidence that he believed it.

Mill's first great philosophical work, which he thought would probably be one of his most enduring, was the *System of Logic* (1843), which defends the position that all knowledge derives from experience, either directly or by the inferences we draw from this experience. Mill argued against the idea that some knowledge was 'self-supporting' and did not depend on the senses for its justification. He extended this view to mathematics, a field where self-supporting knowledge was, and is, sometimes held particularly to exist, but he was also thinking of religion, and the social and political views sometimes, especially in his day, drawn from revelation.

If all knowledge is derived from experience and the inferences we draw from it, this might help to explain how it could be that every average individual is able to achieve as much as J. S. Mill, since every individual is subject to similar influences. At least it shows the value of education.

In the *System of Logic*, Mill's belief in fallibility is also clearly sketched: the inferences drawn by induction are never founded on necessity. Every average individual is perfectible, as far as fallibility will allow. He was distrustful of logical necessity, but perhaps surprisingly in the *Logic* he came down against free will, although in the process argued the controversy more or less out of existence. He believed that the social and moral sciences would progress so far that in the end human actions would be so well understood that it would be possible to predict accurately what a combination of circumstances would produce in terms of a response from a given individual.

Mill wrote a great deal on a tremendous range of subjects, but is best known for his three ethical and political books, published towards the end of his life: *Utilitarianism* (1863), *On Liberty* (1859), and *On Representative Government* (1861). Mill's teacher-father, James, had instilled in his son the ideas of Benthamite utilitarianism, the principle that the morally right action is that which increases the greatest happiness of the greatest number. As the young Mill grew older, he inevitably reacted against his father's teaching (the most poignant passages in the *Autobiography* describe how he suffered a period of depression in early manhood as he was beginning to escape from the hot-house of his father's influence), but in the end like a good son was unwilling to abandon **Bentham**, the great guide of James Mill.

What he did do was to enlarge the scope of utilitarianism considerably, arguing for a qualitative element to be added to the quantitative calculations of the principle of utility. The point now was to maximize the greatest happiness of the greatest number, but also the higher pleasures of the greatest number; higher pleasures being the intellectual rather than carnal ones. Mill has been accused of élitism in this, but as will be recalled he believed (subject to fallibility) in the perfectibility of all the average and above. He hoped that most people would, after sufficient instruction, naturally prefer poetry to ten-pin bowling. But Mill was still worried about the 'tyranny of the majority', to which he felt utilitarianism committed him. In *Representative Government*, Mill therefore advocated proportional representation, plural voting, and a literacy test for the franchise, in order to reduce the influence of the below average.

In *On Liberty*, all these themes come together. The scope of utilitarianism must now include liberty. Complete freedom to express ourselves will enable fallible humans to live with our fallibility and to progress to what perfection it is possible to achieve in a world where there is no logical necessity. Freedom of action is essential for the moral development of individuals, but this development is also impossible if individuals do not live securely in communities. Hence the famous harm principle, which says that the only reason liberty may be interfered with is in order to prevent harm to others.

Mill's work is not without its inconsistencies: liberty, equality and fraternity do not work together as easily as Mill tries to maintain. His idea of progress, taken from Condorcet, the French philosopher, could easily be criticized, and seems to lead him astray. But it is difficult to be harsh on a philosopher whose instincts on so many things were so sound, and whose daring in the field of thought was so great.

Suggested reading
Mill, J. S. 1998. *On Liberty and Other Essays*. Oxford: Oxford University Press.
Mill, J. S. 1989 [1873]. *Autobiography*. Harmondsworth: Penguin.
Thomas, W. 1985. *Mill* (Past Masters). Oxford: Oxford University Press.

Michel Eyquem de Montaigne
1533–1592   **Peter S. Fosl**

Michel Eyquem de Montaigne, sometimes called the 'French Socrates', walked the shifting line between philosophy and literature – or perhaps we should say other forms of literature – inventing what he called 'essays', publishing the first of his own *Essais* in 1580. The word 'essay' originally meant 'attempt', and one might say that in Montaigne's distinctive texts he does not purport to set out the final word on the topics he addresses. Rather, one finds there the exposure and exhibition of something quite personal: the sometimes conflicted thinking processes of a particular man at a particular time and place. One finds concern not only with the arcane and abstruse topics of philosophical thought but also with ordinary and practical matters.

There's something else, however, something not unrelated. One also finds in Montaigne's work a critique of philosophy's vanity in pretending to be a superior, authoritative kind of literature and of philosophers' vanity in pretending to transcend the individual person and the local context of common life. The 'mysteries of philosophy', Montaigne writes, 'have many strange things in common with those of poetry; the human understanding losing its way in trying to sound and examine all things to the utmost.' These sorts of reflections on the limits and pretensions of philosophy are characteristic not only of Montaigne's philosophical style but also of what has perhaps been most influential in his work, his scepticism.

Montaigne was born in 1533 into a century that would be drenched in the blood drawn through struggles between Protestant reformers and Catholic counter-reformers. His father, a Catholic, had found success as a Bordeaux merchant and his mother hailed from a prominent Jewish family that had fled Spain during the vicious anti-Jewish and anti-Muslim attacks of the late 1400s. Having studied law, Montaigne became a magistrate, counsel to the parliament in Toulouse and finally mayor of Bordeaux. He travelled in Switzerland, Germany and Italy, recounting his observations in his *Journal de Voyage* (*Travel Journal*, not published during his lifetime).

Much of Montaigne's adult life, however, was spent in retreat from public life and in devotion to reading and writing. He seems to have been influenced by the classical Hellenistic and Greco-Roman authors that, having become available again, were gripping to many Renaissance and early modern thinkers. Stoics like **Seneca** and Epicureans like Lucretius were important to his eclectic mind. And in his *Essais* one finds him promoting stoical virtues like the mitigation of the passions, and Epicurean themes like the importance of extinguishing the fear of death. But perhaps no authors were more important to Montaigne than the sceptics, in particular the Pyrrhonian sceptic Sextus Empiricus, whose work had been published in Latin in 1562 and 1569.

As **Descartes** would be later, Montaigne became fascinated with sceptical doubt about the abilities of the human mind to acquire knowledge of the self, the world and the divine. Unlike Descartes, however, Montaigne embraced scepticism. Although sceptical ideas surface throughout his work, nowhere is this fascination more evident than in Montaigne's most famous essay, and his longest, 'Apology for Raymond Sebond'. There, in ironically defending Sebond's natural theology (that is, the attempt to gain knowledge of the divine through the use of natural reasoning), Montaigne castigates attempts to establish a dependable criterion for knowledge in either sense experience or reasoning – a classic sceptical strategy. He compares other animals favourably with humans, finding with us no exceptional abilities in cognition or even virtue. (Scandalously, he claimed that elephants seem to exhibit religious behaviour.)

Montaigne also became convinced that scepticism offered a diagnosis and therapy for the pathologies of dogmatism that so afflicted his time. He carved sceptical and other quotations in the rafters of his study so that he could find constant reminders of the importance of avoiding these pathologies. His motto, famously, became, 'Que sçay-je?' ('What do I know?'). Montaigne came to regard tolerance for varying human beliefs, an appreciation of human frailty, and detachment from the violent and puritanical demands of dogma as crucial to the achievement of human well-being. If reason cannot establish final truths, we must accept humans in their error and diversity, we must honour the importance of custom in human life, and we must yield to ungrounded faith in our religion.

It is in his refusal to pursue a project of purportedly transcendent philosophy, his attempt (much like **Hume** in his essays) to bring philosophy back to the ordinary business of common life, and his appreciation for the multiplicity and finitude of human thinking and living, that so many have found inspiration in Montaigne. And it is in these dimensions of his thought that his scepticism is most evident.

Selected reading
Montaigne. M. 1993. *The Complete Essays*. Harmondsworth: Penguin.
Hoffman, G. 2004. *Montaigne: A Biography*. Cambridge: Cambridge University Press.

G. E. Moore
1873–1958   **Bart Schultz**

George Edward Moore's importance as a philosopher is, on the face of it, self-evident. A fellow and then university lecturer at Trinity College, Cambridge, he became a fellow of the British Academy, a legendary stalwart of the Moral Sciences Club, and eventually, in 1925, Professor of Mental Philosophy and Logic. He served as editor of the top journal *Mind* from 1921 to 1947, was awarded the Order of Merit in 1951, and was considered worthy of a volume in the *Library of Living Philosophers* series.

As the legend runs, Moore and **Bertrand Russell** were the dynamic duo who broke the spell of British Idealism, ushering in the age of analytic philosophy. Moore's 'Refutation of Idealism' (1903) supposedly set the philosophical world on fire with its head-on assault on the idealist thesis that everything we know is mental – an idea or a perception. And Russell always credited his friend and fellow apostle with having led the way. Moore was also teacher, colleague and conversational partner to the likes of **Frank Ramsey** and **Ludwig Wittgenstein**.

Beyond serving as philosophical midwife to Russell, Ramsay and Wittgenstein, Moore was revered as a god, the model of moral and mental purity, by the leading members of the Bloomsbury set. An ecstatic Lytton Strachey proclaimed that Moore's classic *Principia Ethica* (1903) marked the birth of the age of reason. Surely, a man who could go down in history as both the philosopher's philosopher, in the age of Russell and Wittgenstein, and the icon of Bloomsbury should not be suspected of leaving too little behind.

Yet a century after the publication of his major works, there is an unusual degree of doubt about the value of his legacy. Across today's philosophical landscape, one can find plenty of Wittgensteinians and a vocal minority of (more or less) Russellians, but no one happily described as 'Moorean'. Moore himself, in his autobiographical statement for the *Living Philosophers* volume, confessed that Wittgenstein 'has made me think that what is required for the solution of philosophical problems which baffle me, is a method quite different from any which I have ever used – a method which he himself uses successfully, but which I have never been able to understand clearly enough to use it myself.'

What were Moore's chief claims? *Principia Ethica*, at least, is often described as combining a substantive theory of ideal utilitarianism (that the rightness of an action can be defined in terms of conducing to maximal goodness) and a metaethics of Platonic intuition (that we can directly perceive or intuit which things possess the quality 'goodness' and to what degree). For Moore, much of past ethical philosophizing – though not his old teacher **Sidgwick**'s – was tainted by a 'Naturalistic Fallacy': the confusion of the 'is' of attribution (for example, 'water is wet') and the 'is' of identity (for example, 'water is H_2O') that supposedly infects, for instance, utilitarian efforts to say that the ultimate good is pleasure. By contrast, Moore argues that goodness is a simple, indefinable, non-natural property or quality or entity, on a par with 'yellow', and that 'good is good' is the not very helpful last word on what good is.

Against reductive definitions which, for example, define good in terms of happiness, one could always sensibly ask whether what they called good was really good. This 'open question' test undercut the ambitions of ethicists from **Aristotle** to **Mill** and Spencer. Yet one can helpfully ask what things possess intrinsic goodness, and on this Moore gives a most eloquent pitch for friendship and art as forming the ideal that utilitarian rules will conduce to maximizing.

It was this appeal to art and friendship as simply and irreducibly good, or intrinsically valuable, that so thrilled Bloomsbury, though Moore gives a fairly sophisticated account of these goods in terms of 'organic unities', more than the sum of the good of the parts. To confirm just

which organic wholes have intrinsic value, apart from their consequences, he invokes the test of imagining the unity in question to exist in
complete isolation and then asking whether this would be better than its
non-existing.

As a type of utilitarian, Moore was more limited than his great
predecessor Sidgwick; his was a utilitarianism without benefit of political
economy or political theory. And his Platonistic view of good as an
objective indefinable property came in for a severe drubbing in the
thirties and forties. Yet Darwall, Gibbard and Railton, in *Moral Discourse
and Practice*, manage to claim that 'it seems impossible to deny that
Moore was on to something' in *Principia Ethica*. If it is scarcely clear from
their generous account how far the 'controversy Moore began' is 'lively
today', because of continuing engagement with Moore, clarification
may well be coming.

Suggested reading
Moore. G. E. 1993 [1903]. *Principia Ethica*. Cambridge: Cambridge Univerity
    Press.
Moore. G. E. ed. Baldwin, T. 1993. *Selected Writings*. London: Routledge.
Baldwin, T. 1992. *G. E. Moore (Arguments of the philosophers)*. London:
    Routledge.

Thomas Nagel
1937–   **Edward Johnson**

Over the last four decades, Thomas Nagel has exerted a profound,
multifaceted and idiosyncratic influence on Anglo-American analytic
philosophy. The two chief arenas of that influence have been philosophy
of mind (where Nagel has insisted on the centrality, and the difficulty, of
the question of the nature of consciousness) and social theory (where he
has subtly analysed, and robustly defended, the moral claims of the
individual). Nagel's work in these areas has concerned the topics, as he
says, 'that have always occupied me: subjectivity and consciousness,
objectivity and ethics, liberalism and reason'.

Best known for his provocative question, 'What is it like to be a bat?' Nagel considers the central problem in the philosophy of mind to be the conundrum of subjective consciousness. It might seem as though all the facts about the world could be stated in the third person: TN thinks x; TN does y. But the fact that I am *this* person, TN (rather than someone else), that these experiences are mine (rather than somebody else's), can only be adequately expressed through the personal perspective, Nagel argues. He holds that attempts by some philosophers (such as **Daniel Dennett** and **Richard Rorty**) to explain away consciousness with theories that expel subjectivity cannot be adequate. And though he is uncertain exactly what an adequate theory would look like, he remains confident that it would have to make room in some way for the subjective character of experience, for what it is like to be me. Unsympathetic naturalists have dismissed such views as 'mysterian,' but Nagel argues against naturalism as the final word, insisting that 'in any process of reasoning or argument there must be some thoughts that one simply thinks from the inside, rather than thinking of them as biologically programmed dispositions.'

In social theory, Nagel has been one of the most thoughtful students of **John Rawls**, and a champion of liberalism's basic values. Nagel figured, along with Rawls and others, as a major force in invigorating the analytic approach to 'applied ethics', beginning in the 1970s. He served for many years as an editor of the influential journal, *Philosophy and Public Affairs*. Like Rawls, Nagel has argued against utilitarian theories which attempt to reduce right action to the promotion of the best consequences. He has also been a critic of conservative, libertarian and Marxist views.

In a recent book co-authored with Liam Murphy, *The Myth of Ownership: Taxes and Justice* (2002), Nagel in effect applies the Rawlsian notion of the natural lottery to policies of taxation, in a way consonant with his approach years earlier to preferential treatment. Ownership of property, like ownership of one's natural talents, must be considered subject to reasonable claims on behalf of the public good, since there is no sense in which one baby can be said to deserve fundamental good fortune more than another.

In his first book, *The Possibility of Altruism* (1970), Nagel argued for the idea that moral justification rests ultimately on objective, rather than merely subjective, reasons. The ability to view one's actions from an impersonal standpoint which 'provides a view of the world without giving one's location in it', he presented as a requirement of practical reason. Just as rational individuals must be able to view their future interests with the same seriousness as present claims, so rationality requires that we be able to see the interests of others as being as compelling as our own. In the contest between **David Hume**, who saw reason as the slave of the passions, and **Immanuel Kant**, who insisted that desire dance to the tune of reason, Nagel defended the Kantian side, and those concerns have persisted throughout his later work.

His second book, *Mortal Questions* (1979), brought together earlier papers on a variety of surprisingly interconnected subjects: what it is that makes death a bad thing, the nature of absurdity, moral luck, the analysis of sexual perversion, the moral limits of action in war, the justification of preferential treatment, the relation between ethics and biology, brain bisection and the unity of consciousness, what it is like to be a bat, panpsychism and other matters. Nagel's charming, quirky, insightful, gracefully-written essays won him a wide audience, which has grown with each subsequent book: *The View from Nowhere* (1986), *Equality and Partiality* (1991), *Other Minds* (1995), *The Last Word* (1997), and *Concealment and Exposure* (2002).

Educated at Cornell, Oxford and Harvard, Nagel taught for three years at Berkeley, fourteen years at Princeton, and for more than two decades at New York University, where he still teaches in the law school and the department of philosophy. He continues to defend the importance of integrating subjectivity into our understanding of consciousness, the necessity of objectivity and reason in the development of moral philosophy as a discipline, and the relevance of a healthy tradition of liberalism to both.

Suggested reading
Nagel, T. 1979. *Mortal Questions*. Cambridge: Cambridge University Press.
Nagel, T. 1986. *The View from Nowhere*. Oxford: Oxford University Press.
Nagel, T. 1997. *The Last Word*. Oxford: Oxford University Press.

Friedrich Nietzsche

1844–1900   **Christopher Budd**

Friedrich Wilhelm Nietzsche was born in Rocken in Prussian Saxony. Nietzsche's father died in 1849, leaving the young Friedrich to be raised by his mother, aunts and older sister. In 1864, Nietzsche left for university in Bonn, and by 1869 was teaching classical philology at the University of Basle. After ten years, he retired due to ill health. He lived on his own, publishing at a steady rate until he suffered a mental breakdown in 1889 in Turin, Italy, that left him completely incapacitated. From 1889 until his death in 1900, Nietzsche remained an invalid, dependent on his mother and then sister to care for him.

It has been said that Nietzsche is one of the best known and yet least understood of philosophers, and the reaction to his best known work, *Also Sprach Zarathustra* (1883-5), amply illustrates this point. Often read by itself, without a firm grasp of Nietzsche's other works, *Zarathustra's* religious imagery and metaphor leave many with the impression that Nietzsche is not a thinker, but a prophet. While Nietzsche chose the style of *Zarathustra* for a purpose, it was not to found a new religion, even an atheistic one. Rather, Nietzsche, who begged not to be made holy in his self-assessment *Ecce Homo* (1888) – the title itself being a tongue-in-cheek reference to the New Testament – uses the language of religion in an attempt to undermine religion. *Zarathustra* epitomizes Nietzsche's plight, as what he saw as the finest, most subtle expression of his thought is misunderstood and interpreted to mean the opposite of what he intended.

While reading Nietzsche is a struggle, it is not a hopeless one. Though his method and language are often oblique, contrary to popular characterization, Nietzsche is not a negative thinker. He has a positive direction towards nothing less than the realization of the genius of humanity. Nietzsche's works can be seen as an ongoing struggle within himself with the fundamental question of what it is to be human, and how humanity can strive to be greater and realize its potential. In this way, his writing is not deliberately obscurantist, but reflects the tensions and difficulties humans face in grappling with a world that is increasingly devoid of objective meaning.

For Nietzsche, the genius of humanity is the ability to create values and beliefs *ex nihilo* – from nothing – and, in so doing, to propel itself to greater heights than would be possible in an anarchic state of nature. Nietzsche does not believe in Christianity as revealed truth: he sees Christianity as one of many instances in history of humans creating values. But, in Nietzsche's opinion, Christianity has expended its last benefits and no longer carries humanity to the heights it once did; instead, all that remains of Christianity are chains that weigh us down. This is one of the subtexts behind his pronouncement that 'God is dead'. For humanity to flourish, it must cast off those values that no longer carry it forward and replace them with new ones that do.

To create new values, Nietzsche applies to values themselves the same analysis and judgement that is at the heart of valuation. Because values are a human construct, indeed *the* human construct, they can themselves be evaluated, and the positive identified and separated from the negative. In measuring values in this way, Nietzsche makes a distinction between those values that ennoble and elevate humanity and those that diminish and reduce humanity. Within this distinction in values lies a difference, not between values that are 'good' or 'evil', but rather between values that are 'good' and 'bad'. Values that give humanity the noble, strong, confident ease we associate with a master are good and to be cultivated. Those that breed the resentment, envy, fear and cowardice we associate with a slave are bad and should be rejected.

But Nietzsche is not a philosopher to propound new values: for values to truly succeed, each person must make them for themselves. Nietzsche provides instruction on how to make the journey, but each person must make the journey and choose the destination for themselves.

It is because of this that Nietzsche's work can seem obscure and oblique: his work provides a testing ground that forces the reader to grapple and struggle on their own. This is why it is not enough to casually read one or two of his works in isolation from the rest of his corpus. Nietzsche never wanted disciples. Indeed, even Zarathustra hopes to see his followers repudiate him in the end. Nietzsche wants thinkers, able and willing to form their own answers for themselves. In this way, Nietzsche is not so much telling his readers *what* to think, but rather *how* to think. His works are meant to convey not a product but a process, and that process is at the heart of what it is to be human.

Suggested reading
Nietzsche, F. 1989 [1886]. *Beyond Good and Evil*. New York: Vintage.
Nietzsche, F. 1988 [1887 & 1888]. *On the Genealogy of Morals and Ecce Homo*.
   New York: Random House.
Kaufmann, W. 1974. *Nietzsche: Philosopher, Psychologist, Antichrist*. Princeton:
   Princeton University Press.

Robert Nozick

1938–2002   **Alan Haworth**

Robert Nozick is mainly remembered for *Anarchy, State, and Utopia*
(1974), the book in which he defends the minimal, or 'nightwatchman',
state of classical liberalism. Under this type of regime, the state's
functions are limited to the protection of the individual against force,
fraud and theft, and to the enforcement of contracts. The allocation of
resources is left to the operation of a free market. There are many well-
rehearsed objections to such arrangements – objections usually raised
by socialists, supporters of the welfare state and other proponents of
'redistributivism'. However, as Nozick saw it, the minimal state is
'inspiring as well as right'.

Anarchy, State, and Utopia made a timely appearance. This was partly
because its publication roughly coincided with a resurgence in the
popularity of robustly anti-state, pro-free market ideology which
persisted until the end of the eighties. Throughout that period, those
who shared Nozick's view were able to refer to *Anarchy, State, and
Utopia* as a demonstration that a fully worked-through, intellectually
sophisticated account of their position was possible. Indeed, Nozick
became something of a guru to the ultras of the 'libertarian' right.
Conversely, those to whom Nozick's standpoint was anathema were
constrained, at the philosophical level, to develop their critique of that
standpoint against the case he makes in the book.

The book appeared only three years after **John Rawls**'s influential
masterpiece, *A Theory of Justice*. In fact, there are similarities between
the two works. For example, both Rawls and Nozick take it as a starting
point that utilitarianism – the view that we should try to maximize the

greatest happiness of the greatest number – is flawed, due to its emphasis on the consequences of actions and policies. Both point out that because utilitarianism emphasizes happiness, or 'utility', within the community considered as a whole, it cannot satisfactorily account for claims, such as claims of right, which individuals are entitled to make upon the behaviour of other individuals. Accordingly, each sets out to develop a political philosophy which adequately reflects what Nozick describes as 'the underlying Kantian principle that individuals are ends and not merely means'.

But from this common starting point, and with this common ambition, each philosopher moves in a completely different direction. While the 'contractualist' Rawls argues for the claims free and equal people are entitled to make upon each other, the 'libertarian' Nozick pictures individuals, the bearers of rights which act as 'side-constraints' upon the behaviour of others, moving freely about in a moral universe within which only uncoerced, consensual exchanges take place. Consequently, whereas Rawls's account of 'justice as fairness' supports redistribution of social goods, so Nozick's 'entitlement theory of justice' yields an argument for the minimal state. It was therefore Nozick's achievement to elaborate an alternative to Rawls's argument, and so demonstrate that there is more than one way to develop a non-utilitarian, 'Kantian', political philosophy.

Time has moved on and 'libertarian' ideology is no longer so fashionable as it once was. Even so, there remain plenty of good reasons for reading *Anarchy, State, and Utopia*. As Nozick once put it, 'It is as though what philosophers want is a way of saying something that will leave the person they're talking to no escape.' But, as he added, 'Well, why should they be bludgeoning people like that? It's not a nice way to behave.' Against this 'coercive' view, it is surely more accurate to think of the philosopher as setting out to 'elaborate a view, to delineate its content'; that is, to explore lines of argument in order to see what they add up to and what they are worth. And that is something Nozick did throughout his life with great skill, elegance, and with the use of 'parallel examples' which engage and challenge the reader. Can there really be a political philosopher, now living, who is unfamiliar with the example featuring Wilt Chamberlain, the basketball champ, or Nozick's 'experience machine' thought experiment? So there is humour too, something especially refreshing in an age when reading through the latest edition of an academic journal can so often feel like reading the phone book, only less exciting.

In an interview, Nozick once remarked that he had no wish to spend the rest of his life writing *Son of Anarchy State and Utopia*, and in his subsequent work he tackled many philosophical problems, in books such as *The Nature of Rationality* (1993) and his last book, *Invariances* (2001), in which he discusses the nature of truth, objectivity, necessity, consciousness and ethics. Quite often, Nozick would boldly go where other, more timidly empiricist philosophical or scientific souls would fear to tread. For an imaginative treatment of one of the great questions you could do worse than turn to the chapter, 'Why is there something rather than nothing?' in Nozick's *Philosophical Explanations*.

Suggested reading

Nozick, R. 1974. *Anarchy, State, and Utopia*. Oxford: Blackwell.
Nozick, R. 1997. *Socratic Puzzles*. Cambridge, Mass.: Harvard University Press.
Schmidtz, D. 2002 (ed.). *Robert Nozick*. Cambridge: Cambridge University Press.

Martha Nussbaum

1947–   **Bart Schultz**

Prolific, provocative and passionate, the philosopher Martha Nussbaum has made significant contributions to many different fields within and beyond philosophy, including classics, political theory, ethics, legal theory, educational theory, public policy and gender studies. Transcending not only disciplinary boundaries but academics in general, she is an influential public intellectual actively championing a wide range of causes, from women's rights in India to civility in political discourse in the US. She is a regular contributor to and editorial board member of *The Boston Review*, a lively forum for promoting a more deliberative and democratic political agenda.

Nussbaum's core project represents a qualified yet still universalistic form of Aristotelianism. In her seminal essay, 'Non-Relative Virtues: An

Aristotelian Approach' (in *The Quality of Life*, co-edited with Amartya Sen in 1993), she describes her own position as akin to **Aristotle**'s view that the main task of politics is to create the conditions under which each and every member of the community has the capability to choose and live a fully good human life. In specifying such capabilities, and the major human functions involved in the good life, she develops a universalism that also recognizes the force of relativism, immersing a general, open-ended conception of the good in the myriad variations of history and culture. The 'nuclei of experience around which the constructions of different societies proceed' include such things as death, the body, pleasure and pain, cognitive capability, practical reason, early infant development, affiliation and humour; though of these she tends to emphasise affiliation and practical reason as playing the lead role in human life, as the deepest and widest of the shared elements of human experience.

Nussbaum allows that her approach can also be seen as close to Rawls's theory of primary goods or, better, as an objectivist interpretation of Sen's 'capabilities' approach. Her focus, as she explains in her powerful *Women and Human Development* (2000), is on 'what people are actually able to do and to be – in a way informed by an intuitive idea of a life that is worthy of the dignity of the human being.' Her Aristotle believed that the good human life in the good human community could be understood and defended on its own terms and need not be grounded on some non-moral source, such as a metaphysical account of the structure of the universe. Whether or not she is right about Aristotle, however, this is certainly the spirit of her own neo-Aristotelianism, which also, and admittedly unlike Aristotle, aims at a practical and political, rather than comprehensive, conception of the good life. The object is to define the basic entitlements of a liberal political society as guaranteeing for each citizen a threshold level of capabilities for functioning in the central areas of human life, affiliation, practical reason etc., though Nussbaum is increasingly concerned to extend this approach to such difficult areas as international justice, the just treatment of people with disabilities, and justice for nonhuman animals

For all her indebtedness to Aristotle, Nussbaum weaves many other influences into her work. Her *Cultivating Humanity* (1997) is an extended tribute to Socratic self-examination as a key element in any curriculum fit for citizens of the world. And she has been instrumental in stimulating recent interest in the ancient Stoics; her own account of human emotion is, she allows, justly described as 'neo-Stoic'. In *Upheavals of Thought* (2001), she argues that emotions are a form of judgement, assigning values to things and persons that are of importance to one's own flourishing but outside of one's control. Even so, she admits that both Aristotelianism and Stoicism may be too hard on human complexity and frailty, demanding 'zealous critical surveillance over desire and emotion'.

Moreover, **Kant**, **Mill** and **Marx** also make frequent appearances in her writings, as providing some of the necessary correctives to the ancients. And in an illuminating exchange with Robert Adams, she contrasts the Platonic-Christian view that transcendent Good or God is at the heart of morality with her own comprehensive, Aristotelian-Kantian-Jewish view of the good life, according to which religion is best understood as highlighting the largely autonomous, primary domain of human moral effort. In this vein, of the ethical rather than political, she writes movingly about how wrong it is to think that the highest moral paradigms are 'people who are not fully natural'. Rather, the good life for humans is defined by their limitations, their finitude: 'It is right for human beings to think as human beings, not as something other than the human.' Nehru, not Gandhi, is her moral hero, and finitude the fount of such compassion as humans are capable of.

Suggested reading

Nussbaum, M. 2000. *Women and Human Development*. Cambridge: Cambridge University Press.

Nussbaum, M. 2001. *Upheavals of Thought: the Intelligence of Emotions*. Cambridge: Cambridge University Press.

Sen, A. & Nussbaum, M. 1993 (eds). *The Quality of Life*. Oxford: Oxford University Press.

Thomas Paine
1737–1809   **Robin Harwood**

Thomas Paine was a political theorist who tried to put his theories into action. His aim was to free human beings from oppressive government, oppressive religions and oppressive poverty. His method was to appeal to reason, so that all people could recognize truth and justice. His achievements were spectacular. Paine invented America, took part in the French Revolution and inspired revolutionary movements in Britain. The American Revolution was a success, the French Revolution was a disaster, and the British Revolution never happened. Even so, Paine's ideas of democracy and social welfare have been at least partly realized not only in these countries, but in many other countries as well.

He was born in England, but his life there was difficult and, on Benjamin Franklin's advice, he emigrated to the New World. Paine arrived in Philadelphia in 1774, and took a job as editor for the *Pennsylvania Magazine*. One of his first essays was a call for the abolition of slavery. Inspired by the first moves of the American Revolution, he wrote the pamphlet 'Common Sense' (1776), in which he argued that independence was both morally justified and the only practical option for the American colonies. The book was massively influential, and converted many waverers, including Thomas Jefferson and George Washington, to the idea of the United States of America (Paine coined the name) as an independent nation.

After the War of Independence was over, he went to France, and then to England, where he wrote *The Rights of Man* (1791–2). Paine's message was clear and powerful.

All individual human beings, he argued, are created with equal rights. However, human beings do not live as isolated individuals, but as members of society. In society we flourish fully, because we can enjoy the company of other people and gain help and support from each other. Nonetheless, human beings are not perfect and so sometimes infringe each other's rights. As individuals we may not have the power to exercise some of our rights, such as the right to protect ourselves. Thus we create the state to protect these rights, and the individual's natural right is transformed into a civil right of protection. Also, as members of the state, we gain additional rights, such as the right to vote and the right to run for office. The only legitimate form of state is a democratic republic. Hereditary monarchy is morally illegitimate, since it denies the current generation the right to choose their own leaders.

Of course, Paine held that we also have duties. We have a duty to protect the rights of our fellow citizens and to maintain society, but we also have to improve, enrich and benefit society. This includes the duty to eliminate poverty as much as we can. Paine proposed a system of welfare to do just this. This welfare was not charity, but a civil right.

The popularity of the book frightened the British Government. Paine had to flee to France and the British revolutionary movements were squashed.

The French elected Paine to a seat in the National Convention. During the Terror he was imprisoned and came close to being executed. After his release, he took little active part in French politics, and concentrated mostly on writing, particularly on religion and economics. He produced *The Age of Reason* (1794–5), arguing for deism and against atheism and Christianity. He argued that Christian theology was unreasonable and the doctrine of redemption was immoral. He also argued that the Bible cannot be divine revelation, and condemned it for its portrayal of God as cruel and vindictive.

In *Agrarian Justice* (1797), he returned to the question of rights and social justice. Civilization, he argued, should not throw people into a worse condition than they would be in if they were uncivilized, and yet in Europe many people were poorer than American Indians. The Earth had been given by God as common property to all men, but the system of land ownership meant that only some could use it. Paine argued that they should compensate the others by paying a ground rent to society.

When Paine finally returned to America in 1802, his writings on religion had made him an unpopular figure. Nonetheless, Paine did yet another great service to his ungrateful country, in proposing that the USA buy the Louisiana territory from Napoleon. Jefferson took Paine's advice and thus more than doubled the size of the United States.

Paine carried on writing to the end, but his old age was miserable and he died in obscurity. Officialdom has preferred to ignore him, even when carrying out his proposals, and his name is seldom on the lists of great men; and yet many of his ideas are common currency now. We can still learn from him.

Suggested reading

Paine, T. 1984 [1791–2]. *The Rights of Man*. Harmondsworth: Penguin.

Foot, M. and Kramnick, I. 1987 (eds). *The Thomas Paine Reader*. Harmondsworth: Penguin.

Keane, J. 1995. *Tom Paine: a political life*. London: Bloomsbury.

Blaise Pascal

1623–1662   **Douglas Groothuis**

Blaise Pascal was many things – a theological controversialist, a superb French stylist, an inventor, a scientist, and a mathematician. But he is most known for being a philosopher of the heart. 'The heart has its reasons of which reason knows nothing; we know this in countless ways,' he wrote in *Pensées* (or *Thoughts*, 1670), his unfinished book commending Christianity to sceptics. Given this and other references to the heart, many take Pascal to be an early religious existentialist who, like **Kierkegaard**, disparaged reason and opted for an emotional leap of faith. One can only wager that God exists for the sake of what can be gained by believing in God if God does exist. This common description is a bit of a caricature. The truth is more interesting.

Pascal was possibly the greatest mind of his day, despite a frail constitution and chronic pain. His mathematical and scientific abilities were prodigious and well known, sparking the envy of the older and eminent philosopher **René Descartes**. Pascal's scientific research proved that, against received opinion, nature did not abhor a vacuum. He designed the first working calculating machine in order to aid his father in assessing taxes. He also engineered the first mass transport system to help the poor of Paris.

When Pascal discussed religion, he did not put aside his exceptional intellect or deny the power of reason. Instead, he employed a variety of arguments in support of Christian faith, despite the fact that he disparaged traditional arguments for God's existence as too abstract and generic. (He distinguished 'the God of the philosophers' from 'the God of Abraham, Isaac, and Jacob'.) Some of his most searching and memorable lines come from his reflections on the human condition contained in the fragments of *Pensées*, which were written with the sceptic's doubts in mind. Speaking for the baffled sceptic, he writes, 'Why have limits been set upon my knowledge, my height, my life, making it a hundred rather than a thousand years?' Pascal wanted the sceptic to be puzzled by his own contingency and to seek out answers to these riddles.

Pascal addressed this sense of cosmic wonder by delving into the condition of the one wondering. 'What sort of freak then is man! How novel, how monstrous, how chaotic, how paradoxical, how prodigious!' This polarity at the heart of humanity, or 'greatness and misery', is both troublesome and resistant to simple explanation. Humans are neither angels nor beasts; neither entirely praiseworthy nor entirely blameworthy. They are, rather, enigmas to themselves. Finding no consolation in human philosophy, Pascal appeals to biblical revelation to solve the riddle. We are great by virtue of our origin as God's creatures, made in the divine image; we are miserable because of original sin. Pascal believed that the evidence for both propositions was abundant once one took them seriously.

Pascal presents this case as an argument for Christianity, but he realized the limitations of unaided human reason. Therefore, he attempts to strike a balance between conceiving Christianity as either an airtight rational system devoid of mystery or as a dark mystery that escapes understanding entirely. Nevertheless, there are 'reasons of the heart', or first principles, which can be known intuitively. These include mathematical, commonsense and religious beliefs.

Pascal realized that some sceptics would not be convinced to embrace Christianity by evidence or rational arguments alone. Therefore, in the famous wager argument, he appealed to the eternal stakes involved in Christianity's truth or falsity with respect to one's belief or unbelief. The wager is not an argument for the existence of God (which the hardcore sceptic would reject), but rather concerns situations where one must make momentous prudential decisions under conditions of uncertainty. Pascal challenges the unbeliever to believe in God, despite the lack of proof, because of the infinite gain (heaven) that accompanies belief if Christianity is true. There is little for the believer to lose if Christianity is false. On the other hand, there is much to lose if Christianity is true and one fails to believe (the loss of heaven). A terse fragment outside the longer wager fragment captures the essence of this proposition: 'I should be much more afraid of being mistaken and then finding out that Christianity is true than of being mistaken in believing it to be true.'

Therefore Pascal advises the unbeliever to become a believer by engaging in certain religious practices that may result in belief and the eventual beatitude. But Pascal thinks the sceptic can in this way find certainty; it is not brainwashing. He may find 'reasons of the heart.' Pascal does not offer the wager as the essence of faith, but as a step toward truer faith.

Because of the fragmentary nature of *Pensées*, interpretations of the wager (and other arguments) differ, but readers of Pascal will, nevertheless, find themselves in for an intellectual adventure.

Suggested reading
Pascal , P. 1995 [1670]. *Pensées*. Harmondsworth: Penguin.
Hammond, N. 2003. *The Cambridge Companion to Pascal*. Cambridge: Cambridge University Press.
Groothuis, D. 2003. *On Pascal*. Belmont, Calif.: Wadsworth/Thomson Learning.

Charles Peirce
1839–1914 **Jack Ritchie**

Few would be willing to concur with Max Fisch's judgement that Charles Sanders Peirce is the 'most original and most versatile intellect the Americas have so far produced'. Peirce remains a little known figure amongst many philosophers, especially in Europe. When he is discussed, it is often fleetingly with regard to one or two of his better known doctrines or to say merely that he was the founder of pragmatism. Even then, he occasionally suffers the ignominy of having his name misspelt or mispronounced. (It should be said like purse.) This ignorance is at least partly attributable to Peirce's failure to write a unified account of his position. Nevertheless, picking through the fragments that Peirce did bequeath, a rich and developed system emerges which is truly worthy of Fisch's high praise.

Peirce was born into a well-to-do and academic Boston family and did his undergraduate studies at Harvard. His eventual position in the class, 79th out of 90, is hardly suggestive of a fledgling genius. After graduating, he had greater success, becoming the first student to graduate *summa cum laude* from the newly founded Lawrence Scientific School. With no obvious career avenues opening up for the young Peirce, his father procured a position for him at the American National Coastal survey.

It is this practical and scientific background which forms the basis of much of Peirce's thought. He described his pragmatism, aptly, as the philosophy of the laboratory scientist. According to Peirce, the search for knowledge, 'inquiry', arises from the need to settle doubt. Peirce did not mean doubt in the Cartesian sense of doubting the very existence of the external world. Only doubt arising from normal inquiry interested Peirce. In 'The fixation of belief' (1877) Peirce argues that only the method of science can guarantee this alleviation of doubt. What is this method? A fallibilistic process in which a community of investigators puts forward theories, tests them and revises them in light of falsifications.

Peirce elaborated upon this methodology, dividing scientific thinking into three modes of inference: abduction – the initial formulation of the hypothesis to explain the phenomena; deduction – the deriving of consequences from this hypothesis; and induction – the testing of the hypothesis against experimental evidence. Peirce spent much time and effort explaining how these modes of inference would lead to the ultimate convergence of opinion and the removal of doubt.

One of Peirce's most notorious contributions to philosophy, his 'pragmatist principle', arises from this scientific attitude. The principle was given various formulations, but in essence it claims that the best way to clarify the content of a thought or hypothesis is by working out its experimental consequences. This principle was supposed to debunk non-empirical disciplines like a priori metaphysics. Combined with his theory of inquiry, the pragmatist principle led Peirce, infamously, to define truth as that which would be agreed upon eventually by the community of (scientific) inquirers.

After 1879, Peirce was able to devote more time to another of his life-long passions at the then recently founded Johns Hopkins University: logic. He developed a system of three categories, uninspiringly labelled firstness, secondness and thirdness. Peirce claimed that all three categories were necessary for an adequate scientific language. Peirce's work with his students eventually culminated in the publication of a book of essays, *Studies in Logic* (1883), in which a logic of quantification (invented quite independently of **Frege**) is outlined.

Logic, though, was just one part of a more general study of thought and representation: Peirce's theory of signs or semiotics. The sign relation is irreducibly triadic, involving the sign, the object signified and the interpretation of the sign. So signs are of the category thirdness. Many issues that are currently live in the philosophy of language are contained in his semiotic writings.

By 1883, what can most politely be described as Peirce's eccentric behaviour led to him being ejected from Johns Hopkins. He was never again to obtain an academic post. With his second wife he moved to Pennsylvania, where he remained, penniless, until his death in 1914.

During these years of seclusion, Peirce's writing became more metaphysical; not the sort of a priori speculation ruled out by the pragmatic principle but a metaphysics that employed the scientific method. In particular, Peirce wished to justify his claim that inquirers would agree in the long run. His answer was an evolutionary cosmology in which all the laws of nature emerged out of a chaos of pure possibility and 'develop' into stricter and stricter laws through time. So everything in the universe, including us, tends towards a unified, perfectly law-governed whole.

Many of his collected writings still lie unpublished at Harvard. We have, I suspect, more to hear from Peirce.

Suggested reading

Hauser, N. and Kloesel, C. 1992 (eds). *The Essential Peirce*. Bloomington: Indiana University Press.

Brent, J. 1998. *Charles Sanders Peirce: A Life*. Bloomington: Indiana University Press.

Hookway, C. 1985. *Peirce (Arguments of the philosophers)*. London: Routledge.

Plato

c. 427–347 BCE   **Roy Jackson**

Plato is one of the founding fathers of philosophy and has had a massive impact on the history of western thought. He was probably born in Athens or the nearby island of Aegina. He was given the name Aristocles, but was called Plato, which means 'broad' or 'flat', a possible reference to his broad shoulders (he used to wrestle).

Although there were a number of outstanding Greek philosophers before Plato, only fragments of their writings survive. However, we are fortunate to possess a great deal of Plato's work. What distinguishes Plato from earlier philosophers is his development of a more cogent and rational approach to philosophy which laid the foundations for all philosophers who came after him. This is why the British philosopher **Alfred North Whitehead** famously said that the history of philosophy is but 'a series of footnotes to Plato'.

During his lifetime, Plato witnessed the decline of Athens and experienced the moral uncertainty that resulted. Plato was born into a wealthy and politically powerful Athenian family, and he was encouraged to enter politics himself. But his experience of unscrupulous politicians and the constant strife amongst various political groupings soon disillusioned him. However, he had a deep concern for the welfare of Athens and its citizens and so it was philosophy he looked to as a way of voicing these concerns.

At around twenty years of age, Plato encountered a remarkable man: **Socrates**. Socrates was deliberately provocative. It was for this reason he jokingly referred to himself as a gadfly, biting away at his victims. However, this also resulted in him making many enemies and, in 399 BCE, he was placed on trial for 'corrupting the youth' with his ideas. He was condemned to die by drinking a cup of hemlock.

Socrates' death had a profound impact upon Plato. Undoubtedly, the fact that his friend and teacher was condemned by democrats was one reason why Plato distrusted democracy and, as he saw it, the rule of the mob. He was determined to keep the spirit of Socrates alive by engaging in philosophy in the Socratic tradition. He set about writing a series of dialogues with Socrates as his mouthpiece.

Plato's works can be divided into three periods: early, middle and late.

The early period was mostly concerned with moral issues and is heavily influenced by the teachings of Socrates. The late period contains works that are less dramatic and original, although they help to show how Plato developed his earlier philosophy. However, it is in the middle period that Plato really comes into his own, dealing with such issues as politics and metaphysics. The best-known work of this period is his *magnum opus*, the *Republic*.

The *Republic* is one of the world's greatest works of philosophy and literature. It set the standards and boundaries for future western philosophy. It is the first major work of political philosophy and presents a comprehensive and radical theory of the state which views its role as not merely an agent of control, but as an agent of virtue. The state is an educational tool to nurture, nourish and develop individual behaviour. In this respect, Plato had great faith in the ability of the state to wield its power wisely.

However, the *Republic* is more than just a political theory, for it is also very personal. It concerns justice in the state and in the individual. Further, the individual is inextricably linked to the state and cannot exist outside of it.

Plato has been criticized, most notably by **Karl Popper**, for presenting us with a utopia, and utopias are always destined to fail because by their nature they are static and therefore unable to adjust to changing circumstances.

Underlying all of Plato's philosophy is his belief in an eternal and unchanging truth, the realm of the 'forms', and that it is possible to have access to these 'forms'. Plato was concerned that if there are no such things as universal standards then we are confronted with moral relativism. For Plato, however, there are such things as 'good' and 'bad', 'beautiful' and 'ugly', and if it is indeed possible to know these things, then those who have this knowledge should be in a position to educate and rule. In this respect, Plato was the founder of political science: the belief that political rule can be studied scientifically.

After over two and a half thousand years, Plato continues to be educative and controversial. A huge achievement considering that he was at the very beginning of western philosophy.

Suggested reading

Plato. 1970. *Republic*. Oxford: Oxford University Press.
Plato. 1993. *The Last Days of Socrates*. Harmondsworth: Penguin.
Jackson, R. 2001. *Plato: A Beginner's Guide*. London: Headway.

Plotinus

c.204–270   **Lewis Owens**

Plotinus was the founder, and most important figure, of the philosophical movement known as Neoplatonism. His work, mainly written after
the age of fifty, survives as the *Enneads*, a collection put together by his
student and fellow neoplatonist, Porphyry.

Plotinus' philosophical system is dominated by the notion of a spiritual
and non-material 'One' that structures all existence. This 'One', as it constitutes the underlying foundation of all existence, is beyond all being
and hence beyond all names. It is therefore beyond all understanding
and thought. Given this, it is clear why Plotinus stresses the inevitable
linguistic problems when attempting to refer to this principle.

Nevertheless, Plotinus attempts to articulate a discourse about the
'One' in which meaning can reside. He claims that the 'One' is all things
but no thing. As the 'One' is no 'thing' there is no conflict with the idea
that it is 'inside' and 'outside' the world at the same time, as it lies
beyond all finite determination. The 'One' comes before 'this' or 'that'
and is paradoxically 'everywhere and nowhere'.

The 'One' is not simply static, however. It is the first, simplest and
highest part of a triad that becomes Mind, Intellect and Soul as it freely
wills itself to become the overflowing source of the lower forms of
being. These lower forms of being are essentially constituted by their
distance away from the 'One'. As the 'One' freely wills itself out to lower
gradations of unity, it becomes increasingly multiple until the negative of
being is formed: matter. An ongoing tension between the ascent and
descent of the soul characterizes the struggle to attain unity with the
'One'. Action, effort and spiritual preparation are required if the soul is
to leave its estranged and isolated existence, its slumber within the body,

and return 'home'; hence the Plotinian reference of the 'flight of the one to the One'.

Despite this emphasis on the 'One' as the fundamental structural principle of existence, Plotinus also gives a prominent place to the individual soul which, although tied to the body and all its physicality, has a greater unity due to its ability to comprehend the intelligible (Platonic) Forms that reside in the Divine Mind. The 'One' is the true source and homeland of the individual soul and is to be reached by sloughing off the multiplicity of the material world and obtaining unity through abstraction and contemplation of these Forms. Following **Plato**, Plotinus sees the apprehension of beauty as a means of lifting the soul upwards and away from material imprisonment. However, the soul, instead of following its true destined ascent towards unity, is often overcome with sensual desires, which are merely temporal and consequently further away from the 'One'.

The 'One' of Plotinus is thus the radically transcendent causal power of the lower forms of being; it is the source of all being, actual and potential. This 'One' is logically prior to the workings of human reason, which traditionally requires a subject and an object with which to operate. The 'One' is therefore an undifferentiated unity, and a Divine Mystery, as it lies beyond all rational conceptualization, which can categorize it only as 'not-being'. The finite cannot grasp the infinite rationally, but in recognizing its limits reason can be led towards the truth of this supra-rational mystery, which may be experienced intuitively. At this moment of intuition, all difference is transcended between the seer and the seen. As the 'One' is the transcendent, unifying principle behind everything, it cannot be said to 'exist'; it lies 'beyond being'.

Nevertheless, Plotinus recognizes the immense difficulty that the individual has in 'letting go' of the certainty of the lower realms of being. This results in a fear of embracing a lack of structure to existence, given the formlessness of the 'One' that is prior to all thought and reflection, which will mean that the soul has nothing by which to declare its individuality. For Plotinus, such a fear is overcome by strength of will.

Suggested reading
Plotinus. 1991. *Enneads*. Harmondsworth: Penguin.
O'Meara, D. J. 1993. *Plotinus: an introduction to the Enneads*. Oxford: Clarendon
    Press.
Gerson, L. P. 1996. (ed.). *The Cambridge Companion to Plotinus*. Cambridge:
    Cambridge University Press.

Karl Popper

1902–1994   **Andrew Talbot**

Karl Popper was born in Vienna, Austria-Hungary. Popper's father was a doctor of law at the University of Vienna. Popper was certainly influenced by his father's love for history and philosophy, and the books that surrounded him. As a teenager, young Karl debated philosophy with his father and formed the following view: 'Never let yourself be goaded into taking seriously problems about words and their meanings. What must be taken seriously are questions of fact and assertions about facts: theories and hypotheses, the problems they solve and the problems they raise.'

Popper studied psychology with Alfred Adler and although he obtained his PhD in 1928, he taught at a secondary school before gaining his first academic post in 1937. By this time he had published *Logik der Forschung* (1934), the English version of which, *The Logic of Scientific Discovery* (1959) was not a translation but a new version prepared by Popper himself. In this work, Popper proposed a new line of demarcation between science and pseudo-science based on the principle of falsifiability. Pseudo-science for Popper included any system of beliefs that relies on predetermined 'laws' of human behaviour. To qualify as science, the claims advanced by a theory must be testable and must be capable of being proven incorrect. This notion was in sharp distinction to the view of most scientists of the day: that science discovers immutable laws by observing nature, developing hypotheses and verifying them through experiment. Instead, Popper described science as trial and error, or 'conjecture and refutation'. Science represents a Darwinian natural selection of the survival of the best-tested ideas, which appear to be true because they have not yet been proven wrong. Science is and must be for ever different from dogmatic forms of thought because its assertions are always tentative.

Popper agreed with Tarski that a statement is true when it corresponds with the facts. Popper said facts are 'reality pinned down by descriptive statements'. Further, 'The success of science is best accounted for by the metaphysical belief that the growth of knowledge consists in progress towards the truth.'

Popper attempted to provide a clearer understanding of what knowledge is with his three worlds theory, which distinguished between the different domains of knowledge. The first world is the physical world, the second is the mental world and the third is the world of ideas in their objective states. All three worlds are objective and real, with the second world performing a mediating function between the first and third worlds.

From 1937 to 1945, Popper taught at the Canterbury University College, Christchurch, New Zealand. In 1945 he accepted a post at the London School of Economics, where he taught until retiring from teaching in 1969.

During the academic year 1946–47, Popper accepted an invitation from the Moral Sciences Club at Cambridge, whose members included **Ludwig Wittgenstein** and **Bertrand Russell**, to 'Read a paper on a philosophical puzzle'. What followed was the famous 'poker incident'. Wittgenstein was apparently angry because Popper said philosophy is about real problems, and this was perceived as a personal slight. Popper never stopped arguing against what he saw as a new form of medieval scholasticism being practised by philosophers who play 'language games'. For him, philosophy is trivialized when it is about the description of meanings, or as **Carnap** and the Vienna Circle held, the 'explication of concepts'.

Popper was a realist who held that a tentative approach to finding truth was the socially responsible position. In *The Open Society and Its Enemies* (1945), Popper argued that the good fight each thinker must wage is against the assault on reason. Popper blamed anti-reason for much of the twentieth century's bloody conflict. The worst calamities befell those who were gulled by various leaders into thinking that their respective movements were truly scientific, and therefore represented historical inevitability. This can be said of all the fascisms as well as Soviet style Marxist-Leninism. Theories of historical inevitability from **Plato** onwards are throwbacks to tribalistic, closed societies and need to be exposed to the clear light of critical method.

Suggested reading
Popper, K. 1945. *The Open Society and Its Enemies*. London: Routledge.
Popper, K. 1945. *The Logic of Scientific Discovery*. London: Hutchinson.
Edmonds, D. & Eidinow, J. 2001. *Wittgenstein's Poker*. London: Faber and Faber.

Hilary Putnam
1926–   Jack Ritchie

The one thing that can definitely be said of Hilary Putnam is that he is not afraid to change his mind. Some might think that this is a weakness, indicating that he bends with the winds of fashion rather than engaging in detailed defence of his theories. This would be a mistake. His changes of philosophical heart always arise from deep critical reflection on the problems and assumptions of his own former views. So to understand Putnam's philosophy, it is vital to see how his later views developed out of his earlier ones.

His early philosophical career was marked by the influence of logical positivism and in particular **Carnap**. But in the sixties and seventies he began to develop a clear and distinct philosophical position all his own. In the philosophy of science, Putnam rejected his positivist past and defended a form of realism, the view that mature scientific theories are (approximately) true. His original contribution was to suggest that scientific realism be understood and defended on the grounds that the best explanation of the success of the mature sciences was that they were approximately true and most of the terms in those theories referred to real entities.

In the philosophy of mind, again Putnam adopted a realist position. He denied that mental states can be reduced to physical, brain states, on the grounds that it is possible to imagine creatures with different physical constitutions – people, aliens, maybe robots – that had the same mental states but different, or no, brains. In its place he suggested a position known as functionalism, which sees the mind as analogous to a computer. Psychology, so understood, is an abstract software description of the thinking organism.

A third influential position which emerged during this realist period was semantic externalism. Putnam asked us to consider a world exactly like ours except that instead of water, it contains a substance with all the same gross properties, it is liquid, refreshing, etc. but has a different microconstitution, XYZ, not H_2O. The inhabitants of this world happen to call this substance water too. Now imagine there is somebody physically identical in all respects to you in this world. You both come across a pool of this refreshing liquid and have the thought 'water is refreshing'. Do you think the same thing? Putnam argues not, since what the thought is about is different in each case. It is about H_2O for you, XYZ for your twin. But since by hypothesis you are physically identical, that difference cannot be accounted for by any internal state. Meanings, as Putnam says, just ain't in the head.

The first doubts about his own brand of realism emerged when Putnam realized that his argument for realism would work using any definition of truth, realist or anti-realist. If that is so, then there seems no more need to regard it as an argument for scientific realism than for anti-realism. In addition, using technical results from model theory, Putnam claimed to prove that one cannot draw a distinction between ideal justification and truth. This led him to adopt 'internal realism': a position that seeks to make sense of notions like truth by employing concepts (such as justification) internal to our non-philosophical practice. Normally, this is interpreted as a version of anti-realism since Putnam appears to be suggesting that there is no more to truth than ideal justification.

His present views reflect a working through of the tensions implicit in his functionalism, semantic externalism and internal realism. For instance, consider the relation between functionalism and externalism. If there is more to meaning than what goes on in the head, then functional states, understood as internal states of the organism, cannot really be mental states.

Putnam now argues for what he calls a deliberate *naïveté* or realism with a small r. The mind is not to be thought of as an organ but as a 'system of object-involving capacities'. Putnam is also anxious to revive the pre-philosophical and metaphysically innocent senses of terms like 'realism' and 'meaning'. Strongly influenced by the work of the later **Wittgenstein**, Putnam today eschews direct philosophical theorizing. Instead he offers descriptions of our use of words like 'meaning' and 'truth' and insists on the importance of considering what role these everyday uses play in our lives.

Suggested reading
Putnam, H. 1992. *Renewing Philosophy*. Cambridge, Mass.: Harvard University Press.
Putnam, H. 1999. *The Threefold Cord: Mind, Body, and World*. New York: Columbia University Press.
Putnam, H. 2002. *The Collapse of the Fact/Value Dichotomy and Other Essays*. Cambridge, Mass.: Harvard University Press.

Pythagoras
c.570–500 BCE   Scott O'Reilly

'Sooner or later,' the philosopher Barbara Amodio writes, 'philosophers turn into mystics.' Many a philosopher would disagree, but there can be little doubt that the origins of western philosophy owe much to an ancient Greek mathematician, philosopher and mystic named Pythagoras.

Pythagoras is a figure shrouded in mystery. So much so that scholars have trouble untangling his own contributions from the ancient sources he undoubtedly borrowed from, as well as ideas developed by his disciples that were later attributed back to him. Nevertheless, the ideas credited to and associated with Pythagoras have proven pivotal in the history of philosophy.

Pythagoras was probably born on the island of Samos in 571 BCE. A good part of his life, however, was spent in Croton, a part of southern Italy, where he established a community of scholars, mathematicians and mystics. A great deal of secrecy surrounded the Pythagoreans, though the report of one Dicaearchus, a student of Aristotle, sheds some light:

His most universally celebrated opinions . . . were that the soul is immortal; then that it migrates into other sorts of living creature; and in addition that after certain periods what has happened once happens again, and nothing is absolutely new; and that one should consider all animate things as akin.

Many scholars believe that Pythagoras' views on the soul may have been influenced by contact with sources in the Near East, particularly Sanskrit and Vedic philosophy. For Pythagoras taught a doctrine called metempsychosis, a form of reincarnation in which the immortal soul of an individual could evolve, through many different incarnations, as a plant, animal, or human. As much a seer as a philosopher, Pythagoras claimed to remember his past lives and further avowed that after philosophical purification he and his followers would be absorbed, after death, within the Divine.

In contrast to these rather questionable metaphysical claims, Pythagoras is credited with important contributions in helping to lay the foundation for mathematics and deductive geometry. The theorem for calculating the length of the hypotenuse of a right-angled triangle based on the sum of the square of the sides, for instance, bears his name.

The mathematical and metaphysical ideas associated with Pythagoras have proven enormously influential, even revolutionary. It was Pythagoras, after all, who is credited with discovering the mathematical basis of music. According to legend, Pythagoras noticed the different pitched sounds that emerged from hammers of different weights used by local blacksmiths. His followers extended his insight by observing how the lengths of the strings of musical instruments corresponded to the various notes that make up a musical scale, and were thereby able to deduce that the language of music was composed from a series of mathematical ratios or proportions. Music was the sensory manifestation, the Pythagoreans believed, of transcendent mathematical patterns or harmonies. This view extended became the doctrine that 'all things are number', a view which interpreted subtly implied that the entire sensible world could be understood as the expression of abstract mathematical principles discernible solely to the intellect.

This was to prove one of the most important ideas in the history of philosophy. As **Bertrand Russell** noted 'The whole conception of an eternal world, revealed to the intellect but not to the senses, is derived from him [Pythagoras].' Like Pythagoras, Russell and **Moore** argued that mathematical ideas were something eternal, immutable, and existed independently whether we thought about them or not.

Whether one accepts or rejects Pythagoras' mystical inclinations, there can be little doubt that Pythagoras helped inaugurate a very important method for philosophy. According to the mathematician Keith Devlin, Pythagoras helped develop and advocate a very specific methodology – the stages of which are observation, abstraction, understanding, description and proof – that has been an essential part of good mathematics and science ever since Pythagoras' day. As Devlin notes, we cannot say that this method originated with Pythagoras himself, since it was a method popular with many Greek minds of the time, but no one did more than Pythagoras to advocate the methodology that is now associated with his name.

In his *A History of Western Philosophy* Bertrand Russell counted Pythagoras as among the most influential thinkers that ever lived. This is because, as he notes, so much of what appears as Platonism, when you get down to it, is in essence Pythagoreanism. Even today it seems that the dreams of many leading philosophers and scientists of the twenty-first century are suffused with Pythagorean themes, for the continuing quest to understand the universe in mathematical and logical terms finds both its source and its goal in the mystical thought of Pythagoras.

Suggested reading
Kahn, C. H. 2001. *Pythagoras and the Pythagoreans*. Cambridge, Mass.: Hackett Publishing.
O'Meara. D. J. 1989. *Pythagoras Revived: Mathematics and Philosophy in Late Antiquity*. Oxford: Clarendon Press.
Strohmeier, J. and Westbrook, P. 2000. *Divine Harmony: The Life and Teachings of Pythagoras*. Berkeley: Berkeley Hills Books.

Willard Van Orman Quine
1908–2000   Chalmers C. Clark

Willard Van Orman Quine underscores a primary feature of his philosophy when he writes: 'We do not adjudicate between our aggregate system of the world and a rival system by appeal to a transcendent standard of truth.' Truth, for Quine, is immanent – embedded in our world, language and practices.

Quine's philosophy can be sharply contrasted to that of **Descartes**. Descartes' ambition was to complete a philosophy of knowledge based upon the absolute certainty of *'cogito ergo sum'* – I think, therefore I exist. Try to doubt it and you only affirm it. Descartes thought this exemplar of knowledge was so certain it would silence 'the most extravagant suppositions of the sceptics'. After Descartes, the grand ambition for empiricists and rationalists alike was a complete justification of our knowledge of the world based on the same absolute certainty as the *cogito*.

By the middle of the twentieth century, Quine saw Descartes' project as barren and deeply flawed. A major problem was its radical subjectivity. How could we justify knowledge of the world from the subjective certainty that we exist? Instead, Quine sought to ground knowledge outside the individual, justifying our picture of the world from what **C. S. Peirce** called 'a community of inquirers'.

As an empiricist – one who thinks all knowledge claims are justified by experience – Quine was committed to the role of sensory experience in knowledge. But since a single mind has no fixed anchor to halt inner experience from 'drifting', Quine argued that in a community, drift would be arrested; we are not apt to drift in the same direction. Thus publicly reinforced language – and not subjective ideas – could check the tendency for drift. 'Safety in numbers' rather than subjective certainty would provide Quine's key to knowledge.

For Quine, this meant philosophy was no longer a tribunal outside and above science. 'Unlike Descartes,' Quine wrote, 'we own and use our beliefs of the moment . . . until by what is vaguely called scientific method we change them here and there for the better.' Critics thought Quine abandoned philosophy for science altogether. Quine said otherwise. True, there was no longer the grand dichotomy between philosophy and science, but there were important differences of degree (as with the more speculative reach of philosophy and greater breadth of its categories).

To explain his total image, Quine invoked 'Neurath's boat': a ship on a landless sea that must be adjusted or repaired piece by piece as it sails.

Similarly, knowledge cannot be snatched from its place in the world to be rebuilt from the bottom up as Descartes had dreamed. For Quine, knowledge is an embedded and interrelated field of force without appeal to the transcendent.

In Quine's most famous paper, 'Two Dogmas of Empiricism' (1951), he challenged the longstanding view that there are truths grounded in meaning (such as 'all bachelors are unmarried') that are independent of truths of experience (such as 'water freezes at 32 degrees Fahrenheit'). In doing so, he had attacked the distinction between 'analytic' and 'synthetic' that played such a crucial role with **Kant** and throughout modern philosophy.

In *Word and Object* (1960) Quine pushed his holistic vision further with a thought experiment in radical translation – interpreting a totally unknown language. Quine argued that linguists might produce translation manuals with terms which are empirically equivalent – they 'pick out the same scattered portion of the world' – yet incompatible in meaning. In his famous example, we could never determine whether it was correct to translate a word used whenever a rabbit appears – 'gavagai' – as 'rabbit' or as 'undetached rabbit part'. Being empirically equivalent, there is no further fact to decide between them. So, like different translation manuals, our embedded view of the world is relative to a frame of reference. Deciding among equivalent systems of the world turns finally on pragmatic grounds such as simplicity, refutability, fecundity and generality; not transcendent metaphysics.

So has absolute truth vanished from Quine's philosophy altogether? Not exactly. While Quine's emerging philosopher 'no longer dreams of a first philosophy, firmer than science', we can still satisfy a longing for the absolute at least in part. For 'within our own totally evolving doctrine,' Quine reminds us, 'we can judge truth as earnestly and absolutely as can be, subject to correction, but this goes without saying.'

Suggested reading

Quine. W. V. O. 1969. *Ontological Relativity and Other Essays*. New York: Columbia.

Quine. W. V. O. 1996. *From a Logical Point of View* (2nd edition). Cambridge, Mass.: Harvard University Press.

Gibson Jr., R. F. 1988. *Enlightened Empiricism: An Examination of W. V. Quine's Theory of Knowledge*. Tampa: University of South Florida Press.

Frank Ramsey

1903–1930   **Peter Cave**

Frank Plumpton Ramsey was a big man – big in body, in intellect and in breadth of interests – but small in life span, dying at the age of 26. Despite his short life and the consequent small output of papers, Ramsey remains an influential figure. He left his mark not solely on philosophy (especially philosophical logic, probability theory and attempts to derive mathematics from logic), but also on economics and mathematics proper.

Ramsey breathed Cambridge college life. His father was president of Magdalene College and the young Ramsey studied at Trinity, became a fellow of King's and lectured in mathematics. Ramsey, as a student and young don, impressed the great economist John Maynard Keynes (despite demolishing his theory of probability), the philosopher **G. E. Moore** and – an unusual achievement here – even the anguished genius **Ludwig Wittgenstein**. Indeed, Wittgenstein wrote, in *Philosophical Investigations*, of how Ramsey helped him – to a degree he is hardly able to estimate – to realize earlier mistakes. It was the young Ramsey who, with C. K. Ogden, first translated Wittgenstein's *Tractatus*, providing the wonderfully elusive last proposition's translation, 'Whereof one cannot speak, thereof one must remain silent.' In criticism of the implied mysticism, Ramsey quipped, 'But what we can't say we can't say, and we can't whistle it either.' Nonsense is just nonsense.

Ramsey, influenced by **Russell** and Wittgenstein, sought an account of how it is that we can speak of the world – an account avoiding the early Wittgensteinian nonsense of some spoken nonsense being important nonsense.

Someone asserts, 'Jemima is growling'. How do those words come to represent the world? We might say that the speaker expresses a proposition which is true when it corresponds to the fact that Jemima is growling; but we now have: propositions, facts, Jemima, the growling and the property of being true. How do they intermesh? Things get worse. Consider: 'Jemima is not growling' and 'Jemima is sitting on the mat or on the cat'. Must there be, then, negative facts and disjunctive (either/or) facts? Do 'not' and 'or' designate odd worldly items? Ramsey sought to avoid mistaking such accidents of language for worldly structures.

While we might assert a relation to hold between Jemima and the mat, *not* is no further relation out there in the world. Negation could be expressed by a sentence being written as a mirror image; double negation would then be seen to be no different from the original. Thus we avoid an infinity of negative facts. As for truth and falsehood, they manifest no properties. To say that it is true that Jemima is growling is just to say that Jemima is growling, albeit with different stylistic emphases. This redundancy theory of truth – where truth is deflated – has much to commend it; and it gives some explanation of why paradoxical statements such as 'This is not true' are ill-formed.

Ramsey does not stop there in puncturing the pretensions of grammar to show us how the world is. Many of us can still spot the subject-predicate form, whereby 'Jemima' is subject and 'is growling' is predicate; but does this show a world populated by irreducible categories – with items such as Jemima being radically different from properties such as growling? Ramsey is sceptical. We might have said, 'Growling is a characteristic of Jemima.' The differences between that sentence and 'Jemima is growling' are accounted for by differing human interests, not by differences in the world. What is it, though, for someone to *believe* that Jemima is growling? Ramsey explained such beliefs in terms of actions, dispositions to act, causes and effects. These days, this popular approach is labelled 'functionalism'.

Links with action – behaviour and consequences – are frequently present in Ramsey's approach. Consider a regularity of nature: 'All growling tigers are hungry.' This statement is not equivalent to, 'this growling tiger is hungry, that one is, that one is . . .' etc. Rather, it is akin to holding the rule: if I meet growling tigers, I shall regard them as hungry. Depending on your system of beliefs and desires, swift flight from a growling tiger scene might follow. Believing is a matter of degree; and one measure of that degree which Ramsey considers is your willingness to place bets. This pragmatic approach is also to be found in his influential thoughts on the nature of scientific theories and what is going on when we consider how things might have been: for example, what makes it true that had I gone out, it would have rained.

Ramsey was no showman and he was somewhat lazy. He was unimpressed by the vastness of the skies, valuing, instead, humanity, thought and love. Despite serious attractions towards psychoanalysis, Ramsey managed a life that lacked both the public display of a Wittgensteinian tortured soul and the publicized womanizing and marriages of a Russell; but, then, Ramsey had few years in which to develop and expose these human, all too human, dispositions to act.

Suggested reading

O'Hear, A. 2002 (ed.). *Cambridge Philosophers.* Notre Dame, IN: St Augustine's Press.

Mellor, D. H. 1990 (ed.). *F. P. Ramsey: Philosophical Papers.* Cambridge: Cambridge University Press.

Sahlin, N-E. 1990. *The Philosophy of F. P. Ramsey.* Cambridge: Cambridge University Press.

John Rawls

1921–2002   **Alex Voorhoeve**

The political and philosophical problems John Rawls set out to solve arise out of the identity and conflicts of interests between citizens. There is identity of interests because social co-operation makes possible for everyone a life that is much better than one outside of society. There are conflicts of interests because people all prefer a larger to a smaller share of the benefits of social co-operation, and people have ideological differences. The problem a theory of justice has to solve is how, in the face of these conflicts, effective social co-operation can come about on terms that are justifiable to all.

Since such interpersonal justification is only possible if we start from some common ground, finding shareable principles of justice requires some shared convictions about right and wrong, and about fairness. Rawls believed we can find such convictions in the culture of liberal democratic societies. These can be organized under three headings.

First among these, Rawls argued, is our view of people as free and equal. This view is rooted in what he called people's 'two moral powers': their capacity to form, revise and pursue their idea of the good life; and their capacity for a sense of justice. Second is an idea of fairness, which means not allowing ourselves to be influenced by our particular interests when agreeing on the distribution of the benefits and burdens of social cooperation. Third, we have shared, firm and well-considered moral judgements about specific cases: that slavery and religious intolerance are wrong, for example.

But though they may command some allegiance from all but the most anti-social or religiously fundamentalist inhabitants of western societies, freedom, equality and fairness are vague notions. What we are looking for is a set of principles that show us what these ideals demand, and that combine our firm judgements on individual cases into a coherent system. As Rawls put it, we want our judgements of cases and our principles to be in 'reflective equilibrium'.

Here, Rawls introduced his great innovation: to have the resolution of these difficulties take place via a device called the 'original position': an imaginary situation in which we place our representatives and charge them with coming up with a social contract. These representatives should be well-informed and look after the interests of those they represent. To ensure the contract they agree is fair, Rawls places the contracting parties behind 'the veil of ignorance' so they do not know their sex, race, social class, talents and abilities, nor their specific values and aims in life. Behind the veil, the parties have to ask themselves: 'Which distribution of the benefits and burdens of social co-operation do I want, given the fact that, though I am ignorant of the person I will be, I will have to be some person in this society?'

Since the parties are denied knowledge of any particular person's values and aims, they must answer this question with reference to some general idea of human interests. Though a liberal theory of justice cannot draw on any elaborate idea of what the good life for individuals is, it can, Rawls argued, draw on a 'thin liberal theory of the good', which holds that the contracting parties have a most fervent desire to secure the material and social conditions which allow them to develop and exercise their 'two moral powers'. This means, Rawls argued, that they will evaluate social contracts in terms of the all-purpose means, or 'primary goods', that they make available to people who occupy different representative positions in society, namely: basic liberties, the powers and prerogatives of offices and jobs, income and wealth, and the social bases of self-respect.

Rawls's idea was that the parties would naturally first think of distributing all primary goods equally, and then consider improvements that render everyone, including the least advantaged, better off. This is what has become known as the 'maximin conception of justice': we assess social contracts by how well a person in the 'least advantaged social position' would fare under them. This is the thinking behind Rawls's famous 'Difference Principle': inequalities of income and wealth are to be arranged so that they are to the greatest benefit of the inhabitants of the social position that is accessible to those who are least advantaged by the distribution of talent and social and family background.

Rawls is sometimes criticized for being utopian. His response is that the task of finding a shareable conception of justice is one we cannot give up on before attempting it. He thought political philosophers should look for bases of agreement where none seem to exist, and should attempt to extend the range of existing consensus. Rawls viewed this task as an exercise in 'realistic utopianism': to probe the limits of practical possibility, taking people and social institutions not as they are, nor as we might naïvely like them to be, but as they can be.

Suggested reading
Rawls. J. 1996. *Political Liberalism* (Second edition). New York: Columbia University Press.
Rawls. J. A. 1999. *A Theory of Justice* (Revised edition). Oxford: Oxford University Press.
Rawls. J. 2001. *Justice as Fairness*. Cambridge, Mass.: Harvard University Press.

Richard Rorty
1931–   Simon Eassom

Richard Rorty is a philosophical hero to some and enemy of philosophy to others. Richard Bernstein has noted that Rorty-bashing has become something of a philosophical sport. There is no doubt that Rorty is one the most influential, controversial, prolific and widely read philosophers in the world. Unlike many of his contemporaries, and following the example of his own heroes **William James** and **John Dewey**, he is a public philosopher writing for a broad audience on a vast range of topics related to social justice and democracy.

Rorty sets out his stall in two early texts, *Philosophy and the Mirror of Nature* (1979) and *Consequences of Pragmatism* (1982). Rorty is a pragmatist. That is, he believes that language cannot claim accurately to represent reality as some sort of 'mirror of nature'. Instead, the best we can hope for is that knowledge provides us with the means to cope effectively with the 'real' world. There is no truth 'out there' to be discovered. For example, the word 'gene' does not necessarily correspond to some sort of real thing. What matters most is whether or not thinking in terms of genes helps us to cope with the particular environment in which gene-talk has an effect. The resultant collapsing of the assumed 'facts' of hard science into the softer discourse of the humanities and the arts means that there is no guaranteed way of getting beyond language and seeing the world as it 'really' is.

Rorty's work shows the clear influence of contemporary philosophers such as Nelson Goodman, **W. V. O. Quine**, **Hilary Putnam** and **Jacques Derrida**. His strong and sometimes idiosyncratic readings of the work of great philosophical figures such as **Hegel** and **Heidegger** have drawn criticism, but there is no denying that Rorty is the complete, rounded thinker whose work in the collected *Philosophical Papers* shows an enormous grasp of the entirety of western philosophy.

In the area of political philosophy Rorty builds on the pragmatic stance defended in *Philosophy and the Mirror of Nature* and deals directly with the significance of the abandonment of the Enlightenment quest for knowledge of all things (including knowledge of how we ought to live). In his later and most accessible work, *Contingency, Irony, and Solidarity* (1989), Rorty argues that the recognition that all claims to truth and knowledge of reality are contingent upon our spatial and temporal position in the world should lead us to speak of what we believe with a strong sense of irony. The committed ironist accepts that the language of any other community could be just as real or true as our own.

This hint at relativism may sound alarm bells. If there are no grounds for determining which community speaks the truth, does that mean we have no intellectual defence against 'might is right', that what is accepted is true is simply that which the stronger community believes? Rorty prescribes what he sees as the only social construction robust enough to avoid the threat of such ethnocentricity: political liberalism.

Part of the problem, as Rorty sees it, is the repeated attempt to fuse the private domain of self-realization, fulfilment and perfectionism with the public domain of morality and justice. The ideal liberal society limits its concerns to the balancing of freedom, wealth and peace whilst allowing its members the scope and opportunity to pursue their own ideas of how they ought to live. Any attempt at a fusion of the private and public tends in fact to privilege the public over the private and either redefine the private in terms of the public – and generally suppress many private practices – or make public the private practice of the strong or the majority.

Rorty denies the possibility that humanity could one day be united by a common realization of the truth of how we ought to live. Indeed, he accepts that the best we can possibly hope for is a consensus amongst a very large percentage of the population. What matters most is that we are open to the possibility of changing our historical, contingent beliefs to include those of others. Liberalism is the only political philosophy, to Rorty's mind, that allows alternative worldviews to co-exist side by side and thus keep open the possibility of us hearing and incorporating the 'unfamiliar noises' of others. Inevitably then, he has drawn the wrath of neo-Marxists in particular. However, Rorty has continually rebutted and refuted his 'enemies' and, in public debate, he is a formidable opponent, well worth handing over real money to see and hear.

Suggested reading
Rorty, R. 1979. *Philosophy and the Mirror of Nature*. Princeton: Princeton University Press.
Rorty, R. 1989. *Contingency, Irony, and Solidarity*. Cambridge: Cambridge University Press.
Rorty, R. 2000. *Philosophy and Social Hope*. New York: Penguin.

Jean-Jacques Rousseau
1712–1778   **Terri Collier**

Jean-Jacques Rousseau was one of the most enigmatic thinkers of the eighteenth century. His colourful life and consistent defiance of social conventions are reflected in his political writings. He was born in Geneva in 1712. His mother died in childbirth and his father, a watchmaker, left his son to the care of relatives when he was exiled from the city for brawling in 1722. As a young man Rousseau was forced to take several menial positions, but through self-education and the patronage of wealthy women he established himself as a talented musician and intellectual. In Paris in 1745, Rousseau first made the acquaintance of Diderot and the Paris *encyclopédistes*. Thus began his uneasy relationship with Enlightenment thought.

In 1750 Rousseau wrote his 'Discourse on the Sciences and the Arts' for a competition at the academy of Dijon, in which he established the themes which he was to develop in much of his subsequent political philosophy. The competition had asked for an essay on the impact of the arts and sciences on human morals. Rousseau argued that these were merely the seductive characteristics of a modern society in which mankind had lost his natural liberty and entered a moral decline. Rousseau equated virtue with innocence which once lost could never be regained.

The controversy surrounding this essay established Rousseau's place in the intellectual life of Paris. His contemptuous distaste for the mannered salons in which philosophical debate was conducted, however, resulted in his remaining something of an outsider. In 1755 he published the *Discourse on the Origin of Inequality*. His argument that the institution of private property was the prime source of all moral corruption presented a direct challenge to the modernist doctrines of **Locke**, Grotius and Pufendorf. The *encyclopédistes* understood the romanticism of Rousseau's developing position as anti-Enlightenment and broke their connections with him.

Rousseau's greatest and most influential work, *The Social Contract,* was published in 1762. The earlier discourses had established a problem. Natural man, he believed, had been innocent but unfulfilled and incapable of morality. The process by which morality might be achieved was the same process which seemed inevitably to corrupt and degrade him. Since the return to innocence was impossible, how was man best to live in society? In *The Social Contract* Rousseau presented his answer. His account of the social contract differs radically from earlier contract theories in that when individuals contract to enter society, each makes that contract simultaneously with the others and with himself. Each is a part of the sovereign which he is contracted to obey. From the isolated selves of individuals a collective entity is formed which can both legislate for and embody its individual members. Most significantly, freedom is changed by the act of contract. Before contracting, man's freedom lies in pursuing his individual interests; afterwards freedom consists in obeying the general will.

Probably the most elusive and criticized aspect of Rousseau's political philosophy, the general will is that policy or action which will be to the greatest benefit of the society as a whole. This can be discovered only when the citizens act as members of the sovereign, setting aside their personal interests or sectarian affiliations. The general will is that which the sovereign assembly of citizens ought to decide, not necessarily what they do decide. For Rousseau the general will is not created by the sovereign but discovered by it.

His political philosophy centres on developing political institutions that facilitate discovery of and adherence to the general will. The resulting state is one that is regarded by Rousseau's critics as totalitarian. Since freedom consists in obedience to the general will, those who do not obey must be 'forced to be free'. Membership of interest groups is forbidden and the legislator is extremely powerful. However, Rousseau insisted that the object of political might must be liberty and equality, and it is to these ends that his philosophy was directed.

Despite his pessimistic view of society and his hope that a revolutionary age could be prevented, a decade after his death Rousseau's writings inspired many of the leaders of the French Revolution. The same characteristic zeal that had led the *encyclopédistes* to reject Rousseau's philosophy has been found inspirational by many who have shared his sense of outrage at the inequalities present within their own societies. Fidel Castro is said to have carried a copy of *The Social Contract* throughout his days as a revolutionary. And despite the undisciplined character of his work, philosophers such as **Kant** and **Hegel** acknowledged their debt to Rousseau.

Suggested reading
Rousseau, J. 1974 [1762]. *The Social Contract*. Harmondsworth: Penguin.
Rousseau, J. 2001 [1762]. *Emile, or on Education*. Harmondsworth: Penguin.
Rousseau, J. 1953 [1782]. *The Confessions*. Harmondsworth: Penguin.

Bertrand Russell

1872–1970   **Peter Cave**

One day, in Cambridge in 1894, Bertrand Russell went to buy a tin of tobacco. Walking back along Trinity Lane, he threw the tin into the air, exclaiming, 'Great God in boots! – the ontological argument is sound!' The ontological argument seeks to establish God's existence by reason alone – by analysing the concepts of God and existence. Russell soon overcame any such belief, with or without the boots; and he was soon showing where the ontological argument goes wrong. He remained thereafter an atheist, quipping that were he wrong, he would plead that the deity provided insufficient evidence to justify belief. The story illustrates Russell's eagerness for eternal truths yet also his empirical and rational stance, a stance in line with his secular godfather – **John Stuart Mill**.

Russell was born into the aristocracy, but his parents were progressive, supporting birth control, universal suffrage and much more. Within Russell's first few years, his uncle went mad; his mother died, followed by his sister, father, then grandfather; and, despite his parents' wills, the person who secured custody over him was his grandmother, an austere Scottish Presbyterian. Who knows how this affected him, but Russell became fascinated by the pristine purity of mathematics.

At Cambridge, disappointed by mathematics' lack of rigour, he turned to philosophy, devoting over a decade to 'logicism', that is, deriving pure mathematics from logical foundations. For example, statements involving numbers are analysed by means of logical concepts such as identity. The proposition that there are two and only two philosophers becomes: there is an item x that philosophizes and there is an item y that philosophizes, and x is not identical with y, and concerning any item z, if z philosophizes, then z is either identical with x or with y.

A basic premise of Russell's logicism is that numbers are classes of equally numerous classes. Yet here Russell spotted troubling paradoxes. Classes can sometimes be members of themselves. The class of ants is no ant and so is no member of itself; but the class of countable things is countable and so is a member of itself. Now, consider the class of classes that are not members of themselves. Is it a member of itself? Whether we answer 'yes' or 'no' we end up with a contradiction. Russell created his theory of types to try and solve this problem, but ultimately his logicism failed. Yet his work indicates his boldness, genius and commitment to logical analyses.

Another one of Russell's major theories arose in response to a puzzle of language. It is not true that the King of France is bald, for there is no such king. So how can we grasp such a claim, if there is nothing identified by the term 'the King of France'? Russell's theory of descriptions – a paradigm of philosophical analysis for some, rejected by others – shows the true form of such statements. The form is: it is not the case that there is one and only one item that rules royally over France and whatever rules thus is bald. Grasp of this requires no relationship to non-existent entities, but to properties such as 'ruling'. Russell vacillates over what the ultimate items reached through these analyses are; they must be simples with which we are acquainted and which give our words meanings. Coloured patches form one possible set of examples; we denote such items directly with 'this' and 'that'.

Through logical analyses – through respect for scientific results and a robust sense of reality – Russell brought philosophy down to earth, with clarity and wit. Although many now reject the letter of his work, much Anglo-American philosophy continues in his analytical spirit. During his lifetime, his influence extended far beyond logic and metaphysics, into politics, science and education. He was politically active and, mostly, anti-war. His civil disobedience led to dismissal from Trinity College Cambridge and arrival in Brixton gaol in 1918. He founded a progressive school, popularized philosophy – and himself – and in later years worked with Einstein against nuclear weapons. He was gaoled again.

Russell valued reason and evidence, yet was frequently swept away by sexual desires and jealousies, by changes of mind and wives. A New York lecturing appointment was revoked because he was deemed morally unfit, given his advocacy of sexual freedom; yet he was awarded the Nobel Prize and Order of Merit. He said that three passions dominated him: love, knowledge and pity for mankind's suffering. He did his best about all three, eventually living the life of a provocative and prolific personality – a life he fancied living again.

Suggested reading

Russell, B. 1967 [1912]. *The Problems of Philosophy*. Oxford: Oxford University
    Press.
Russell, B., ed. Mumford, S. 2003. *Russell on Metaphysics: Selections from the
    Writings of Bertrand Russell*. London: Routledge.
Ayer, A. J. 1972. *Bertrand Russell*. Chicago: University of Chicago Press.

Gilbert Ryle

1900–1976   **Peter Cave**

Le style, c'est Ryle, quipped colleagues; and whatever the merits of Ryle's
philosophy, Ryle's style has style. He writes with verve and audacity,
example upon example culled from games and illnesses, circuses and
law, ramblings and pretendings. He uses knockabout and spin, jokes and
sound-bites; almost everything is thrown in – and understandably so, for
Ryle is slaying dragons, well, ghosts, of philosophy.

In *The Concept of Mind* (1949), a twentieth-century classic, he boasts
a deliberate abusiveness, when speaking of the 'ghost in the machine',
whereby he rejects dualism – the dogma that mind and body are two
radically distinct, yet interacting, substances. Through *The Concept of
Mind*, the philosophical lexicon became peppered with Rylean terms,
from the 'ghost' to 'category mistakes', from 'privileged access' to
'knowing-how' to 'logical geography'.

In the 1920s, Gilbert Ryle was a young Oxford lecturer at a time when
Oxford philosophy was moribund and blinkered while Cambridge's was
sparkling and fertile, thanks to luminaries **Russell**, **Moore**, Keynes,
Ramsey and **Wittgenstein**. Ryle, challenging Oxford's hostility, studied
Russell and befriended Wittgenstein through walking holidays. Ryle's
thinking developed along these new analytical lines, changing Oxford's
philosophy for good. Through this – and, later, Ryle's promotion of new
postgraduate studies – he filled Oxford with philosophers who respected
clarity, analysis and ordinary language. Ryle, now professorial, became
kingmaker, getting his students philosophy jobs throughout English-
speaking universities.

The *deus ex machina* is the unexpected and mysterious power that
appears in plays, to salvage something from hopeless situations. For

Ryle, minds, conceived as distinct from bodies, are equally mysterious and unjustified intrusions, for which we must blame **Descartes**. It is mistaken to think of minds as things, albeit immaterial things, paralleling the world's material items. It is a 'category mistake' – a radical mistake – as mistaken as thinking that if someone goes home in a sedan chair and tears then they go home in two things. Hiding minds behind bodies – and thoughts, feelings and intentions behind bodily behaviours – generates the problem of how we know what others are thinking, feeling or intending. Indeed, how do we know there even are other minds? And if actions, such as buying whisky, require some mental action, such as intending to buy, then why does that intending not require yet another action – and so on?

Ryle's answer is that the mind's workings are not shadowy operations behind bodily performances; they are the performances. Boswell described Johnson's mind, according to Ryle, when he described how he wrote, talked, fidgeted and fumed. Of course, Johnson kept some thoughts to himself: there were some silent babblings which Johnson could have recorded and only a James Joyce would wish to have recorded. Thus, Ryle looks like a logical behaviourist: what it is for people to be happy, thinking, or intending to get drunk, is for them to behave, or be disposed to behave, in a certain way, as circumstances dictate.

One objection to this position is that while we use people's behaviour to tell us what they are thinking and intentionally doing, that behaviour and related behavioural dispositions need not constitute the thinkings and doings. Indeed we are sometimes disposed not to say what we think. Happily, Ryle is no thoroughgoing behaviourist: neither tingles, tickles nor, ultimately, pensive states receive complete behavioural analyses – though, throughout, he resists Descartes' dualistic delights.

Occam's Razor says that entities should not be multiplied beyond necessity. Ryle shaves off minds as distinct from bodies – we deal with human beings, not dualistic compounds – and shaves off mental events understood as typically possessing privileged access for their subjects. Ryle believes that ordinary language has systematically misleading expressions, expressions that in ordinary discourse give no problem but can mislead under philosophical reflection. 'Virtue is its own reward' might suggest that some abstract entity or Platonic form – virtue – exists over and above virtuous individuals; but virtue is no recipient of rewards.

The meaning is simply that anyone who is virtuous is thereby benefited. Hence Ryle's Occamizing zeal rids us of abstract entities as well as immaterial minds.

Ryle learnt much from Wittgenstein, though maybe an insufficient amount. Ryle – certainly, the early Ryle – can make philosophy seem too easy, even shallow. Although, when speaking of *The Concept of Mind*, Wittgenstein exaggerated in saying, 'All the magic has gone', Ryle offers scant feeling of bewitchment by – and Wittgensteinian-type battle with – the perennial philosophical perplexities. For all that, what Ryle sought to do was admirable; and the way that he did it enchanting. Le style, c'est Ryle – and, sadly, that style of clarity, combined with elegance and humour, is rare amongst today's more technically minded philosophers.

Suggested reading
Ryle, G. 1949. *The Concept of Mind*. London: Hutchinson.
Ryle, G. 1954. *Dilemmas*. Cambridge: Cambridge University Press.
Wood, O. P. and Pitcher, G. 1971 (eds). *Ryle: A Collection of Critical Essays*. London: Macmillan.

George Santayana
1863–1952   Diego Lawler

George Santayana was born in Madrid in 1863 and educated in the United States. Although he is held to be one of the principal figures in classical American philosophy, he never gave up his Spanish citizenship, which was a way of expressing and keeping his distance from American culture.

Santayana taught philosophy at Harvard University as a contemporary of **William James**, Josiah Royce and, briefly, **C. S. Peirce**. Although he was a popular teacher and highly respected by his colleagues and students (which included poets like Aiken, T. S. Eliot and Wallace Stevens), he was driven by strong anti-academic convictions. Santayana believed that such commitments restricted his freedom to pursue his intellectual interests. These anti-academic feelings led him to drop his promising professional career, retiring from Harvard in 1912 at the age of forty-eight and rejecting other academic posts offered at different universities during the rest of his life. He left the US for Europe shortly after in order to concentrate on his writing. He preferred to perceive himself as an intellectual vagabond, rather than as an intellectual engaged in social and cultural policy formulation.

Despite the clear influence of James and Royce in Santayana's thought, he was much more than a mere follower. His philosophy developed more along Greek and European lines than in the American tradition, which he thought was both markedly derivative and greatly tied to the expansion of capitalism.

Santayana's philosophical stance is often called 'pragmatic naturalism'. Its historical roots lie in **Aristotle**'s practical philosophy, **Spinoza**'s metaphysics and the pragmatic approach to knowledge and action elaborated in a continuous conscious and unconsciousness dialogue with the pragmatism of both James and Peirce.

Spinoza's influence is most evident when Santayana writes on the spiritual life. Santayana attempted to develop Spinoza's pantheism – the view that God and nature are one – in a way which makes it consonant with contemporary understanding. Central to Santayana's pragmatic naturalism is his conviction that both scientific and philosophical explanations are deeply rooted in the natural world. Nonetheless, although the only reality is matter itself and all else arises from humanity's experience of and response to matter, we need to avoid a reductive materialism in which everything is explained in the term of mechanistic science.

His mature philosophy is powerfully expressed in *Scepticism and Animal Faith* (1923). According to Santayana, we, as animals, have an irresistible impetus or urge to believe in the independence of the external world. Philosophical reflection must begin by taking into account this urge, which he calls 'animal faith'. Animal faith generates a set of inescapable belief structures that plays an essential role in our actions, by which we understand and transform the world we live in. This set of belief structures is a result of the interaction between our physical makeup and our material environment. These beliefs are incapable of proof. Rather, they operate as the condition of the possibility of others' beliefs. Hence, these beliefs capture our vital constitutional necessity as biological beings in a material setting. Our animal faith is thus an expression of our rational instinct, and constitutes a basis for any knowledge claims and purposeful action.

Santayana's naturalism underlies his moral philosophy. He could be portrayed as a moral relativist who gives all individual moral views an equal standing. This is because each individual is a result of the interplay between environment and 'psyche' – Santayana's name for our physical makeup – and in this sense pursues different goods. Moral philosophical reflection must therefore celebrate the fact that the good life encompasses a diversity of individual goods.

Santayana was not only an innovator philosopher, but also a poet and a famous writer. His novel *The Last Puritan* (1936) was nominated for a Pulitzer Prize. These multiple talents allowed him to think in different arenas of intellectual work. Indeed, he was one of the first philosophers to think of philosophy as literature.

Suggested reading

Santayana, G. 1923. *Scepticism and Animal Faith: Introduction to a System of Philosophy*. New York: Scribner's.

Saatkamp Jr, H. J. and Holzberger, W. G. 1986 (eds). *The Works of George Santayana, Volume 1*. Cambridge, Mass.: MIT Press.

Sprigge, T. 1974. *Santayana: An examination of his philosophy*. London: Routledge.

Jean-Paul Sartre

1905–1980   **Jeremy Stangroom**

Jean-Paul Sartre is the philosopher whose work – certainly in the English speaking world – largely defined the existentialist movement in the twentieth century. The themes which he explored in his writings – particularly the primacy of individual existence, human freedom, and the lack of objective values – are precisely those of existentialism. Consequently, a common view about Sartre is that he is a kind of humanist, concerned with the necessity that individuals face to choose their own lives and the morals that they espouse. However, although there is something right about this view, the truth about Sartre's philosophy is stranger than might at first be supposed.

Some of this strangeness derives from the way that he conceptualized consciousness and the human subject. In *Being and Nothingness* (1943), his major existential work, Sartre divided being into two primary realms: being for-itself, which is consciousness; and being in-itself, which is everything else. He argued that the for-itself is characterized by nothingness – that is, that emptiness lies right at the heart of being. What did he mean by this? In simple terms, he meant that there is no human essence. Consciousness is permanently detached from the given order of things. It is pure empty possibility, and therein lies its freedom.

This is a complicated idea. Some light can be shed on it by considering Sartre's treatment of the concept of negation. This concerns the capacity to conceive of what is not the case. It is manifest in a whole series of attitudes that the for-itself can adopt towards the objects to which it is directed. Perhaps most significant is the ability of the for-itself to project beyond the given present to an open future of unrealized possibilities – to imagine what *might* be the case. In this sense, the freedom of the for-itself is the permanent possibility that things might be other than they are.

Human beings do not find this freedom easy to live with. With the realization that the future is always radically in doubt comes anguish. Sartre argued that in order to escape anguish individuals adopt strategies of bad faith; that is, they seek to deny the freedom that is inevitably theirs. They might do so, for example, by adopting an attitude of seriousness towards a perceived moral sphere. That is, they might portray their actions as entirely governed by a binding moral code – 'I'd like to help you, but I can't, it would be wrong'. Of course, as far as Sartre is concerned, this is just so much rationalization. As he argued in his popular *Existentialism and Humanism* (1946), there are no binding moral codes. The moral choices that individuals make are theirs and theirs alone, and they are fully responsible for them. All people can do is to choose authentically in the full recognition that they choose freely.

However, the fact that the for-itself is always and inevitably free does not mean that individuals make their choices in a vacuum. Rather, they face up to the specifics of the situations that they confront – for example, that the bank-robber has a gun in his hand – and the 'facticity' of their particular lives. Facticity here refers to all the things about an individual that cannot be changed at any given point in time – for example, their age, sex and genetic dispositions. Choices then are made against a particular background, so freedom of consciousness does not translate into the idea that people are free to do absolutely anything at the drop of a hat.

Interesting in this regard is the role of the self and its relation to human freedom (the self was first properly discussed in an early work, *The Transcendence of the Ego,* 1936). Sartre denied that individuals have essential selves. Indeed, part of what defines his philosophy as existentialist is his claim that existence precedes essence. We exist first – the self that we subsequently become is a construct that is built and rebuilt out of experiences and behaviour. In principle, then, the self is something which can be changed, it can be reconstructed. However, in practice, it is not easy to choose a course of action that is out of character with the fundamental project of the self. Consequently, the self that we have become imposes another limit on the practice of the freedom that belongs inevitably to the for-itself.

Concentrating on the philosophical foundations of Sartre's idea of freedom can make his philosophy look almost entirely individualist. This is something of a distortion. It would have been possible to have entered Sartre's work at a different point – for example, with his later book, *Critique of Dialectical Reason* (1960) – and to have painted a different kind of picture. Nevertheless, his early existentialist work has proved to be of the most enduring interest, and underpinning this work is the idea that the individual consciousness is always and inevitably free.

Suggested reading
Sartre, J-P. 1969 [1943]. *Being and Nothingness*. London: Routledge.
Sartre, J-P. 1974 [1946]. *Existentialism and Humanism*. London: Methuen.
Sartre, J-P. 2000 [1938]. *Nausea*. Harmondsworth: Penguin Modern Classics.

Ferdinand de Saussure

1857–1913   **Christopher Norris**

Ferdinand de Saussure was a Swiss linguist whose thinking laid the conceptual foundations for what later emerged as the structuralist movement in his own and other disciplines. His ideas were developed in lectures at the University of Geneva and later published from student transcripts under the title *Course in General Linguistics* (1916).

Saussure's chief aim was to place the study of language on a more scientific basis by breaking with traditional, historically-oriented or 'diachronic' (across time) approaches of the kind that had dominated nineteenth-century philology, his own earlier work included. Instead, it should treat language synchronically (at a time) as a system of con-trastive or differential features, a system 'without positive terms' since the relationship between *signifier* and *signified* (or word and concept) cannot be understood on the model of a straightforward, one-to-one correspondence. Rather it consists in the complex structure of inter-articulated differences which enables a mere handful of phonemes – minimal distinctive sound-units – to serve as the basis for a vast (potentially infinite) range of significations.

At the semantic level (the level of meaning), the precondition for language is its structural capacity to distinguish various concepts one from another and thereby impose an intelligible order on the otherwise inchoate flux of human experience. Moreover, different languages impose different orders through their various, culture-specific resources. Language should thus be treated from a structural-synchronic standpoint that acknowledges the 'arbitrary' character of the sign or the absence of any 'natural', other than conventional, link between signifier and signified.

Two further Saussurean distinctions are of crucial relevance with regard to the aims and scope of the structuralist enterprise. First is that between *langue* and *parole*, the former applying to the system of language in its structural-synchronic aspect, the latter to the open-ended variety of speech-acts or particular (context-specific) items of utterance. Related to this is the 'syntagmatic'/'paradigmatic' distinction. The syn-tagmatic concerns how discourse unfolds 'horizontally' in accordance with certain linear (e.g., grammatical) rules of combination. The paradig-matic concerns the selection of lexical units from a contrast-class of possible alternatives (synonyms, antonyms, near-equivalents, metaphoric substitutes, etc.) conceived as belonging to a 'vertical' dimension from point to point along the syntagmatic chain.

The syntagmatic/paradigmatic distinction has come to exert great influence on later developments in literary criticism, narrative poetics, anthropology, cultural studies, and the human sciences at large. For it offers a means of analysing texts – 'texts' in the broadest sense of that term, taken to include (say) poems, novels, myths, kinship-systems, culinary codes, fashions in dress, cinematic conventions, or musical styles and genres – on the basis of certain structural features involving the interplay or relative predominance of syntagmatic and paradigmatic elements. Hence also certain heterodox readings of the texts of philosophy (among them deconstructive readings by analysts such as Jacques Derrida and Paul de Man) which emphasize their complex rhetorical structures and moments of logico-semantic undecidability.

Philosophically speaking, Saussurean linguistics would seem to be at odds with any approach (like Frege's) that lays chief stress on the referential aspect of language, that is, the idea that propositions or statements acquire their truth-value through picking out certain real-world or factual (including historical) objects, events, or states of affairs. On Saussure's account, conversely, it is the two-term signifier/signified relationship – i.e., that between word and concept – that is the focus of theoretical attention rather than the three-term relationship between word, concept and referent. Still, the contrast is liable to be exaggerated by those, post-structuralists among them, who raise Saussure's notion of the arbitrary sign to a high point of radical doctrine and take it to explain how 'revolutionary' texts, such as Mallarmé's poems or Joyce's *Finnegans Wake*, can disrupt or subvert all the codes that govern our conventional, acculturated meanings and beliefs. What these theorists ignore, firstly, is the fact that Saussure doesn't so much reject the notion of linguistic reference as suspend or bracket that notion for his own distinctive methodological purposes; and, secondly, his frequent insistence that meanings can and do become stabilized through usage or custom despite the lack of any natural (non-'arbitrary') link between signifier and signified.

Moreover, Frege's philosophy of language converges with Saussure's on one point at least, namely the principle that 'sense determines reference', i.e., that when we pick out a certain object we do so via some reference-fixing range of associated attributes, descriptive features, identifying traits etc. Still, it can scarcely be denied that philosophies of language in the 'two traditions', post-Saussurean continental and post-Fregean analytic, have tended to develop along very different lines, most of all with regard to this issue concerning the centrality (or otherwise) of linguistic reference.

Suggested reading

Saussure, F. de. 1983 [1926]. *Course in General Linguistics*. London: Duckworth.
Harris, R. 1987. *Reading Saussure*. London: Duckworth.
Holdcroft, D. 1991. *Saussure: signs, system and arbitrariness*. Cambridge: Cambridge University Press.

F. W. J. Schelling
1775–1854   Lewis Owens

Schelling's philosophical development can generally be split into three periods: *Ich* (I) related philosophy and *Naturphilosophie* (philosophy of nature, 1794–1800); *Identitätsphilosophie* (philosophy of identity, 1800–1806); and the so-called middle and later philosophy of 1807 onwards.

In his earlier work Schelling, echoing **Spinoza**, speculated that nature was a self-contained and organized unity. Schelling saw God not as existing 'outside' the world, but as part of nature; the absolute Subject, the infinite 'I am' of Exodus 3:14. Hence the world participates in God rather than remaining 'outside' him.

However, it is Schelling's two later periods that capture the essence of his philosophical speculations. Schelling's middle and later philosophy was strongly characterized by an emphasis on history and the end of the world, the latter being the culmination of the former and the means by which the self-revelation of God is manifested. His later thought was dominated by an insistence that history is an epic composed within the Christian Trinity, with the second person of this Trinity – the Word made flesh – being the template or paradigm for the physical world.

It was largely from the somewhat obscure thought of the mystic Jacob Boehme that Schelling shifted his thought to a mystical theology that he believed accounted for problems inherent in his previous *Naturphiloso-phie*. Schelling developed a theory of evolution as a self-manifestation of

God in history and nature, fulfilling the scriptural passage of 1 Corin-
thians 15:28: 'in order that God may be all in all'. It was a theory of
evolution in which God was revealed in physical and visible forms.
Schelling was also heavily influenced by F. C. Oetinger, who drew on the
Jewish mystical tradition of the cabbala, which attempted to account for
God's self-manifestation in this world. This 'unfolding' of God is what
Schelling referred to as 'theogony': the manifestation of the eternal God
into time and space. Indeed, the universe is called by Schelling the
'heartbeat' of God.

Drawing on the notion of the deity largely expressed by Boehme, both
Schelling and **Hegel** agree that God is an 'ens manifestativum sui'; a self-
manifesting being. However, whereas Hegel's emphasis was on a more
precise law of historical progression that followed a strict rational formula,
Schelling was more concerned to highlight the free will and liberty of God
in his self-revelation. Boehme's stress on the psychology of the Godhead,
which claimed that God actually desires consciousness, provides the possibility for God's free will to create out of his own 'nothingness'.

Like Boehme, Schelling came to see creation as a 'fall' away from the
divine unity, resulting in finite creatures that, although having their true
source in the infinite absolute of God, are now alienated or estranged
from their homeland. Their emphasis on the divine will prior to divine
being enabled Boehme and Schelling to stress the priority of the
'nothingness' from which creation issued forth. This creation from
'nothingness' also guaranteed human freedom. For Boehme and
Schelling, therefore, 'nothingness' or 'non-being' has a very real
existence within God. Although God is able to overcome this power of
non-being, it becomes the source of evil when manifested in creation.
This enables Boehme and Schelling to give evil a very real existence
whilst denying that it limits God in any way.

Furthermore, the idea of God in a process of realizing himself through
finite nature enables the possibility of creaturely, existential freedom. The
individual mind, made in the image of God and a microcosm of the
whole, is embroiled in the struggle to overcome darkness and in so
doing gives external form to the inner conflict of God. It is the duty of
mankind, and indeed the goal of history, to move from darkness to light
and awaken the slumbering spirit that will lead man back to the true
source of his being: the 'odyssey' of history.

Schelling's emphasis on the inner psychology of God, and his belief that at the very core of God's essence is a non-rational will to achieve consciousness, had a strong influence on the emergence of later existential thought. Indeed, it is fair to call Schelling one of the fore-runners of religious existential thought, which reacted against the closed, largely rational system of Hegel and stressed the importance of human freedom that issues forth as a result of God's free creation. For example, the German philosopher **Martin Heidegger** posits similar ideas with his claim that 'being' is not subjected to human categories but reveals itself through humanity.

Suggested reading

Schelling, F. W. J. 1993 [1800]. *System of Transcendental Idealism*. Charlottesville: University of Virginia Press.

Schelling, F. W. J. 2000 [1811–15]. *The Ages of the World*. New York: State University of New York Press.

Heidegger, M. 1984 [1936]. *Schelling's Treatise on the Essence of Human Freedom*. Athens, Ohio: Ohio University Press.

Arthur Schopenhauer

1788–1860   Matthew Ray

Arthur Schopenhauer presented his interconnected philosophical theories in the major systematic work *The World as Will and Representation*, which was first published in 1819 and then revised twice, in 1844 and 1859. (These 'changes' are in fact largely additions and constitute a second volume.) Schopenhauer also published collections of short essays and longer monographs on such traditional philosophical themes as ethics and the problem of free will, but, unusually, these essays largely stick to the conclusions that Schopenhauer had already reached in his *magnum opus*. Schopenhauer, therefore, is that fairly rare thing: a philosopher whose thought barely developed and therefore need not be examined chronologically. This lack of alteration in his thought seems to have been in keeping with his stubborn personality.

Schopenhauer's main philosophical theories follow on from the thought of his chief predecessor, **Immanuel Kant**, without whom Schopenhauer's system would be unthinkable. Explicitly following Kant, Schopenhauer believed that our world of space and time was merely the 'phenomenal' world of appearances and that the world as it really is, outside of the way we represent it to ourselves, is timeless and spaceless. We subjectively add space and time to the world just as, to re-use a well-known metaphor, in wearing red-lensed glasses we add the colour red to all our (visual) experience. Because time and space are the way that we necessarily picture things, however, we cannot see the way the world really is in itself (in terms of the earlier metaphor: we cannot take the glasses off).

Kant thought that we could say nothing more about the nature of the world in itself, but Schopenhauer radically innovated at this point and argued that the world as it is in itself is essentially 'will', a kind of blind, striving desire. How do we know this? Because when we consider our 'inner' experience of our body we supposedly feel it to be will. Since this inner experience of will has shed one of our two subjective forms of representation (the experience of will is not in space), it is presumably – a big 'presumably' – nearer to the world as it is in itself. This, in its essentials, is Schopenhauer's basic philosophy: the world is made up of our representations in space and time and the 'will'. This fairly simple ontology (account of being) has consequences for both Schopenhauer's ethics and his aesthetics, which actually follow on quite straight-forwardly from this metaphysical picture.

In his ethics, Schopenhauer argues that we should be compassionate to other people because deep down we are really all one being. Less metaphorically, beyond space and time, in which we are separate individuals, there is only *one* will. So harming another person is, when viewed philosophically (i.e. through Schopenhauer's system), actually just harming oneself. Some commentators, however, have argued that this ultimately reduces morality to prudence.

Schopenhauer's aesthetics, although it too follows on from his ontology, is rather more complicated than his ethics and should probably be split into two domains. First, there is his aesthetics of music, which argues that music, because it takes place only in time and not space, actually 'mirrors' the world of will. Exactly how it does so is not explained, however. This perhaps goes some way towards explaining why music is so bound up with our emotions but nonetheless leaves unexplained why other non-spatial experiences, such as hearing another person talking, do not similarly mirror will. (Incidentally, the importance granted to music by Schopenhauer in his aesthetics would be one of the most profound influences on **Nietzsche**'s first book, *The Birth of Tragedy from the Spirit of Music*).

Second, Schopenhauer appears to believe that all the other non-musical arts aim to represent Platonic ideas or forms. In other words, a painting of a tree is beautiful in so far as it reflects the eternal idea of a tree. Furthermore, under the influence of Kant (who thought that artistic appreciation should be 'disinterested'), Schopenhauer argues that such contemplation of eternal ideas takes us out of our earthly world of strife and desire and gives us a moment of calm. The aim of art, Schopenhauer contends, is to quell the stirrings of desire (the will) we all feel inside us. The problem with this line of Schopenhauerian argument is, however, that paintings of nudes and the art of dance exhibited in, say, ballet, cannot be, and are not, admitted to be art by Schopenhauer, being directed, as he put it, 'more to lasciviousness than to aesthetic pleasure'.

Suggested reading

Schopenhauer, A. 1970. *Essays and Aphorisms*. Harmondsworth: Penguin.
Schopenhauer, A. 1969. *The World as Will and Representation (Volume 1)*. New York: Dover Publications.
Janaway, C. 2002. *Schopenhauer: A Very Short Introduction*. Oxford: Oxford University Press.

John Duns Scotus

c.1266–1308   Peter S. Fosl

Little is known about the life of John Duns Scotus. He was probably born in Scotland in about 1266. Some accounts place Scotus on the beautiful and lonely island of North Uist in the Outer Hebrides. He studied at Oxford and then Paris, where he became a master and regent until being transferred to Cologne. It seems likely that he died there in Germany, his death traditionally dated as 8 November 1308.

Scotus's accomplishments are legion, and indeed in many ways Scotus defined the terms with which institutional philosophy would be engaged during the fourteenth century. One of Scotus's main preoccupations was with the 'transcendental', both in the sense of rising above or beyond ordinary experience to reach something divine, and in **Immanuel Kant**'s sense of investigations into the necessary conditions for the possibility of knowledge and experience. Scotus's doctrine of transcendentals describes certain special features of reality, features different from those that characterize ordinary and natural things as ordinary and natural. Transcendental features of reality are those that are shared by all beings, the divine and supernatural as well as the ordinary and natural.

Importantly, through this doctrine Scotus attempted to secure the project of natural theology: using natural powers of human perception, cognition and reason to know the divine. Revealed theologians and illuminationists, such as **Augustine**, Al-farabi and Henry of Ghent, held that human knowledge of God, and indeed of anything at all, requires revelation or illumination of the natural faculties of mind by something supernatural, namely God. Natural theologians, by contrast, while not excluding revelation, maintained that the work of natural, unaided human faculties could themselves acquire knowledge of the divine. One could accomplish this either negatively, by considering what God is not (Maimonides), or more positively by working to acquire an understanding of what God is through the exercise of natural thinking (**Aquinas**).

Negative or positive, natural theologian or illuminationist, however, nearly all medieval thinkers held that human understanding of God must remain significantly limited. In Aquinas's case, he maintained that we can think and speak of God at best 'analogically'. That is, whenever we attribute qualities to God (for example that God is 'good') we cannot do so in precisely the same manner in which we make those attributions to ordinary things. We can, however, through analogy still acquire some positive understanding of the deity.

Scotus argued that these views risk the conclusion that we cannot in fact know God at all. It is only if, Scotus argued, we can think and speak 'univocally', that is in precisely the same way, about God and creatures that we can really know the divine. Moreover, it makes greater sense in attempting to know God to appeal only to our natural faculties than it does to 'illumination'. Scotus, however, like his predecessors, is clear that our knowledge of God remains incomplete. While we can know that God is a being and that God is good, we cannot know God's particular essence.

Scotus's arguments about the univocity of the transcendentals were devastating to illuminationism. They also foreshadow the wider, modern naturalistic shift in focus from divine intercession to the natural powers of mind as a source of knowledge and understanding.

Scotus not only departed from the scholastic tradition through his doctrine of the univocity of the transcendentals, he also broke with it on the relation of universal 'forms' (such as 'dog') to individuals (such as any particular dog). He closed the gap between universals and particulars by claiming that forms carry with them a principle of individuation or 'thisness', which he called 'haecceitas'.

Finally, Scotus's doctrine of the will changed philosophy's conceptions both of humans and of God. Scotus held that God's activity in creating the world is not fully determined by the demands of reason and may always exceed them. Similarly, the human will is free not simply because it can change, and not simply because it can act independently of both the causal order of nature and the rational order of intellect, but because at any moment it is capable of acting contrary to the course it is presently set upon. Even the intellect lacks this sort of freedom. Fortunately for us, the will according to Scotus is intrinsically inclined to the good.

Suggested reading
Duns Scotus, J. 1987. *Philosophical Writings: A Selection*. Indianapolis: Hackett
    Publishing Company.
Cross, R. 1999. *Duns Scotus*. New York: Oxford University Press.
Williams, T. 2002. (ed.) *The Cambridge Companion to Dun Scotus*. Cambridge:
    Cambridge University Press.

John Searle

1932–   **Christopher Norris**

John Searle has published on topics in the philosophy of mind, language and cognitive psychology. His work has been highly controversial, no doubt as a result of Searle's uncompromising stance on various issues and his taste for the intellectual equivalent of 'see you outside, jackets off'. This has led him to engage opponents on multiple fronts, among them speech-act theory (where he has sought to provide a more systematic treatment of issues first raised by J. L. Austin) and artificial intelligence (where Searle has vigorously contested the claim of 'strong' AI theorists that computer-run programs could manifest the same powers and capacities as the human brain). He has also locked horns with sociologists of knowledge who argue that 'reality' is socially constructed and that all 'truths' (scientific or other) are the product of cultural or ideological interests. The shrewdly-aimed title of his 1995 book *The Construction of Social Reality* (cf. Berger and Luckmann, *The Social Construction of Reality*) makes the point that this applies only to certain aspects of communal life where understanding depends on the existence of shared codes, values, or conventions. Where it doesn't apply is in the physical sciences or other disciplines which have to do with objective, non-culture-relative truths about the world.

These interests are linked via Searle's emphasis on 'intentionality' as the uniquely distinguishing feature of human thought, language and experience in general. What the term 'intentional' signifies here is not the obvious sense in which speech-acts like promising or ordering depend for their efficacy on our grasping the utterer's intent. Rather, the 'intentionality of the mind' refers to the fact that there is a certain property of 'aboutness' intrinsic to all mental states and that conscious experience is always directed toward something or other. Such items might be objects of perceptual acquaintance but would also include abstract items like numbers, concepts, or even imaginary entities such as centaurs or golden mountains. The concept of intentionality had previously been developed by philosophers in the phenomenological line of descent from Meinong and **Brentano** to **Husserl**. This lineage is one that Searle very largely ignores since he is keen to play the role of a hard-headed 'analytic' philosopher with no time for such forms of 'continental' (= waffly metaphysical) talk. All the same, as his nifty antagonist **Jacques Derrida** has pointed out, there is a lot more in common than Searle would have us believe between his way of thinking and theirs. Thus Searle's case against 'strong' AI involves an appeal to precisely those aspects of mind, meaning and intentionality which thinkers like Husserl brought to light.

Searle's most famous contribution to this debate is his 'Chinese room' thought-experiment. Here we are asked to imagine that someone outside the room hands in a series of written messages in Chinese which are then replied to with other Chinese expressions through a process that involves nothing more than mechanically sifting through a database of lexical items and substitution rules. Searle's point is that there is no reason to suppose that the inside goings-on manifest any kind of linguistic intelligence, much less any sign of conscious awareness, beyond the mere capacity to check things off in a purely automatic way.

This analogy to how computers work shows what is wrong with the Turing Test for artificial intelligence, namely, the idea that if a human interlocutor failed to distinguish reliably between the answers delivered by a human respondent and those delivered by a computational device, then the case that the device has intelligence and consciousness has been made beyond any reasonable doubt. Of course it might appear to display intelligence, if programmed with sufficient ingenuity. Yet this would always leave room for the alternative explanation that it was just churning out responses in accordance with a rule-based decision procedure and with no understanding of what the responses meant, just like the person in the Chinese room. From this Searle concludes that the AI project is utterly misconceived, since no experiment along these lines could establish the existence of intelligent or conscious thought in systems other than the human brain.

There have been many counter-arguments to Searle's thesis, most of which he has answered in typically robust style. Among them is the standard objection that the brain *just is* a complex computational device which in the case of human beings happens to require certain carbon-based neurophysiological structures but whose workings could in principle be replicated by some other (e.g. silicon-based) system of equivalent complexity. At any rate there seems something premature, even dogmatic, about any argument like Searle's that would rule out such possibilities in principle.

Suggested reading

Searle, J. 1983. *Intentionality: an essay in the philosophy of mind*. Cambridge:
  Cambridge University Press.
Searle, J. 1984. *Minds, Brains, and Science*. Cambridge, Mass.: Harvard University
  Press.
Searle, J. 1998. *Mind, Language and Society*. New York: Basic Books.

Lucius Annaeus Seneca

c.4 BCE–65   **Robin Wood**

Seneca was the second son of Seneca the Elder, born at Córdoba in
Spain but brought up as a child in Rome by an aunt and educated there
in rhetoric and philosophy. He was particularly drawn to philosophy and
deeply influenced by the Stoic doctrine, which he himself later
developed. He became quaestor (chief revenue officer) and a senator
and, under Claudius, he occupied a position at court. He was accused of
an intrigue with Julia, the daughter of Germanicus, and banished to
Corsica in 41. He was recalled eight years later in 49 by Agrippina to be
the tutor of her son Nero because of his literary reputation, which he
had achieved during his exile. When Nero became Emperor in 54 CE the
influence of Seneca and Burrus (prefect of the guard) kept the young
emperor temporarily under control. Later, after the death of Burrus,
Nero's conduct worsened and Seneca asked permission to withdraw
from court and lived in retirement devoting himself to literature. But in
65, on a charge of complicity in Piso's conspiracy, he was ordered to take
his own life. Tacitus records the calm and dignity with which he did this.

Seneca was one of the most important and prolific writers of his day,
both in prose and in verse. Ten books of ethical essays (miscalled
'*Dialogi*') survive on subjects such as anger, the constancy of the stoic
sage, and tranquillity of mind. Three of them are 'consolations' to the
bereaved. He presented to Nero, early in his reign, a treatise called *De
Clementia* (*On Clemency*) in which he commended this quality to the
autocrat. It is possible that Shakespeare had it in mind when composing
Portia's great speech on the quality of mercy. He also wrote the *De
Beneficiis* (*On Benefits*) in seven books. His *Naturales Quaestiones*

(*Studies into Nature*), eight books on physical science, achieved great popularity. The *Epistolae Morales* (*Moral Epistles*), of which 124 survive, give philosophical and ethical advice to a friend. He is almost certainly the author of the *Apocolocyntosis* (*The Pumpkinification of the Emperor Claudius*), a bitter satire on the deification of Claudius. Seneca also wrote nine tragedies on Greek mythological subjects, more designed to be recited or read than acted. They are somewhat melodramatic and violent and had an influence on Elizabethan and Jacobean tragedy in England out of all proportion to their merits.

Seneca's moral writings greatly influenced or at least gained the respect of later Christian writers, to the extent that before 400 CE a forged correspondence between him and St Paul had been composed. This was possible because of his broad humanitarian outlook. He was a Stoic and shared the cosmopolitan Stoic view of life and in many ways, in theory at least, he was in advance of his contemporaries. He condemned false values engendered by wealth, he denounced the cruelty of the Games and the stupidity of much in the official religion. He showed compassion to slaves and in principle rejected the concept of slavery, although in practice he did not really do anything towards its abolition. He believed that some portion of the divine spirit dwelt in each and every person.

The problem remains, however, that there seems to be a serious discrepancy between his ethical ideals and his actual life (such as we do not find, for example, in Socrates). To some, he appears as unduly morally complacent, and to others as a loathsome hypocrite. He had wide financial interests and was very rich. So how could, as one modern historian of Rome has put it, 'the millionaire who flattered Polybius and showed such spite to the dead Claudius and drafted Nero's justification for the murder of his mother, at the same time preach virtue and the simple life?'

Maybe the circumstances of his life proved too burdensome and he did what he could but has been harshly judged by some. Perhaps, as Nero's tutor, he hoped to turn the young aspiring emperor to true virtue. In *De Clementia* he urged the ruler to limit his autocratic powers by self-regulation. But, as Nero became more callous, Seneca's influence over him began to decline and he weakly condoned one excess after another, perhaps hoping to prevent worse.

Like Cicero, in retirement he devoted himself to philosophical writing, particularly the *Moral Epistles*, seeking inner freedom of spirit and the virtue that leads to it. Although a notable expounder of Stoic doctrine and a significant Latin writer, he cannot be said to rank with the great philosophers of ancient Greece.

Suggested reading
Cooper, J. M. & Procope, J. F. 1995 (eds). *Seneca: Moral and Political Essays*. Cambridge: Cambridge University Press.
Griffin, M. 1992. *Seneca: A Philosopher in Politics* Oxford: Clarendon Press.
Seneca. 1969. *Letters from a Stoic: Epistolae Morales Ad Lucilium.* Harmondsworth: Penguin.

Henry Sidgwick
1838–1900   **Bart Schultz**

Rivalling **Jeremy Bentham** and **John Stuart Mill** as an architect of the classical utilitarian doctrine that ethics and politics ought to involve maximizing happiness, Henry Sidgwick was also a guiding spirit in the causes of women's higher education and of parapsychology, a founder of Newnham College, Cambridge, and the Society for Psychical Research.

Sidgwick's *The Methods of Ethics* (1874) reflected not only an advance in utilitarianism, but also a sensitive engagement with and appropriation of the leading mid-Victorian alternatives. For instance, following William Whewell, Sidgwick came to think that intuitions had to be invoked as the rational ground of fundamental principles. Moreover, he went beyond J. S. Mill in arguing that many of the commonsense moral rules that the intuitionists sought to refine and defend, for example that promises ought to be kept, could be defended as by and large conducing to the greatest happiness, at least for the ordinary purposes of ordinary people.

But Sidgwick was nervous about his views. Often cited as one of those Victorians whose religious doubts did not undermine their ethical rectitude, he actually worried endlessly that without a defensible, religious conception of the moral order of the world, philosophical ethics

ended up in a conflict, a 'dualism of practical reason', between the utilitarian view that reason dictates promoting the general happiness and
the egoistic view that it dictates promoting one's own happiness. This
concern motivated both his parapsychological investigations into the
possibility that the human personality might somehow survive physical
death, which would provide some evidence for a divine moral order, and
his determined refusal to promulgate the sceptical arguments that led to
his religious and ethical agnosticism, since such conclusions were not, he
thought, likely to contribute to human happiness and could well imperil
social order.

Still, agnosticism and egoism were not the only subjects on which
Sidgwick was less than forthcoming, and his psychical research was not
the only matter his philosophical reception avoided. Sidgwick was very
much a part of the intimate circle of John Addington Symonds, the
controversial poet, literary critic and cultural historian, who became a
pioneer of gay studies. Symonds's candid explorations of the nature of
homosexual identity – such as his collaboration with Havelock Ellis on
the book *Sexual Inversion* (1897), or his remarkable, long unpublished
Memoirs, detailing his struggles with his own tendencies, which he
thought inherent – set the agenda for twentieth-century debates over
nature versus nurture in questions of sexual identity.

Sidgwick's support for Symonds was admirable. This cannot be said of
his support for such figures as Sir John Seeley and Charles Henry
Pearson. Seeley promoted one of the most influential legitimating
philosophies of British imperialism. His *The Expansion of England* (1883),
stressing England's civilizing, cultural mission in the world, was a prime
text for the new, liberal imperialists of the 1880s. Sidgwick's political
theory drew heavily on the views of his Cambridge colleague, and he
edited and introduced Seeley's posthumous *Introduction to Political
Science* (1896).

Pearson had been brought to Cambridge by Sidgwick in the late
1860s, to lecture in history, and he went on to become a leading figure
in Australian politics and educational administration. His *National Life
and Character* (1893) was praised by Sidgwick as the 'most impressive
book of a prophetic nature which has appeared in England in many
years'. What Sidgwick did not do, amidst his criticisms of the book's
method, was distance himself from Pearson's racist thesis that 'Our

science, our civilisation, our great and real advance in the practice of government are only bringing us nearer to the day when the lower races will predominate in the world, when the higher races will lose their noblest elements, when we shall ask nothing from the day but to live, nor from the future but that we may not deteriorate.' Pearson fanned Australian fears about the 'Yellow Peril'.

Sidgwick's publications never descended into such crude prejudice, but on the other side, they never plainly disclaimed it. His *Elements of Politics* (1891) only managed a guarded, evasive agnosticism when it came to the subject of 'debasement of the race' and the claims for segregative measures. Consequently, it would appear that Sidgwick's agnostic silences had a more sinister turn than his philosophical admirers have heretofore been willing to admit.

Suggested reading
Sidgwick, H. 1981 [1874]. *The Methods of Ethics*. Indianapolis: Hackett Publishing.
Sidgwick, H. 1988 [1886]. *Outlines of the History of Ethics for English Readers*. Indianapolis: Hackett Publishing.
Schultz, B. 2004. *Henry Sidgwick – Eye of the Universe*. Cambridge University Press.

Peter Singer
1946–   **Edward Johnson**

Peter Singer has been called the most important and most influential moral philosopher of his time. An indefatigable public speaker and a prolific author, Singer, an Australian who did his advanced study under R. M. Hare at Oxford University, has published more than 18 books, many more if we count his numerous edited volumes, and hundreds of essays over the last three decades. Aiming his work at both professional and popular audiences, Singer has exemplified his own ideal of the philosopher as 'moral expert', bringing reason to bear on controversial issues that demand both value analysis and empirical assessment.

Early in his career, Singer gained attention by arguing, in a famous 1972 essay, that citizens in well-off societies have a moral obligation to make extensive sacrifices to aid the poor of other nations. Displaying a refined ability to apply his simple utilitarian intuitions – that morality requires us to increase people's abilities to satisfy their preferences – to complex circumstances, Singer offered the hope that philosophical answers to practical questions might be possible. We all agree that (other things being equal) it is worse to lose a little finger than to lose a hand. Does that not remain true even if the hand is yours, and the finger mine?

Singer has a fair claim to be the individual most responsible for the contemporary prominence of the debate over the moral status of non-human animals. His essay on 'Animal Liberation', published in the *New York Review of Books* in 1973, christened a social movement. Expanded to book length in 1975, *Animal Liberation* became the bible of the 'animal rights' movement (though, as a utilitarian, Singer spoke of 'rights' loosely, whether for humans or non-humans). It is perhaps the only philosophical treatise ever to include a cookbook. Attacking the 'speciesism' of traditional views that exalted human beings, Singer argued against meat eating and 'factory farming', as well as the exploitation of animal subjects in experimental research.

In fact, Singer's defence of animals was part of a much larger project of 'unsanctifying human life', as became clear in many later books, such as *Practical Ethics* (1979), *Rethinking Life and Death: The Collapse of Our Traditional Ethics* (1994), and *Unsanctifying Human Life* (2001). This project has predictably inspired Nazi comparisons. In a 1991 account of the stiff resistance his views were encountering in Germany, Singer expressed concern about the health of the field of 'applied ethics' in a country where professors using his books found their courses disrupted by protesters who attributed Singer's views to *Menschenverachtung* (contempt for humanity).

In the United States, his 1999 appointment as DeCamp Professor of Bioethics at Princeton's University Center for Human Values sparked disability-rights protests, as well as pressure from figures such as Princeton trustee, major donor and ex-presidential candidate Steve Forbes. The passions show no signs of fading away. A *New York Times Magazine* cover story about Singer in February 2003 displayed disability-rights lawyer Harriet McBryde Johnson seated in her wheelchair, asking 'Should I Have Been Killed at Birth?' Another disability-rights activist, Stephen Drake, once complained that Singer 'is extremely charming and engaging, and is able to give a rational veneer to what is actually a genocidal agenda'.

The charge of contempt for humanity must, of course, be painful to Singer, who lost relatives in the Holocaust, as he reminds us in *Pushing Time Away* (2003), an account of his grandfather and 'the tragedy of Jewish Vienna'. And it is frustrating to have three decades' worth of careful philosophical argument dismissed as 'a rational veneer'. But one cannot influentially criticize traditional ideas and avoid impassioned responses.

In fact, as a critic of 'traditional ethics', Singer can be attacked both when he deviates from tradition in his ideas and when he conforms to it in his behaviour. Despite the fact that he has apparently given substantial financial support to moral causes he espouses, the revelation in 2000 that he had purchased expensive nursing care for his mother, an Alzheimer's patient, outraged some. To many, it flagrantly contradicted his view that ethics demands impartiality and not directing resources to those who happen to be related to us or share our nationality, ethnicity or even species membership.

In 2001, Singer outraged both friend and foe anew by criticizing the traditional taboo against sexual contact between humans and animals. The following year he returned, in *One World: The Ethics of Globalization* to his early topic of moral obligations across national boundaries. The reach of the most influential ethicist of the old century bids fair to extend wider still in the new one.

Suggested reading

Singer, P. 1993. *Practical Ethics* (2nd edition). Cambridge: Cambridge University Press.
Singer, P. 2000. *Writings on an Ethical Life*. New York: Ecco.
Jamieson, D. 1999 (ed.). *Singer and His Critics*. Oxford: Blackwell.

Socrates

470–399 BCE   **Robin Wood**

Socrates was born the son of a stonemason and a midwife, the latter being an intellectual image that he applied to himself when in conversation (which he initiated) a new understanding came to birth. Cicero said that he brought philosophy down from heaven and planted it on earth. Socrates was concerned with humanity and how it should live. He turned aside from the physical speculations of the earlier philosophers and directed his attention to issues concerning the knowledge of virtue.

He could be said to be the founder of moral philosophy. He wanted to know what virtue is and was aware of his own ignorance. Indeed, the story goes that a friend asked the Delphic oracle whether there was anyone wiser than Socrates and the oracle said No. So Socrates started asking questions and found that others could not give adequate answers any more than he could. When he asked a soldier 'What is courage?' or a religious leader 'What is piety?' and discovered that they did not know he concluded that he really was the wisest man in Greece because he knew that he did not know. This is part of the famous Socratic 'irony' which, while genuine at one level (demonstrating Socrates' humility), was also a weapon in debate to elicit from others, for his own and their edification, the truth latent in their minds.

He sought, from a moral point of view, to probe conventional ideas and detect errors, and so to arrive at true ideas on the subject by a new method. He analysed the definitions of such things as virtue by particular cases and examples. The resulting contradictions showed the errors of those definitions, the truth of a definition being proved by the consistency of its result. This analysis was carried on by a system of question-and-answer (the distinctive 'Socratic method' or *elenchus*) in which each point in succession was accepted or rejected by the interlocutor, who was thus gradually led to the conclusion at which Socrates wished to arrive.

Both **Plato** and Xenophon agree that it was Socrates' view that virtue is knowledge, that no one is willingly wicked, because true happiness lies in virtue. Socrates' concern was to discover what the good is because if a person is wicked it is essentially due to their ignorance.

On a wider philosophical front **Aristotle** claimed that two things may be credited to Socrates, 'inductive argument and universal definition'. By these he meant the ability to discern patterns, to pick out the general principle underlying a set of events or similar objects. All scientific practice consists in this.

While this is important there can be no doubt that Socrates' great and lasting legacy lies not just in what he said or did but in what he was. Socrates was a martyr and died for his beliefs. In 399 BCE, after a trial described in the *Apology* of Plato and in that of Xenophon, he was sentenced to death on a charge, brought by Meletus, Anytus and Lycon, of introducing new deities and corrupting the youth. He had made enemies by interrogating those who had a reputation for wisdom and refuting them. His perception of the weak points in democratic government was unpopular with the Athenians, who attributed to his influence the misdeeds of Alcibiades, Charmides and Critias, who had been his disciples but abused the essence of his teaching.

His execution was postponed for a month because the sacred trireme had just been dispatched to Delos and during its absence no execution was allowed to pollute the city. When it returned, in a scene described by Plato in the *Phaedo*, where Socrates discusses the immortality of the soul, surrounded by his faithful companions he drank with great courage, as required, the draught of hemlock.

Socrates was at once a rationalist, a mystic (he believed that he was the recipient of warnings addressed to him on occasion by the Divine Voice), an active citizen in public affairs, a soldier of courage, and indeed a lover of the city and society that executed him because it could not bear his questionings. His greatness consists firstly in just that, his relentless efforts to get at the truth; secondly in his influence on Plato who surely gives us the most authentic 'picture' of him (for Socrates himself wrote nothing); and finally in his dying for the truth in which he believed.

Suggested reading

Plato. 1993. *The Last Days of Socrates*. Harmondsworth: Penguin.
Gottlieb, A. 1997. *Socrates*. London: Weidenfeld & Nicholson.
Macdonald Cornford, F. 1932. *Before and After Socrates*. Cambridge: Cambridge University Press.

Baruch Spinoza

1632–1677   **Margaret Gullan-Whur**

Spinoza is acknowledged in all philosophical traditions as a great thinker, yet his work is seldom studied. Here is a paradox that, like his doctrines, is explicable on several levels, each giving rise to further paradoxes. Small wonder that those who think the beautiful theory is the simple one shun him.

Some textual ambiguities spring from the complexity of his cultural background. Born in Amsterdam in 1632 of Portuguese Jews who had fled the Inquisition, Spinoza was expelled at twenty-four from his orthodox community for 'horrendous heresies'. Bento de Espinosa (Baruch in the synagogue and seminary) became Benedictus, western scholar and opinionated proponent of the 'new philosophy' that threatened all theistic religions with its assertion of a mechanistic universe. Yet Spinoza would never speak good Dutch, or marry, and in some ways remained a thinker in the Jewish rationalist tradition. His largely self-taught classical education never displaced his love for Hebrew studies and Spanish mystical literature. His *Theologico-Political Treatise* (1670), challenging **Hobbes**'s pronouncements in *De Cive* on human nature and reason, is presented through the medium of biblical exegesis, in the style of his forebears.

Most of his texts, but especially the early *Short Treatise* (unpublished until 1899), contain esoteric themes and assumptions that baffled even those who regularly debated or corresponded with him. While enigmatic enough to be labelled both atheist and spiritual guru, he insisted from the start that he combated confused thinking and supernaturalism solely through deductive reasoning. After explaining his cognitive 'method' in his *The Treatise on the Emendation of the Intellect* (1677), and testing formal arguments on friends, he wrote his masterwork *Ethics* (1677) as a Euclidean demonstration in which propositions and proofs are accompanied by insightful, tortuous or impassioned explanatory notes.

Spinoza's first published bid to knock the recently-dead **Descartes** (himself one of Holland's religious refugees) off his philosophical pedestal came in his *Principles of Descartes' Philosophy* (1663). Here, dissension intrudes with subtle wit, necessarily subtle because Spinoza's belief that there existed just one absolutely infinite substance, named

God, or Nature, entailed that God could not lie outside the material world, a heresy that eclipsed Descartes'. For Spinoza, every existing thing is an aspect or mode of the one substance, God or Nature, and every mode has thinking and material aspects. This doctrine, expounded in *Ethics*, would be published only posthumously.

Why should such a dated thesis, or any of the extrapolations Spinoza makes from it, interest people today? Spinoza's work is perennially important because many tensions in his texts represent genuine and still-unresolved philosophical problems, on which he sets useful agendas for inquiry.

In the case of the mind-body problem he presses the claims of mental irreducibility: the impossibility of explaining mind in terms of matter, or vice-versa. His non-reductive monism entails that while mind and body are 'the same thing', mind and body must be two really existing aspects of this thing and not merely two ways of seeing that thing. We must stipulate unique and diverse real properties for mental and physical phenomena if the mind is not to dissolve into body, or body into mind.

The doctrine of 'common notions' asks us to concentrate on what any thinking and material thing must have in common with all other modes of its kind, and thereby how we discover laws of nature. Once we start working with basic principles grounded in knowledge of common properties, we can begin to dissolve divisions artificially created by human convention and subjective observation. Spinoza claims that his deductive method surpasses the shaky empirical generalizations often used in sciences like biology and physics. He also demonstrates the usefulness of common notions in such arenas as politics, religion and psychology, all of which he equally regards as sciences. *Ethics* treats emotions as natural phenomena governed by laws of human nature, extending Descartes' theory of basic human passions into a system of mental causes and effects to be understood through a science similar to our modern cognitive therapy.

Among Spinoza's political arguments, his 'social contract' theory of the *Theologico-Political Treatise* stands apart as one of the earliest to have collapsed under the strain of trying to preserve, within a general will theory, the right of the individual to pursue self-interest or dissent on rational or ethical grounds.

Still considering the individual as a member of society, Spinoza's own life invites reflection. In one dimension a study in elected loneliness, it also displays the unquestioning self-regard conferred by accepting determinism: the thesis that everything happens as a matter of absolute necessity. The obstacle this creates for a scholarly exchange of ideas is evident in his letters. In *Ethics* we also see a tension in Spinoza between reason, which unites minds, and private intellectual satisfaction.

Suggested reading

Spinoza, B. 1951 [1670]. *The Theologico-Political Treatise*. New York: Dover Publications.

Spinoza, B. 1951 [1677]. *The Ethics, Treatise on the Emendation of the Intellect, and Selected Letters*. Indiana: Hackett.

Gullan-Whur, M. 1998. *Within Reason: A Life of Spinoza*. London: Jonathan Cape.

Charles Taylor

1931–   **Deane-Peter Baker**

Charles Taylor's *Sources of the Self* (1989) established him as one of the major figures of contemporary philosophy. *Sources of the Self* is a rarity in that it is a book of philosophy that achieved a wide readership outside of philosophical circles, as did his *The Ethics of Authenticity* (1992), an extended version of the 1991 Massey lectures which were broadcast as part of CBC Radio's *Ideas* series.

Taylor is part of what is often called the 'neo-Aristotelian revival', a school of thought that has arisen, as much as for any other reason, out of a perceived failure of ethical thought in the post-Enlightenment world. Taylor's specific approach to this often focuses on a rejection of what he calls 'naturalism', by which he means not just the unobjectionable view that man is in some sense part of nature, but that 'the nature of which he is a part is to be understood according to the canons which emerged in the seventeenth-century revolution in natural science'. Indeed, Taylor calls himself a monomaniac in this regard, and Isaiah Berlin labelled him a 'hedgehog' because of this consistent thread in Taylor's broad-ranging philosophy.

In taking on 'naturalism' in its various forms, Taylor perceives himself as challenging one of the key sources of what he calls the 'modern malaise', which manifests itself primarily in a 'centring on the self'. This 'flattens and narrows our lives, makes them poorer in meaning, and less concerned with others or society' and can lead even further, to a disorientating dislocation from those things that give our lives meaning and sense.

In *Sources of the Self*, Taylor argues that the self is essentially defined by its relation to the framework of goods that define the 'good life' (in the Aristotelian sense) for that self. Further, these moral frameworks are presided over by 'hypergoods', which are not only incomparably more important than other goods but which also provide the measure against which these goods must be judged.

Taylor then goes on to develop a magnificent account of the philo- sophical sources of the modern western self, starting with **Plato**'s self-mastery and working his way through to what he calls the 'epiphanies of modernism'. Taylor's efforts at 'philosophical archaeology' in *Sources of the Self* follow from his claim that articulation of the self's sources is an essential part of the antidote to the malaise of modernity.

Taylor has been described as a paradigm case of a 'post-analytic' philosopher, someone who retains the rigour and clarity characteristic of the analytic tradition, but draws on sources and addresses subjects that fall beyond the analytic-continental divide. He is particularly noteworthy for his willingness to move beyond the ahistorical ethos characteristic of analytic analysis. While some of the continental influences on Taylor are fairly obvious, such as **Hegel**, it is interesting to note that he has been strongly influenced by the work of phenomenologist **Maurice Merleau- Ponty**.

The political scene has long been a central focus of activity for Taylor. Taylor has spent a great deal of time and effort in a struggle to prevent the break-up of the Canadian federation, both through his position as a philosopher and through direct political involvement in the New Democratic Party.

One of the key assumptions that characterizes Taylor's political philosophy is that the age of modernity and post-modernity is a plural- istic age. Taylor criticizes contemporary philosophers such as **Jürgen Habermas** and **John Rawls** who, he believes, have failed to take this sufficiently into account. Taylor takes a kind of communitarian point of view, claiming that it is essential to human identity that one's community be recognized both politically and socially, and he warns that certain forms of political liberalism endanger that recognition and promote homogeneity rather than recognizing plurality. However, this plurality is not something Taylor thinks we must simply accept at face value. He argues that we cannot assume that all cultures are intrinsically valuable, and we must instead work towards a 'fusion of horizons' that grows out of recognizing the qualitative contrast between cultures.

Taylor's recent work has focused mostly on the relationship between religion, Catholic Christianity in particular, and modernity. Many of his contemporaries are expecting him to produce another work on the scale of *Sources of the Self*, focused on the sources of contemporary secularity.

Strangely, Taylor has not attained as wide a degree of recognition as the quality of his work would seem to justify, though thankfully a number of recent books focusing on his work have gone some way to rectifying this. Taylor has been praised by some of the foremost philosophers of our day. The late Isaiah Berlin said, 'Whatever one may think of his central beliefs, [they] cannot fail to broaden the outlook of anyone who reads his works or listens to his lectures or, indeed, talks to him.'

Suggested reading

Taylor, C. 1989. *Sources of the Self*. Cambridge, Mass.: Harvard University Press.
Taylor, C. 1992. *The Ethics of Authenticity*. Cambridge, Mass.: Harvard University Press.
Tully, J. 1994 (ed.). *Philosophy in an Age of Pluralism: The Philosophy of Charles Taylor in Question*. Cambridge: Cambridge University Press.

Alan Turing

1912–1954   **Peter Cave**

On 7 June 1954, Alan Turing, aged 41, ate an apple injected with cyanide. Thus died a man who laid the foundations for computer science; who, through his secret cryptological work, significantly contributed to the Allied victory in the Second World War; and who founded the artificial intelligence programme, a source for much of today's philosophy of psychology. Nobody can be sure of the exact reason for the suicide, but his homosexuality was the key. Such sexual activity was, for some, almost *de rigueur* where Turing studied at King's College, Cambridge, whose Keynes had earlier promoted the ethics of higher sodomy. In the wider world, though, homosexuals received public vilification, predictions of eternal damnation, and even earthly imprisonment; and in 1952, a Turing sexual affair was exposed to the police. Turing was dismissed from his cryptological post and to avoid imprisonment he submitted to chemical treatment to submerge his sexuality.

Turing read mathematics at Cambridge, finding King's life congenial, with its progressive intellectualism and libertarianism. He turned specifically to mathematical logic and computability. After his wartime success in breaking the Enigma code, he moved to Manchester, pioneering further computer development. What has captivated many philosophers is Turing's belief that, one day, we will have engineered machines that think. What counts as engineering here? The answer 'when by mechanical means' is no help: sexual copulation is often mechanical, yet churns out people.

Investigating ideas of effective procedures, Turing conceived of 'Turing machines' – hypothetical abstract devices, with infinite storage, but finite rules or algorithms which determine, given a prior state and input, subsequent states and output. Manifestations of Turing machines, therefore, would behave predictably. There are also abstract universal Turing machines – machines that mimic basic Turing machines and each other. Although (physical) computers these days look pretty different from machinery with cogs and pistons, they follow determinate procedures. Computers, like humans, lack infinite memory storage, of course; but they operate according to finite algorithms and can mimic.

If computers can be constructed to think as intelligently as humans, then it is possible that our thinking operates mechanically and that we are part of the physical, causal world. It remains a practical matter about what stuff can realize the algorithms. Silicone chips can do so; biological brains too – but maybe they do much more in human thinking? After all, machine intelligence seems contradictory, for we contrast mechanical behaviour with intelligent. To deal with this, Turing devised a discriminatory test – The Turing Test.

An interrogator, receiving only printed answers, interrogates two hidden individuals, one intelligent human, one machine. If he cannot tell which is the machine, then the machine is intelligent. Of course, the interrogator needs intelligence himself. Asking simple arithmetical questions alone, for example, would lead to no difference being identified between persons and pocket calculators with suitable interfaces. Further, the machines need to be intelligently programmed to avoid tell-tale signs of their non-human nature: so they can, for example, delay answers to complex questions, print out hesitant 'er's and even make mistakes. Turing anticipates that, once we grow accustomed to intelligent machines, their programmes could give quirky outputs, leading us to note, 'My machine said such a funny thing yesterday.'

Even if machines pass Turing's test (some have, but were their interrogators sufficiently discerning?) they might be merely simulating or modelling. After all, computers can model weather changes, but there's no danger of computers raining. In contrast, simulating steps of reasoning to right answers, with right answers given – as also, sometimes, acting sex scenes in films – amounts to the real thing. So, are machines that pass Turing's test akin to weather modelling or to realistic sex acting?

The Turing Test hides seeming irrelevancies, such as whether the 'thinker' is metallic or flesh; but it hides much more. Our thinking engages a fleshy life – riding bicycles, coaxing lovers with headaches, using chairs as coat-hangers. Simply knowing *that* something or other, about bicycles, coat-hangers and lovers, captures neither our thoughts' richness concerning these items, nor our knowing how to use them, nor how to judge what is relevant to say about them; so maybe algorithms could not account for all our thinkings. If robotic computers could be constructed, engaging headachy, mouse-fearing lives, we should need to think further – and perhaps grant them the vote. Computation, however, is symbol manipulation – symbols that *we* interpret as meaningful. Pocket calculators churn out symbols, but have no understanding of the numbers symbolically represented. Can we even grasp how sheer computational complexity could give rise to interpreting symbols, to understanding their meaning?

Turing's ideas continue to stimulate research into mentality as nothing but functional relationships between inputs and outputs, with the mind akin to software, not hardware. This gives rise to controversial and fertile thought experiments – from replications of oneself to tales of Chinese rooms and of brains consisting of the Chinese nation. Turing, with his yen for the provocative, radical and comic, would surely have approved.

Suggested reading

Boden, M. 1990 (ed). *The Philosophy of Artificial Intelligence*. Oxford: Oxford University Press
Hodges, A. 1992. *Alan Turing: The Enigma*. London: Vintage.
Hinsley, F. H. and Stripp, A. 1993 (eds). *Codebreakers.* Oxford: Oxford University Press.

Giambattista Vico

1668–1744   **Giorgio Baruchello**

The Neapolitan philosopher Giambattista Vico is one of those thinkers of whom much is heard and little is read. Perhaps because he has been depicted mainly as the forerunner of other, more famous thinkers (especially **Hegel** and Herder), and of following established currents of thought, many acknowledge his contribution to the history of western philosophy, but few actually read his writings. Still, this relegation to the periphery of the philosophical canon reflects somehow the unorthodox character of his life and of his scholarly achievements, which, as Gramsci stated, moved from 'a small, dead corner of history'.

Vico spent his life tormented by indigence and illness. Nevertheless, he succeeded in gaining a vast, comprehensive erudition in law, philology and philosophy, as he worked as a lawyer, a tutor and a professor of rhetoric at the University of Naples. He believed it a fundamental trait of human nature that we long for knowledge. Why that is the case, however, is unknown to us: we can only observe that it is so. There are limits, in other words, to that which we can know.

In *De antiquissima Italorum sapientia* (*On the Most Ancient Wisdom of the Italians*, 1710) we find Vico's most forceful expression of this realization: '*verum ipsum factum*': only that which is made by the human being can be known in depth. Exhaustive knowledge can be gained only in the human sciences. Human beings cannot know the reasons which lie behind the existence of the realities they observe in nature; so only a partial, hypothetical knowledge is possible of those things of which the human being is not the author. Human reason is severely limited when dealing with the understanding of the natural world, whose author is, presumably, God.

Vico was writing against the well-established intellectual faith of his time, which proclaimed the natural sciences as the highest expression of human reason (logic and mathematics were included in this privileged disciplinary group). Vico intended to defend the humanistic tradition with its curriculum of studies comprising classical literature, jurisprudence, history, oratory and foreign languages. Throughout his writings, Vico tried to show how human reason cannot work ahistorically, as a pure, neutral instrument of discovery, which does not depend upon the motives, aims, expectations and prejudices of people. For Vico, the truth may be achieved, but not by letting reason operate in the void: context is required.

In his best-known work, *The New Science* (1725), Vico stresses the centrality of culture in and for any intellectual endeavour, the natural sciences included. Knowledge relies upon understanding and, in turn, understanding relies upon tacit beliefs, which are the result of the history of one's personal development within a variously-layered historical reality. *Sensus communis* (common sense) is, for Vico, the fundamental ground out of which all forms of human knowledge spring and to which, ultimately, they are bound to return. *Sensus communis*, in his words, is 'judgement without reflection, shared by an entire class, an entire people, an entire nation, or the entire human race'.

This fundamental cultural ground is contained already in the myths, traditions and poetical metaphors of human culture. They anticipate, inform and sustain any explicit act of intellectual scrutiny of reality, thus providing the any implicit background justifying the choice, worth and communicability of inquiry. For Vico, much modern scientific knowledge is contained already in the allegories of poetry, the insights of religion, the images of art. Moreover, these involve an ability of which science is devoid, namely the ability to address and involve in the cognitive process the human body and the human heart.

In his *New Science*, Vico specifies a fundamental 'dialectical' structure regulating the historical development of human knowledge. This structure can be represented as a moving spiral of occurrences and recurrences (*corsi e ricorsi storici*), along which moments of collapse and of regress in the human understanding of the universe are as unavoidable as the overall progress of the human species from the bestial state to the civilized state. For Vico, history repeats itself, but never in an identical fashion and always along a necessary path of amelioration, which adds new steps to the old ones and never erases any. Taken as a whole, human culture advances through the centuries in the same fashion as the individual person matures through the years. Both start from the 'age of the senses' (or 'divine age'), and, via the 'age of fantasy' (or 'heroic age'), they reach the 'age of reason' (or 'human age'), yet without ever discarding completely either that which had been previously experienced by means of the 'non-' or 'pre-rational' faculties, or these faculties themselves.

Suggested reading
Vico, G. 1710 [1993]. *On the Most Ancient Wisdom of the Italians.* Ithaca, NY: Cornell University Press.
Vico, G. 1709 [1990]. *On the Study Methods of our Times.* Ithaca, NY: Cornell University Press.
Vico, G. 1725 [1993]. *The New Science.* Ithaca, NY: Cornell University Press.

Simone Weil
1909–1943   **Megan Laverty**

Simone Weil is an original and complex thinker. She can be classified as a twentieth-century Christian Platonist and is studied by philosophers and theologians alike. They agree that understanding Weil's philosophy is helped by understanding her life, and vice versa. Weil was born in 1909 to a middle class Jewish French family. She was educated at Lycée Henry IV and École Normale Supérieure in philosophy, where her fellow students included **Simone de Beauvoir** and **Jean-Paul Sartre**. She began teaching philosophy in 1931 (a student's class notes were later published as *Lectures on Philosophy,* 1959).

Weil's particular philosophical preoccupations compelled her to become involved in political activism – educating workers, engaging in factory and farm labour, joining the Republican forces in the Spanish Civil War in 1936 and then the Free French forces in 1942 – which shaped and informed her philosophical development. Her lifestyle was characterized by a strict asceticism and she claimed to have had three vital contacts with Christianity (one of them a visit from Christ) although she was never recorded as being baptized. Weil died of tuberculosis in 1943, at the age of 34.

Simone Weil's major works were published posthumously, including *Waiting for God* (1950), *Gravity and Grace* (1947), and *The Need for Roots* (1952). During her life she wrote mainly essays, the most famous of these being 'The *Iliad*, Poem of Might' and 'Human Personality'. Although Weil's writing ranged over issues from religion, literature, work and the organization of factories, central to her thought is her theory of human affliction, the primary 'uprooting of life'. Affliction, she argues, includes but is more profound than physical suffering because of its total and overwhelming impact upon the soul: it is unwillingly endured and robs life of inherent meaning, which is the same as saying that it negates the possibility of consolation. Although our natural response to affliction is one of dread, Weil thought it a privileged position of enlightenment because, for her, to understand affliction is to understand the human condition. The human condition is one of affliction because to be human is to be separated from God, which is to be subject to blind necessity. This is because God created the world by withdrawing from it – his ultimate act of love.

Weil characterizes the human condition as having two dimensions: the natural (gravity) and the supernatural (grace). As natural beings, our actions are principally governed by our needs (biological, psychological, intellectual etc.). It is the relentless constancy of these needs and our attempts to fulfil them that inform the way in which we read the world and our attachment to it. 'Reading' characterizes our experience of the world as necessarily interpretive and 'attachment' characterizes the self-centred quality of this 'reading', causing us to value some situations and individuals more than others. Attachment combines with contingency to produce our greatest happiness and greatest suffering. Weil refers to this as the force of 'gravity' so as to draw on the analogous relationship that she sees between the operation of the human soul and the laws of gravity governing the natural world.

Given that human beings cannot escape the laws of gravity, their only recourse is to accept them; that is, to love blind necessity and the world's beauty as love reveals it. Such love requires that one disengage from reading and attend to the world. Attention involves detaching oneself from what one desires or values and ultimately the function of desire itself, including one's desire for God and eternal salvation. It is a 'decreation' of the self on the model of God's original decreation. It is, in essence, to love God as he loves us: indirectly or implicitly. Our capacity for attention is, according to Weil, a testament to the other defining feature of the human condition, namely grace.

Simone Weil believed that philosophy was best evaluated in terms of the actions and broader societal changes which it produces, hence her interest in ethical and political philosophy. She thought that the purpose of ethics and politics is to alleviate human affliction, whilst at the same time accepting that affliction is the unique occasion of profound insight. Weil acknowledged this contradiction, to eradicate that which is the occasion for grace, but thought it a sign of truth. She maintained that to do this we need to move away from talk of human rights to talk of obligations; that we need to organize work so it becomes more meaningful; and that we need to love our neighbour, including the most afflicted and those seemingly most lacking in goodness. Hers is a radical philosophy indeed.

Suggested reading
Weil, S. 2002 [1947]. *Gravity and Grace*. London: Routledge.
Panichas, G. A. 1985 (ed.). *Simone Weil Reader*. Rhode Island: Moyer Bell Limited.
Winch, P. 1989. *Simone Weil: The Just Balance*. Cambridge: Cambridge University
    Press.

Alfred North Whitehead

1861–1947 V. Alan White

Twentieth-century Anglo-American philosophy, born with a stern and focused analytical face, took on a humbler, pluralistic countenance as it aged, and the careers of certain philosophers such as **Wittgenstein** and Whitehead were living embodiments of that fact.

In the case of Whitehead, an initial career in mathematics at Trinity College, Cambridge, allied him with **Bertrand Russell**, with whom he collaborated from 1901–1913 to produce the influential logical study *Principia Mathematica*. The *Principia* attempted to complete an ambitious project conceived by **Gottlob Frege** to reduce mathematics to its pure logical foundations. This monumental work set the stage for the philosophical dominance of logic and philosophy of language throughout the century, but also blazed the trail for its own unravelling in 1931, when **Kurt Gödel** proved that no logical system such as the *Principia*'s can be entirely self-contained and complete. Today the intricate analytical machine of the *Principia* is still taught and admired, but the asterisk appended to it by Gödel is a constant reminder of the difficulty of achieving conceptual closure even in basic matters of rational thought.

Buoyed by this achievement and while at University College London, Whitehead gravitated to an intensive study of science, publishing such acclaimed works as *An Enquiry Concerning the Principles of Natural Knowledge* (1919) and *The Concept of Nature* (1920). Whitehead systematically stressed the importance of interpreting the universe using the **Einstein**-Minkowski concept of four-dimensional space-time events to describe all phenomena, thus displacing more traditional descriptions involving substance 'stuff' that problematically fits into three-dimensional spaces at certain times. Whitehead's single-mindedness about the fundamental nature of events eventually led him to delineate a conceptually distinct view of Einstein's theories in his *Principle of Relativity* (1922). Unfortunately this work suffered the same stillbirth from the press that **David Hume** attributed to his first *Treatise*, and Whitehead's reputation as philosopher of science lapsed into dark eclipse.

In a literal sea-change of later life, in 1924 and at the age of 63, Whitehead accepted an offer to teach at Harvard University, where he finished his career. In that same year *Science and the Modern World* appeared, heralding a new philosophical interest: metaphysics. In this book Whitehead continued his previous arguments that nature should not be split by science into matter and mind 'things'. However, here he also argued for the first time that the universe must be accounted for in more holistic terms that embrace a theory of knowledge and ontology (account of being) co-ordinated with ordinary experience, aesthetics, values and all sundry furniture of reality right down to subatomic quanta. Whatever expectations Harvard might have had for the heralded logician/philosopher of science they hired, with *Science and the Modern World* Whitehead served notice that he intended to rival the broad metaphysical scope of the likes of **Descartes** and **Leibniz**.

Science and its heirs greatly expanded an already familiar trend in Whiteheadian exposition as well – neologism. That same work introduced among others the term 'actual occasion' as a synonym for 'event', and as well first explicitly spelled out the 'quantized' nature of events, so that from then on for Whitehead all events in nature are irreducible droplets of time and space that actually cannot be infinitely subdivided in the familiar Euclidean fashion, even though they may be so analysed abstractly and mathematically.

Science and the Modern World also introduced another startling turn in Whiteheadian thought–interest in religion. With a chapter on 'God' this minister's son, who earlier had explicitly repudiated his devotional legacy by selling his entire theological library, invoked deity as a final ground of metaphysical explanation. In 1926, further ruminations on the nature of God and faith appeared in *Religion in the Making*. These and later reflections on religion, always highly conceptual and dispassionate in tone, have ironically turned out to be some of Whitehead's most enduring contributions.

An invitation by the University of Edinburgh for the Gifford Lectures of 1927 provided Whitehead with the opportunity to gather his new metaphysical and epistemological perspectives into a systematic whole, later expanded in 1929 into his triumphant *Process and Reality*.

Arguably, *Process* remains the last grand metaphysical treatise elaborated in the history of philosophy. It describes in excruciating detail and almost arcane language how actual occasions 'prehend' and compose one another by a form of complex internal relatedness involving 'eternal objects' that are much like Platonic ideas retained in the 'primordial nature' of God. Brilliantly integrating science, philosophy and religion, this work christened contemporary studies of 'process philosophy' and 'process theology', which in their own domains equally stress the fundamental role of time in explaining how things are.

A truly gentle man of convivial spirit, Whitehead stands remembered as much as an admirable person as for his sweeping intellectual accomplishments.

Suggested reading

Whitehead, A. N. 1985 [1924]. *Science and the Modern World*. London: Free Association Books.
Whitehead, A. N. 1996 [1926]. *Religion in the Making*. New York: Fordham University Press.
Whitehead, A. N. 1979 [1929]. *Process and Reality*. New York: Macmillan.

Ludwig Wittgenstein

1889–1951   **Rupert Read**

Central to Wittgenstein's work was the nature of language and its role in the process of philosophizing. He played a leading role in the 'linguistic turn' of modern philosophy, away from ideas and toward sentences in contexts. But his iconoclasm and deep distrust of any theory makes it misleading to classify him as a 'philosopher of language'.

The brilliant, gnomic and influential *Tractatus Logico-Philosophicus* (1921) was the only book Wittgenstein published in his lifetime. This book offered an elaboration of its prefatory dictum, 'What can be said at all can be said clearly; and whereof one cannot speak thereof one must be silent.' Many philosophers have argued that Wittgenstein believed that the truths which one could not speak – those supposedly found in ethics, religion and philosophy itself, for example – could still be 'shown'. A new, alternative interpretation, associated especially with Cora Diamond and James Conant, is that Wittgenstein meant the dictum quoted above quite austerely and resolutely – that there was simply nothing to be said about what cannot be said. On this interpretation,

Wittgenstein was quite in earnest when he wrote that the *Tractatus* itself was nonsense. The illusions of sense that it produced would be thrown away by one who, in reading it, understood his point in writing it.

After completing the *Tractatus*, Wittgenstein was silent on the subject of philosophy for some years, before returning to it publicly at the close of the 1920s with a renewed interest and some strikingly new formulations. In contrast to the crystalline simplicity of the *Tractatus*'s apparent depiction of an ideal language, Wittgenstein's later thought was expressed as a motley of considerations about the motley that language actually is. In contrast to the early focus on the 'essential form' of logic and language, the later philosophy chiefly works by pointing out differences within and between real or imagined 'language-games'. The *Tractatus* gave the appearance of being a magisterial theory of logical form. *Philosophical Investigations*, the masterpiece of his later period, was fashioned rather after a dialogue with interlocutors or students.

Wittgenstein held throughout his life that clarity of thought and expression were hard to obtain because we fail to notice that we are always doing things with language. Uses of language have to be contextualized within living practice if they are to be understood, and there is all the difference in the world between the contexts of significant use of sentences which appear extremely similar – for example, consider 'Swifts fly very fast', 'How time flies!', and 'The boat flew down the rapids'. He summed this up thus: 'Philosophy is a battle against the bewitchment of our intelligence by means of language.'

As it stands, this proposition is perhaps ambiguous: does it mean that it is language itself that befuddles our intelligence; or does it mean that we can combat philosophical confusions through particular clarificatory uses of language? Arguably, both. Wittgenstein thought that it was indeed only through investigation of what it made sense to say, and of the sources of the compulsion to misunderstand, that philosophers could begin to put an end to conceptual confusions and pacify perturbed reflective minds. He also thought that it was precisely conceptual (i.e. linguistic) confusions, such as that which might be engendered by the failure to distinguish different uses of 'fly', which led to philosophical perturbation in the first place. In this way, language (and our relation to it) is both the cure and the disease.

Finding methods of 'cure' was far more important for Wittgenstein than arriving at dogmatic philosophical theses. Indeed, the very quest for and defence of theses was for Wittgenstein a symptom of philosophical confusion, because he held that only in scientific and other empirical disciplines could meaningful assertions about 'how things are' be made. This methodological precept, together with his lack of interest in giving arguments, has contributed to his being hard to absorb within any professional thought-community, including the discipline of philosophy.

Thus his philosophical 'position' might be described as evanescent. Wittgenstein hoped to get us to see how most philosophical questions, and the positions which we take up in response to those questions, are based in an unsatisfactory relationship between us and our words, a kind of linguistic confusion in which we want to say things that don't make any sense.

In fact, the challenge which Wittgenstein makes to philosophy today can perhaps best be put precisely thus: try to philosophize, to think, without putting forward any 'position' at all.

Suggested reading

Wittgenstein, L. 2001 [1921]. *Tractatus Logico Philosophicus*. London: Routledge.
Wittgenstein, L. 1973 [1953]. *Philosophical Investigations*. Oxford: Blackwell.
Monk, R. 1990. *Ludwig Wittgenstein: The Duty of Genius*. London: Jonathan Cape.

Chronological Index

Thematic Guides

The aim of these guides is to provide a suggested selection of readings from this volume for those wishing to trace the trajectory of some of the major strands in western philosophical thought. The introduction provides an overview of these themes. The lists are selective and reflect which aspects of the various philosophers' thought have been given most attention in this volume. Hence, it should not be assumed that a philosopher not listed under one of the headings has nothing to say on that subject.

Theory of Knowledge
1 Socrates
2 Bacon
3 Descartes
4 Locke
5 Hume
6 Kant
7 Comte
8 Peirce
9 Dewey
10 Ayer
11 Quine
12 Rorty

Metaphysics
1 Pythagoras
2 Aristotle
3 Spinoza
4 Berkeley
5 Kant
6 Hegel

7 Schopenhauer
8 Bergson
9 Santayana
10 Lewis

Moral philosophy
1 Seneca
2 Hume
3 Bentham
4 Mill
5 Sidgwick
6 Nietzsche
7 Gandhi
8 Moore
9 Levinas
10 Singer

Political philosophy
1 Plato
2 Machiavelli
3 Hobbes

4 Rousseau
5 Paine
6 Bentham
7 Marx
8 Gandhi
9 Adorno
10 Rawls
11 Foucault
12 Nozick

Philosophy of Religion
1 Augustine
2 Avicenna
3 Duns Scotus
4 Pascal
5 Spinoza
6 Vico
7 Butler
8 Schelling
9 Santayana
10 Gandhi

Phenomenology
1 Dilthey
2 Brentano
3 Husserl
4 Bergson
5 Heidegger
6 Sartre
7 Merleau-Ponty
8 Beauvoir

Philosophy of Language
1 Frege
2 Saussure
3 Russell
4 Wittgenstein
5 Ryle
6 Lacan
7 Quine
8 Chomsky
9 Derrida
10 Kripke

Philosophy of mind
1 Descartes
2 Spinoza
3 Brentano
4 Ryle
5 Turing
6 Putnam
7 Searle
8 Nagel
9 Churchland
10 Dennett

Philosophy and Science
1 Bacon
2 Comte
3 Darwin
4 Peirce
5 Einstein
6 Whitehead
7 Carnap
8 Popper
9 Turing
10 Kuhn

Notes on Contributors

Douglas Allen is Professor of Philosophy at the University of Maine and author of *Myth and Religion in Mircea Eliade* (Routledge) and *Culture and Self* (Westview).

Julian Baggini is an editor of *The Philosophers' Magazine* and author of *Making Sense; Philosophy Behind the Headlines* and *Atheism: A Very Short Introduction* (both Oxford University Press).

Sanghamitra Bandyopadhyay is Lecturer of Development Economics at Queen Elizabeth House, Oxford University.

Deane-Peter Baker is Lecturer in Philosophy at the University of Kwa Zulu-Natal and co-editor of *Explorations in Contemporary Continental Philosophy of Religion* (Rodopi).

Giorgio Baruchello is Adjunct Lecturer at the University of Akureyi.

Steven F. Bernstein was Adjunct Lecturer at Ithaca College New York and is currently writing a research thesis on Butler's moral theory.

Charles Booth is Principal Lecturer at the University of the West of England and co-author of *Making Sense of Management Research: A Critical Approach* (Sage).

Jan Broadway is Deputy Director of the AHRB Centre for Editing Lives and Letters, Queen Mary, University of London.

Christopher Budd is an independent scholar.

Peter Cave is Associate Lecturer in Philosophy at the Open University and Visiting Lecturer in Philosophy at City University London.

Chalmers C. Clark is Visiting Scholar at the Institute for Social and Policy Studies, Bioethics Project, Yale University.

William Clohesy is Associate Professor of Philosophy at the University of Northern Iowa and editor of *Ethics at Work: A Symposium on the Worker and the Workplace* (Iowa Humanities Board).

Terri Collier has been incommunicado since completing her graduate studies at York University.

Hans Dooremalen is a philosopher at the University of Groningen.

Guy Douglas has a PhD in the philosophy of mind from the University of Western Australia.

Laura Duhan Kaplan is Professor and Chair of Philosophy at the University of North Carolina at Charlotte and author of *Philosophy and Everyday Life* (Seven Bridges Press) and *Family Pictures: A Philosopher Explores the Familiar* (Open Court).

Robert Eaglestone is Lecturer in Twentieth Century Literature at Royal Holloway, University of London, and author of *Ethical Criticism* (Edinburgh University Press) and *Doing English* (Routledge).

Simon Eassom is Principal Lecturer and Teacher Fellow at De Montfort University and author of *Cyborg Sport – Primate Play* (Routledge).

James Gordon Finlayson is Lecturer in Philosophy at the University of York and author of *Habermas: A Very Short Introduction* (Oxford University Press).

Peter S. Fosl is Associate Professor of Philosophy and Department Chair at Transylvania University, co-author of *The Philosopher's Toolkit* (Blackwell) and editor of the *Dictionary of Literary Biography: British Philosophers* (Gale).

Jack Furlong is Professor of Philosophy at Transylvania University and co-author of *The Search For the Individual* and *Essays on Ancient and Medieval Philosophy* (both Peter Lang).

Douglas Groothuis is Professor of Philosophy at Denver Seminary and author of *On Jesus* and *On Pascal* (both Wadsworth).

Margaret Gullan-Whur is Visiting Research Fellow at the University of East Anglia and author of *Within Reason: A Life of Spinoza* (Cape) and *The Four Elements* (Century Hutchinson).

Robin Harwood is the author of *The Survival of the Self* (Ashgate).

Lawrence R. Harvey is completing a PhD thesis on Levinas and representation at the University of Wales, Aberystwyth.

Alan Haworth is Senior Lecturer in Philosophy at London Metropolitan University and author of *Understanding the Political Philosophers* and *Free Speech* (both Routledge).

Peter Herrisone-Kelly is Research Assistant at the University of Central Lancashire and is working on a PhD thesis on Kant and rational agency.

Marc A. Hight is Assistant Professor of Philosophy at Hampden-Sydney College.

Peter Holmes is head of Political and Social Sciences at Hills Road Sixth Form College and author of *Resistance and Compromise* (Cambridge University Press) and *Elizabethan Casuistry* (CRS).

Roy Jackson is Lecturer in Theology and Religious Studies, Kings College London and author of *Plato: A Beginner's Guide* (Hodder) and *The God of Philosophy* (TPM).

Edward Johnson is Professor of Philosophy at the University of New Orleans.

Glen Koehn is Adjunct Associate Professor of Philosophy at University College, the University of Maryland.

Irving Krakow is Associate Professor of Philosophy at Camden County College, Blackwood, New Jersey and author of *Why the Mind-Body Problem Cannot Be Solved* (University Press of America).

Michael C. LaBossiere is Associate Professor of Philosophy at Florida A&M University.

Megan Laverty is Assistant Professor at Montclair State University and editor of *What's in an Issue: Perspectives on Contemporary Australian Concerns* and *What's at Issue Now? Perspectives on Contemporary Australian Concerns* (both Oxford University Press).

William F. Lawhead is Professor of Philosophy at the University of Mississippi and author of *The Voyage of Discovery* (Wadsworth) and *Philosophical Journey* (McGraw-Hill).

Diego Lawler is Associate Professor at the University of Salamanca and author of *Las acciones técnicas y sus valores* (Universidad de Salamanca).

Chris Lawn is Lecturer in Philosophy at the University of Limerick.

Orlan Lee is Adjunct Professor of Law at Hong Kong University of Science and Technology, author of *Hong Kong Business Law in a Nutshell* (Juris Publications) and co-author of *'Moral Order' and the Criminal Law* (Martinus Nijhoff).

Jeff Mason is Adjunct Professor at California State University, Fullerton and author of *Philosophical Rhetoric* and *The Philosophers' Address* (both Routledge).

Christopher Norris is Distinguished Research Professor in Philosophy at Cardiff University and author of *Truth Matters: realism, anti-realism and response-dependence* (Edinburgh University Press) and *Philosophy of Language and the Challenge to Scientific Realism* (Routledge).

Scott O'Reilly is author of *The Philosophy of Robert Ettinger* (Universal Publishers/Ria University).

Lewis Owens is author of *Creative Destruction: Nikos Kazantzakis and the Literature of Responsibility* (Mercer University Press).

Frank Pajares is Winship Distinguished Research Professor at Emory University and author of *Adolescence and Education* (Information Age Publishers).

Mark Paterson is Lecturer in Cultural Studies at the University of the West of England.

Jon Phelan teaches philosophy at Hills Road Sixth Form College and is author of *Philosophy: Themes and Thinkers* (Cambridge University Press).

Rosalind Rawnsley has a PhD in the philosophy of Education from Manchester University.

Matthew Ray is the author of *Subjectivity and Irreligion* (Ashgate).

Rupert Read is Senior Lecturer and Head of Philosophy at the University of East Anglia, co-author of *Kuhn: The Philosopher of the Scientific Revolution* (Polity) and co-editor of *The New Wittgenstein* (Routledge)

Jack Ritchie is Lecturer in Philosophy at University College Dublin.

Sajjad Rivzi is Research Associate and Lecturer in Islamic Philosophy at the University of Bristol.

Stewart Saunders is writing his PhD thesis on the philosophy of mind at the Australian National University.

Sally J. Scholz is Associate Professor of Philosophy at Villanova University and author of *On de Beauvoir* and *On Rousseau* (both Wadsworth).

Bart Schultz is Fellow and Lecturer at the University of Chicago and author of *Essays on Henry Sidgwick* and *Henry Sidgwick: Eye of the Universe* (both Cambridge University Press).

Jeremy Stangroom is an editor of *The Philosophers' Magazine* and co-editor (with Julian Baggini) of *New British Philosophy: The Interviews* (Routledge) and *What Philosophers Think* (Continuum).

Alison Stone is Lecturer in Philosophy at Lancaster University and author of *Petrified Intelligence: Nature in Hegel's Philosophy* (SUNY Press).

Andrew H. Talbot is an independent scholar.

Roger Taylor was Lecturer in Philosophy at Sussex University and is author of *Art an Enemy of the People* (Harvester Press) and *Beyond Art* (Barnes & Noble).

Iain Thomson is Assistant Professor of Philosophy at the University of New Mexico.

Alex Voorhoeve is writing a PhD thesis on equal opportunity at University College London and has published in *Economics and Philosophy* and *Philosophy and Public Affairs*.

Jonathan Walmsley has a PhD on John Locke's natural philosophy from King's College London and has published in *The British Journal for the History of Philosophy* and *The Journal of the History of Ideas*.

V. Alan White is Professor of Philosophy at the University of Wisconsin Manitowoc.

Julian Willard has a PhD on the Epistemology of William Alston and Alvin Plantinga from King's College London.

Robin Wood is a Methodist Minister and Lecturer in ethics.

Index